As the host of the Computers and Technology section of AARP Webplace, Sandy Berger has led thousands of AARP members through the electronic wilderness of the Internet. Now, she is using her skills to guide grown-ups on a journey of discovery through the many facets of AOL and the Internet. Whether you simply want to see what the e-revolution is all about, learn about e-commerce, or just send e-mail to your kids and grandkids, Sandy Berger can help you get the most out of your e-experience.

Horace B. Deets
AARP Executive Director

Your Official Grown-Up's Guide to AOL® and the Internet

Sandy Berger

AOL Press

Dulles, VA

**Your Official Grown-up's Guide to AOL®
and the Internet**

Published by
AOL Press
An imprint of IDG Books Worldwide, Inc.
An International Data Group Company
919 E. Hillsdale Blvd., Suite 400
Foster City, CA 94404
www.aol.com (America Online Web site)

ISBN: 0-7645-3417-3

Printed in the United States of America

10 9 8 7 6 5 4 3 2 1

1B/SR/RS/ZZ/FC

Distributed in the United States by IDG Books Worldwide,
Inc. and America Online, Inc.

For general information on IDG Books Worldwide's books
in the U.S., please call our Consumer Customer Service department at 800-762-2974. For reseller information, including discounts and premium sales, please call our Reseller
Customer Service department at 800-434-3422.

Library of Congress Cataloging-in-Publication Data
Berger, Sandy.
    Your Official Grown-up's Guide to AOL and the
Internet, 3rd Edition / Sandy Berger.
        p.   cm.
    Includes index.
    ISBN 0-7645-3417-3 (alk. paper)
    1. America Online (Online service) 2. Internet
(Computer network)
    I. Title.
    QA76.57.A43 B47   1999
    025.04–dc21   99-051485
                                                   CIP

While every precaution has been taken in the preparation of this book, the authors, publisher, and America Online assume
no responsibility for errors or omissions, or for damages resulting from the use of the information or instructions contained
herein.

Trademarks: All brand names and product names used in this book are trade names, service marks, trademarks, or registered
trademarks of their respective owners. IDG Books Worldwide is not associated with any product or vendor mentioned in this
book.

 is a trademark of
America Online, Inc.

 is a registered trademark or trademark under exclusive license
to IDG Books Worldwide, Inc. from International Data Group, Inc.
in the United States and/or other countries.

Welcome to AOL Press™

AOL Press books provide timely guides to getting the most out of your online life. AOL Press was formed as part of the AOL family to create a complete series of official references for using America Online as well as the entire Internet — all designed to help you enjoy a fun, easy, and rewarding online experience.

AOL Press is an exciting partnership between two companies at the forefront of the knowledge and communications revolution — AOL and IDG Books Worldwide. AOL is committed to quality, ease of use, and value and IDG Books excels at helping people understand technology.

To meet these high standards, all our books are authored by experts with the full participation of and exhaustive review by AOL's own development, technical, managerial, and marketing staff. Together, AOL and IDG Books have implemented an ambitious publishing program to develop new publications that serve every aspect of your online life.

We hope you enjoy reading this AOL Press title and find it useful. We welcome your feedback at AOL keyword: **Contact Shop Direct** so we can keep providing information the way you want it.

AOLPress

About the Author

Sandy Berger, nationally respected computer authority, radio host, and author, is a seasoned 30-year computer expert and is president of Computer Living Corp., a computer consulting and training company with headquarters in Pinehurst, NC. Her company specializes in hardware and software selection, implementation, and training for individuals and small businesses.

Sandy also hosts the "Computers and Technology" section of AARP's Web site, www.aarp.org/comptech, where she provides feature stories, product reviews, daily tips, and more for cyber-rookies. To get expert advice from one of the country's most respected computer consultants and easy-to-understand information on personal computing, visit Sandy's Web site at www.compukiss.com.

Credits

America Online

Technical Editor
Judy Karpinski

Cover Design
DKG Design, Inc.

IDG Books Worldwide

Acquisitions Editor
Kathy Yankton

Development Editor
Katharine Dvorak

Technical Editor
Susan Glinert

Copy Editors
Bill McManus
Ami Knox

Project Coordinator
Linda Marousek

Graphics and Production Specialists
Mario Amador
Jude Levinson
Dina F Quan
Ramses Ramirez

Quality Control Specialists
Laura Taflinger
Chris Weisbart

Book Designer
Evan Deerfield

This book is dedicated to the special group of curious and courageous "Grown-Ups" who find themselves with years of living and working experience but no formal computer education. To all the soon-to-be Internet explorers who missed growing up in the digital years, your efforts to explore AOL and the Internet's new and exciting world are sure to be rewarding.

Preface

The other day, I saw a three-year-old child approaching her family's computer. With teddy bear and pink blanket in one hand, she plopped herself in front of the computer, grabbed the mouse with her free hand, and started clicking away.

Not all of us have had the privilege that this child will have of growing up with computers. Although I have worked with computers for the past 30 years, I was 20 years old before I saw my first computer. Many of the adults in the world today only recently realized the pervasiveness of computers in their lives or heard terminology such as *www* or *dot-com*, the interesting combination of letters that has become so popular. How, then, can our generation be expected to be as comfortable with computers as the three-year-old child that I just mentioned?

Yet, as we enter the new millennium, our world is becoming so saturated with computers and high-tech equipment that the average grown-up today can no longer avoid becoming part of the world of digital technology. Many young people have trouble understanding why some of us enter the computer world with a certain amount of fear and trepidation, but I understand. If you haven't grown up with technology, and computers weren't the norm in your classrooms, plunging into this new and unknown world can be difficult.

So, I have written this book for anyone who hasn't grown up with computers and now wants to enter the world of technology and become a confident and comfortable computer user. No one should miss the knowledge, companionship, and entertainment that the Internet offers.

America Online provides one of the easiest ways to become part of the cyberworld, and this book will be your guide to the riches of AOL and the Internet. So, welcome aboard to all you cyber-rookies. We'll turn you into professional players in no time at all.

What's Inside

This book is filled with step-by-step instructions and illustrations to help you master AOL and the Internet. To avoid geek-speak and to make everything easy to understand, I have employed my own personal *Compu-Kiss* technique: I explain the computer world, but I always *Keep It Short and Simple*.

At the beginning of this book, you will find a Jump Start guide. If you are new to the computer, this is where you will want to start your surfing experience. It provides details on using a mouse and moving around in the Windows or Macintosh operating systems.

If you are a fairly seasoned computer user, you can skip the Jump Start and dive right into the first section, Part I, which will explain how online communications work. This section will gently guide you to the pleasures of communicating through e-mail, chatting, newsgroups, message boards, Instant Messenger, and Buddy Lists.

Part II will teach you how to get around AOL and the Internet and will, above all else, explain how to find and organize everything so that your surfing experience will be a pleasant one.

After you learn how to communicate and navigate, you will be ready to start your exploration of the riches of AOL and the Internet in Part III. Do you like to travel? Garden? Cook? Whatever your passion, we have a section for you. Whether you are thinking of retiring, considering using the Internet to track your investments, or just trying to learn more about the computer, you'll find it all here. This book will be your guide to learning about everything from how to keep healthy to how to use AOL and the Internet to research any topic.

To take advantage of the many wonders of AOL and the Internet, you also need to know how to download files and work with graphics and photo-graphs, so we have included Part IV, which will help you do just that. And, who couldn't use a few shortcuts and helpful hints? Don't miss this section, where you can learn some "tricks of the trade" to make your computing life easier.

Conventions

To make this book easier to navigate, we use several different icons to indicate various points of interest that you won't want to miss:

Tip icons call your attention to shortcuts, useful resources, and smarter ways to work

Note icons point out a fact or other short piece of information worthy of further mention.

Caution icons advise you of something *not* to do.

Definition icons define a new term that is used in the text.

Find It Online icons list AOL keywords and Internet addresses.

Feedback

I welcome your comments, questions, and feedback on this book. Contact me, Sandy Berger, at `compukiss@aol.com` or in care of IDG Books Worldwide.

Acknowledgments

Thanks to my husband, Dave, whose unfailing support and encouragement has made everything in my life possible and who has kept things running smoothly both at home and at the office while I took time out to write this book.

Special thanks to Martha Tattersall for her energetic assistance when her part-time job suddenly turned into a 50-hour-a-week job.

Thanks to America Online and IDG Books Worldwide who embraced my vision for this book and helped to make it a reality.

Also, thanks to the supportive team at Computer Living Corp., who kept all the pots simmering while this book was on the front burner.

Contents at a Glance

Contents

Part IV: Shortcuts and Helpful Hints   353

Jump Start

Do you already know how to move around in windows? Do you feel comfortable with toolbars, icons, and keywords? If you do, just skip this section and move right into Chapter 1.

Don't know much about computers? Want to figure out what it's all about? Want to learn how to get around? Ready for a Jump Start? You've come to the right place. I'll explain a few of the basics, and we'll be on our way.

Let's get started.

Mousing Around

A computer *mouse* controls the pointer on the computer screen. The first mouse was a rectangular wooden box. The wire leading from the mouse to the computer gave the little tool its resemblance to the animal that it is named after. You might have chased a few live rodents in your day, but now you must conquer this little computer rodent.

Even if you have never used a mouse before, don't worry: it's easy. Rest your hand on the mouse. Your thumb should be resting on the mouse's side, with your index and middle fingers resting on top of the mouse buttons (or *button,* if you are using a Mac). Your two outside fingers should rest on the side of the mouse opposite the side where your thumb rests. Use your thumb and two outside fingers to move the mouse around without lifting it up. Use your index and middle fingers to press the mouse buttons.

Tip

When working on the computer, each skill builds on the previous one, and each new skill that you acquire will be useful in other programs, as well. So, keep practicing, and soon you'll be an expert!

Definition

A *mouse* is a pointing device connected to your computer by a cable that is used to control an on-screen cursor. A typical computer mouse is a flat-bottomed device with a button (or two or three) on the top and a rollerball on the bottom.

Move the mouse around without picking it up, and you will see the pointer move on the screen. If you run out of room on your desk or mouse pad when using your mouse, simply pick it up and move it where there is more room. The pointer doesn't move when you pick up the mouse.

Four basic types of mouse functions exist for PC users:

- ▶ **Click:** To press and release the left mouse button. (Mac users will find that their mouse has only one button, so pressing and releasing that button is "clicking the mouse.")
- ▶ **Double-click:** To press and release the left mouse button twice in quick succession. (Mac users quickly click the only mouse button twice.)
- ▶ **Right-click:** To press and release the right mouse button. (Mac users simulate the right-click function by holding down the Option key on the keyboard and clicking their mouse button.)
- ▶ **Drag:** To position the mouse pointer over an object on your screen and then press and hold down the left mouse button. While holding down the button, move the mouse to where you want to place the object and then release the button. (This technique is often called "clicking and dragging" or simply "click and drag.")

PC users may find that they have a mouse with three buttons. Some also have a wheel between the buttons. The other button and the wheel may be used to navigate in certain programs. They are additional features and are not needed for ordinary mouse movements.

Customizing Your Mouse

If you are left-handed, you may be more comfortable keeping your mouse on the left side of the keyboard and using your left hand to control it. You can also switch the mouse buttons to accommodate the left hand. Click the Start button on the main Windows screen. Choose Settings, and then choose Control Panel. Double-click the mouse icon. Then, click the word Left-handed and click Apply on the bottom of the screen (see Figure JS-1). The functions of the two mouse buttons will now be reversed:

Definition

A *cursor* or *pointer* is a symbol, usually a solid horizontal or vertical blinking line or an arrow, that signifies on the screen where the next entry will occur.

Tip

If you are having trouble double-clicking, you are probably moving the mouse slightly between the clicks. The mouse must remain stationary between mouse clicks.

Left-handed Button

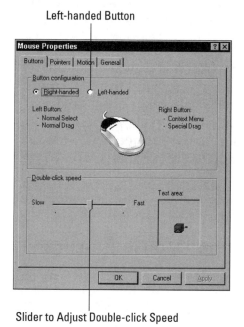

Slider to Adjust Double-click Speed

Figure JS-1. "Lefties" can reverse the functions of the two mouse buttons to accommodate their left hand.

The shape of a mouse may limit its use to only right-handed people, so when you purchase your computer, make sure that you get a mouse that can be used with either hand.

Definition

An *icon* is a small picture
that represents a program,
file, or command in your
computer system. Moving
the cursor or pointer over
the icon and pressing a
button or key activates
the icon.

If you are having trouble double-clicking the mouse,
follow the preceding instructions, but instead of
changing the button configuration, look at the bottom of the screen just shown, where you will see a
Double-click speed box. Place your cursor on the
slider and drag it to the right to slow down the
speed of the double-click action. Then, double-click
the jack-in-the-box icon in the test area to see
whether the speed of the double-click feels right to
you. You can continue to adjust the slider and to test
until you are happy with the results. When you are
finished, click Apply to make the changes permanent. (Depending on the type of mouse your computer is using, your screen may be slightly different.)

Don't let arthritis, Parkinson's disease, or other fin-
ger-dexterity problems keep you away from the
computer. If you or a loved one has trouble using a
mouse, be sure to investigate other input devices,
such as large trackballs, touch pads, pointer sticks,
foot pedals, and other mouse-replacement devices
that are specially made to enable almost everyone
to use a computer.

Let's Play Solitaire: Mouse Practice for PC Users

Want to practice your mouse skills? Windows comes
with an excellent tool — the game of Solitaire.

To practice your mouse-maneuvering skills, start
your computer and, when the Windows screen
appears, click your mouse on the Start button, located on the lower-left side of the screen. A menu
of choices pops up. This type of menu is generally
called a *drop-down box*; however, in this case, it
goes *up*. (Just skip over this inconsistency; it's too

early in the game to get upset about details.) From the list you see on the screen, choose Programs. Another menu of choices will appear. Choose Accessories from that menu, and another will appear. Choose Games and then Solitaire from the next two lists that appear.

A preset game appears in the window (see Figure JS-2). To start playing, click once on the deck of cards. If you see a move, click the card once and use the drag technique to move the card to its proper position. If you see an ace, double-click it to move it into position. Repeat this until you can't go any further. Then, click the word Game. A drop-down box will appear. Choose Deal to start a new game. Or, you can choose Deck to change the look of the cards. If you need help, click the word Help and choose Help Topics. After you play a few games, you will be a proficient "mouser" and will also understand more about how Windows works.

Note

By the way, when you get all 52 cards up to the top, the game puts on a great little display. It may be worth your while to play until you win!

Figure JS-2. Solitaire is preset and ready to challenge you; to start, click once on the deck of cards.

Mouse Skills: Mouse Practice for Mac Users

Unfortunately, the Mac doesn't have a Solitaire game; however, you can still practice your mouse skills and become more comfortable with the computer by clicking your mouse on the word Help at the top of the computer screen. Choose Tutorial from the drop-down box and then click the button that says Mouse Skills (see Figure JS-3). You will be escorted through a tutorial that will enable you to become proficient with the mouse.

Figure JS-3. Mac users can work on becoming proficient with the mouse by using the Mouse Skills portion of their tutorial.

Working with Windows (for Mac Users, Too)

Whether you are working on a PC or a Mac, much of the information on your computer screen will appear in a rectangular box called a *window*. You can have several windows open at the same time.

PC Users

In the upper-right corner of each window, you will see three small icons (see Figure JS-4):

Definition

- ▶ Clicking the button on the left minimizes the window or makes it smaller. When you click this button, the window folds up and becomes a rectangle on the task bar at the bottom of your screen.

- ▶ Clicking the button in the center adjusts the size of any window. If the window is full size, clicking this button reduces it to cover only part of your screen. Clicking the center button again restores the window to its full size. (Note that the icon on the button changes depending on whether the window is partial or full size.)

- ▶ Clicking the button on the right, labeled X, closes the window.

A *window*, in computer-speak, is a portion of the screen in which a document or a message appears. In a graphical user interface (GUI), everything appears within its own window. You can open and close, resize, and hide windows.

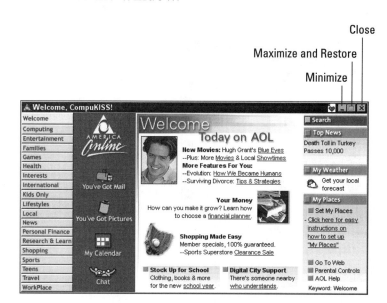

Figure JS-4. The minimize, maximize, and close buttons are found in the upper-right corner of each window.

Mac Users

Click your mouse on a blank area inside of any window. On the top of each window, you will see three small icons (see Figure JS-5):

▶ Clicking the button on the left side of the window closes the window.

▶ Clicking the left button on the right side of the window, called the *zoom button,* changes the size of the window. The window zooms either open or closed, depending on whether it's already open or closed.

▶ Clicking the button on the far right, called the *collapse box,* rolls up the window like a window shade. The title bar of that window will still be visible, and you can move it around by dragging it.

Tip

It is a good idea to close unwanted windows on your screen. This maximizes your screen space and prevents the screen from becoming overly cluttered and hard to navigate. Windows users click the X in the upper-right corner of the title bar to close the window; Mac users click the little box in the upper-left corner of the title bar.

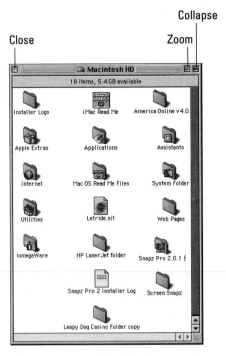

Figure JS-5. Mac users will find three small icons on the top of each window that can be used to close and change the size of their screens.

Look for the Keywords

You can get anywhere on America Online just by pointing and clicking with the mouse — but it's often quicker to get around by using a keyword.

Here's how to use keywords: Click in the text box just to the right of the Find button on your AOL Navigation bar. (You can't miss it — it's the box that says "Type Keyword or Web Address here and click Go." When you click it, that whole phrase is highlighted.) Simply type the keyword you want, and then click the Go button at the right end of the text box. And you're off!

The keyword for an AOL area generally is listed in the bottom-right corner of the area's main screen. The Find tool will also help you find places to explore — but more about that shortly. You can also get a complete listing of all AOL keywords at the Keyword: **Keyword**.

For those of you who like to use the keyboard, just press the key marked Ctrl and hold it down while you press the K key. (For Mac users, hold down the Apple key and press K.) When you do this, a small box in which you can type the keyword pops up on the screen.

Definition

A *keyword* is a shortcut that AOL uses to take you instantly to a specific area of information.

Now, we are almost ready to start our first project, but first you need to know a little about how to use AOL and the Internet.

What Surfing the Web Is All About

One of the key technologies behind Web surfing is something called *hyperlinks.* Both America Online

Definition

A *hyperlink* is a picture, icon, or portion of text within a Web site that you can click with your mouse to take you to another portion of the Web site or to another Web site altogether.

and the Internet use these amazing shortcuts. A hyperlink is a picture, icon, or portion of text within a Web site that you can click with your mouse to take you to another portion of the Web site or to another Web site altogether. To access a hyperlink, click your mouse once over the link. After you click, the area connected to that link will appear.

How do you know where the hyperlinks are located on a Web page? Your pointer (or cursor) will change from an arrow to a little hand when it passes over a hyperlink. A hyperlink can be any text, including words, sentences, or numbers. Most hyperlink text is underlined and appears in blue. However, text may be a hyperlink even if it is not underlined in blue. To find out, simply place your pointer over the words. If the pointer turns into a hand, that item is a hyperlink.

A picture or icon can also be a hyperlink. After a while, you will get a feeling for what may or may not be a hyperlink. In the meantime, you can click everything you see. If what you click is not a hyper-link, nothing will happen. No harm done.

Starting Your Online Adventure

After you install America Online by following the instructions that are on the AOL disk or CD-ROM, you are ready to start your online adventure. Just double-click the AOL icon on your computer screen. If you have not yet set up your AOL account, the instructions on the computer screen will walk you through the setup procedure. If you need any help, don't be afraid to call AOL's toll-free number. America Online is used to dealing with cyber-rookies, so don't worry about asking questions.

When you sign up for AOL service, you will create a screen name and a password. Be sure to write these down and keep them in a safe place. You will need them to access your America Online account.

When you double-click the America Online icon, the AOL Sign On screen will appear (see Figure JS-6). Check to make sure that your screen name appears in the box that says Select Screen Name. If your screen name does not appear, click the down arrow next to the Select Screen Name box, and choose your screen name from the list by clicking it with your mouse. If you are working at a different computer than the one on which you signed up for your account, you may have to choose Guest from the list.

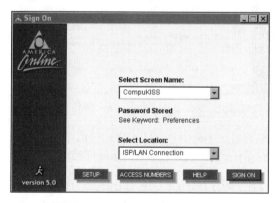

Figure JS-6. When you double-click the America Online icon, the Sign On screen appears with your screen name in the Select Screen Name field.

After your screen name appears in the box, click the button that says Sign On. Type your password when prompted. If this is your first time on AOL, you will hear the soon-to-be-familiar words "You've Got Mail." Don't be afraid to look around and check out a few things, if you like, but you don't have to worry about the mail. I'll explain how to retrieve it in Chapter 1. In the meantime, to learn more about how everything works, just read on.

Toolbars, Title Bars, and Menu Bars

You are now ready to learn about America Online's main screen, its Welcome screen, which gives you icons and shortcuts to help you move around in AOL.

A Welcome screen appears when you start AOL (see Figure JS-7).

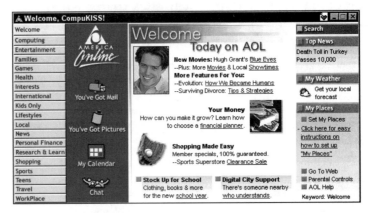

Figure JS-7. The Welcome screen appears when you start AOL.

Look at the top of the page on the Welcome screen and you will see four function bars (see Figure JS-8):

- ▸ **Title bar:** The top bar of the window that constantly displays the name of the current window.

- ▸ **Menu bar:** The second bar, offering the following functions: File, Edit, Window, Sign Off, and the ever-popular Help.

- ▸ **Toolbar:** The third bar, which has a row of colorful icons that are handy "getting around" tools.

- ▸ **Navigation bar:** The bottom bar, containing the browser buttons, Keyword button, address box, Go button, and Search button.

Navigation Bar

Title bar   Menu bar   Toolbar

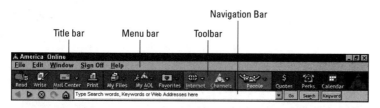

Figure JS-8. AOL divides its function bars into four areas: title bar, menu bar, toolbar, and Navigation bar.

Practice Moving Windows Around

You can move a window around by clicking any blank area of the title bar, as shown in Figure JS-9, and dragging the window to a new location. Vertical movement on your computer screen is accomplished by using either the up and down arrows or the drag box on the scroll bar, found on the right side of your screen (see the following sidebar, "Scroll Bars"). Try it and see.

Menu Bar Shortcuts

An underlined letter in a name on the menu bar represents a keyboard shortcut for that item. Holding down the Alt key while pressing the underlined letter will produce the same result as clicking the word with your mouse.

For example:

<u>F</u>ile = Alt + f

<u>E</u>dit = Alt + e

<u>W</u>indow = Alt + w

<u>S</u>ign Off = Alt + s

<u>H</u>elp = Alt + h

After you press one of these keys, a vertical list of choices, called a *drop-down menu,* appears. Press the key of the underlined letter or click the mouse on the word to choose one of these menu options.

Note

The use of keyboard shortcuts and underlined letters is not prevalent in Mac software, and is used in only a smattering of Mac programs.

Jump Start

As each new window opens, the previous window that was on the screen may still be visible. This can be helpful. If you want to jump from one window to another, you simply click your mouse inside the window that you want to see and it pops up on top of the other open windows.

To delete text, click your mouse at the beginning of the text that you want to remove, and drag the mouse to highlight it. Then, press the key marked Del or Delete on your keyboard.

Scroll Bar or Drag Box

Up Arrow

Down Arrow

Figure JS-9. Click any blank area of the title bar and drag the window to a new location. Vertical movement on your computer screen is accomplished by using either the up and down arrows or the drag box.

Send a Greeting Card

Let's put this high-tech toy to use and get some practice surfing and scrolling at the same time. Our project today will be to send an e-mail greeting card. After you master this simple task, you will be able to send your children or grandchildren birthday cards or brighten the day of any loved one with a spontaneous greeting that will be delivered almost instantly. Are you ready to send your first online greeting card? To do so, follow these steps:

1. Start your computer.
2. Double-click the America Online icon.

Scroll Bars

Sometimes, the entire window does not fit on your computer screen. If that is the case, you will see a scroll bar on the right side of your screen (see also Figure JS-9). The scroll bar is a vertical bar with arrows on either end, and a moveable small box in between. Click the box and drag it down to see the bottom of the screen. You can drag the box on the scroll bar up or down at any time. (Mac users will find both up and down arrows at the bottom of their scroll bar.) To accomplish the same task, you can click the up and down arrows on the top or bottom of the scroll bar, to move up or down one line at a time. However, if you are scrolling up or down several screens, the box is a much faster way of moving than using the up and down arrows. If a window is too wide to be fully visible, you may also see a scroll bar on the bottom of the screen that enables you to scroll both from right to left and from left to right.

3. Click the button on the Navigation bar that says Keyword.

4. When the pop-up box appears, type the Keyword: **American Greetings**.

5. Click the word Go (or press the Enter key on your keyboard).

6. The American Greetings Online Greeting window appears.

7. At the window that says American Greetings Online Greetings on the title bar, click the featured Free Greeting card, shown in Figure JS-10, which takes you to the screen in which you can fill in the form to send the greeting card.

Featured Free Greeting Card Button

Tip

AOL screen names, also used as e-mail addresses, are neither case-sensitive nor space-sensitive.

Definition

Field is a space allocated for a certain type of information.

Figure JS-10. American Greetings Online Greetings offers a free greeting card to send online to your friends or family.

8. Click your mouse in the box to fill in the screen name or e-mail address. If you don't have anyone's screen name or e-mail address handy, then send me a card. Type in my screen name, **CompuKISS**. (My screen name is my trademark and it stands for The Computer World — Keeping It Short and Simple.)

9. Click your mouse in the next empty box, which is the e-mail subject box.

10. Type a subject for the e-mail card.

11. Click your mouse inside the last box and type a personal message, if you like.

12. Click the Send button.

Congratulations, you have just completed your first e-mail greeting card!

Let's Get Started

Now you know how to play Solitaire and send greeting cards! But, unless your expectations for the powerful technology of your computer and the Internet are very low, you probably have the suspicion that you should be able to do much more. As a matter of fact, the basic skills of harnessing your computer's capabilities through its mouse and windows are essential to nearly everything else you'll be doing with this electronic tool.

Get ready to explore some of those possibilities with the rest of this book. I've tried to organize it in a way that will be clear and useful to most users, and — as we've seen — what you learn in one area of computing is likely to help you in another. So, work on the basics, but feel free to jump ahead to other chapters of interest, as you wish.

PART

I

ONLINE COMMUNICATION

CHAPTER

1

COMMUNICATING THROUGH E-MAIL

Quick Look

▶ **AOL Mail Extras**   **page 34**

You can easily jazz up the main message of an AOL e-mail message with some
creative formatting. AOL Mail Extras, accessed in version 5.0 by clicking the
Mail Extras button on the AOL toolbar (click Mail Central and select Mail
Extras from the pull-down menu if you are using version 4.0) enables you to
add photos, smileys, colors, style, and hyperlinks to your e-mail. Ever thought
about sending a picture of your grandchild to other members of your family
via e-mail? Or quickly passing along an interesting news article or link to a
great Web site? You can also use this button to send online greeting cards
and create your own personalized stationery.

▶ **E-Mail Emoticons**   **page 39**

E-mail is usually short and to the point, so including any emotional sentiment
in e-mail messages can be difficult. However, a new way to denote emotions
has also developed that is easy and fun to use. Many e-mail users include small
symbols called *emoticons* in their messages. The most common emoticon is a
smiley :-). This indicates a happy state. If you turn your head to the left while
you view the smiley, you will see why.

▶ **E-Mail on the Road**   **page 42**

With AOL, you can access your e-mail account even if you are away from your
own computer. For example, when visiting a friend who has AOL installed
on her computer, just sign in as a guest at the Welcome screen to check your
e-mail. You can also access your mail from any computer that has Internet
access, even if it doesn't have AOL installed. Just log on to the Internet, go
to www.aol.com, and choose AOL NetMail. Another method would be to
type the address http://netmail.web.aol.com/. Fill in your screen name
and password, and you would then be able to access your mail.

▶ **Automatic AOL**   **page 49**

Automatic AOL is a nifty feature that enables your computer to access AOL,
send unsent mail, and get all of your new mail without requiring you to do
anything, other than leave your computer on. With Automatic AOL you can
be sure to get important e-mail messages as soon as they arrive without having
to log on and off of AOL. Automatic AOL is easy to set up from the Mail Center
icon on the AOL toolbar. Just click Mail Center, select Set up Automatic AOL,
and follow the instructions on the screen.

Chapter 1

Communicating Through E-Mail

Understanding How E-Mail Works

One of the biggest attractions about owning a computer is the ability to send and receive e-mail. E-mail is quickly becoming a standard method of communication because it's fast, fun, easy, and inexpensive.

E-mail travels from one computer to another until it reaches its destination. In most cases, e-mail moves efficiently, arriving within minutes. E-mail that is sent between AOL users is transmitted using only AOL computers and is delivered especially quickly. Only in unusual circumstances does e-mail take more than a few minutes to be delivered.

1

Communicating Through E-Mail

America Online handles nearly one half of the Internet's e-mail traffic and makes e-mail easy to use. An e-mail account is part of your AOL subscription. No extra cost is involved no matter how many messages you send or receive. What a bargain! The postal system is finding e-mail business to be some stiff competition.

To use AOL's e-mail, you must first start your computer and sign on to AOL. You sign on to AOL using the screen name and password that you chose when you first set up AOL. Every AOL account includes the use of up to seven screen names. Each of these screen names has a separate mailbox, so each member of your family can have his or her own screen name and private e-mail mailbox.

Choosing a Screen Name

Your AOL screen name is your unique identifier. It is wise to take your time when choosing a name. Your first selection may already be in use by someone else, so before you begin, make a list of ten or twenty names that you would like. Try to make your screen name easy to identify and easy to remember. You may get a faster response to an e-mail if the recipient recognizes who you are by your screen name, so it is always smart to try to link your screen name to something about yourself. A cute and clever name may seem irresistible, but may not be appropriate for all the different circumstances you may experience using e-mail in the future.

Definition

E-mail is short for *electronic mail*. E-mail uses online computers and communication networks to transmit messages and attached files electronically across the entire world.

Definition

Snail mail is the slang term e-mailers use for the regular postal mail.

Cross-Reference

See Chapter 4 for more about AOL's Welcome screen, the first screen you see after signing on to AOL.

Note

Every AOL account includes the use of up to seven screen names.

Definition

A *screen name* is a unique label that identifies you when you are connected to AOL.

The Basics of E-Mail

Definition

Cyberworld (also called *cyberspace*) is a reference to the electronic universe of the Internet.

The basic e-mail functions for Macintosh and Windows operating systems are similar, but not identical. I have noted where obvious differences exist. Most of the figures and descriptions in this book are based on the Windows operating system. Mac users please note that your screens may look slightly different than my descriptions or the figures shown.

You've Got Mail

When you log on to AOL and the Welcome screen appears, you may hear the familiar, "You've got mail!" notification. Seeing and hearing this message is truly exciting. Now you are really a part of the cyberworld!

Several ways exist to determine whether you have mail waiting in your e-mail box:

▶ You will hear the computer say, "You've got mail!" when you sign on to AOL. (If you don't hear this, make sure that your speakers are turned on.)

▶ The mailbox on the Welcome screen has its red flag up and mail is sticking out of the box. Under the mailbox, instead of Mail Center, you now see You've Got Mail, as shown in Figure 1-1.

▶ The mailbox appears with mail in it on the left side of the toolbar at the top of the screen, as shown in Figure 1-2.

▶ If you are using a Mac, a mailbox flashes in the upper-right corner of your screen. This mailbox will flash on and off even if you are working in another program — a great feature for Mac users that is not available to PC users.

Red Flag and Mail in Box

Figure 1-1. The red flag flying and the mail peeking out of the mailbox is especially exciting for new AOL members. This means that you have mail.

Mail Delivery Alert

Figure 1-2. A second mail delivery alert (red flag flying and mail peeking out of the box) appears at the top left of your screen on the toolbar at the same time a letter appears in the mailbox on the Welcome screen.

All new members have mail from AOL waiting for them the very first time they log on to AOL after setting up their screen name and password. You can see your mail by opening your e-mail box in any of the following ways:

> ▶ Click the mailbox picture on your Welcome screen (refer to Figure 1-1).
>
> ▶ Click the mailbox button on the left side of the toolbar (refer to Figure 1-2).
>
> ▶ Click the Mail Center button on the toolbar and select Read Mail from the drop-down menu.

Definition

The *toolbar* is the row of colorful pictures (called *icons*) at the top of the AOL screen. These icons are handy "getting around" tools. Each icon is a shortcut to an AOL feature or area.

Cross-Reference

Refer to the Jump Start for more information on navigating through AOL's toolbars, title bars, and menu bars.

Definition

A *keyboard shortcut* is a key combination that is pressed in lieu of clicking buttons and menu choices with the mouse. Using a keyboard shortcut involves pressing and holding down two keys at the same time. On a PC, the keys most often used are the Ctrl key, the Alt key, and the Windows key, which has the Microsoft Windows design on it. A Mac shortcut usually involves using the keys marked Command or Control, or the key with the Apple (or cloverleaf) on it. All of these keys are located near the spacebar.

▶ Simultaneously press and hold down the Ctrl key and the R key. (Mac users should press the Command key and the R key.) This is a *keyboard shortcut*, as explained in the Definition in the margin.

Reading E-Mail

When your e-mail box opens, you will see three tabs: New Mail, Old Mail, and Sent Mail. The mailbox will open with the New Mail page visible on the screen (see Figure 1-3). On this screen, you will see one line for each piece of mail in your box. The sealed yellow envelope at the beginning of the line indicates that the mail has not yet been opened. If the envelope contains a small snapshot (for Windows users) or a flash bulb (for Mac users), it means that the e-mail has an embedded photo or graphic. If the envelope has a small disk on it, it means that a file is attached. (We'll talk more about attachments later in this chapter.) Next to the envelope, you will see the date the message was originally transmitted (adjusted for your local time zone), the address of the sender, and the subject of the e-mail.

The name of the sender will give you the screen name of the person who sent the mail, if that person is using AOL. If your mail comes from someone on the Internet, you will see the sender's e-mail address. The main difference between the two types of addresses is that an Internet address will have an @ sign in the name.

Several ways exist to open a piece of e-mail. The easiest way is to double-click the item that you want to read. Or, you can select or highlight the item by clicking it and then clicking the Read button at the bottom of the window.

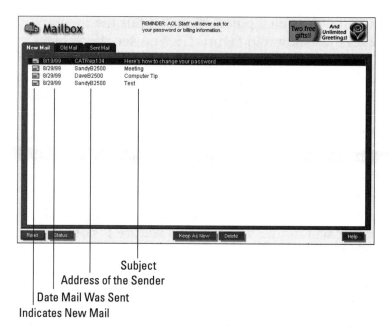

Subject
Address of the Sender
Date Mail Was Sent
Indicates New Mail

Note

On AOL everyone has both a screen name and an Internet address. Your Internet address is your screen name with *@aol* after it. For instance, my screen name is Compukiss and my Internet address is compukiss@aol.com. You will note that screen names can have capital letters in them, but Internet addresses are generally written all in lower case letters.

Figure 1-3. Your e-mail box opens with the New Mail page visible. You can see one line for each piece of e-mail in your box.

Maximize Button

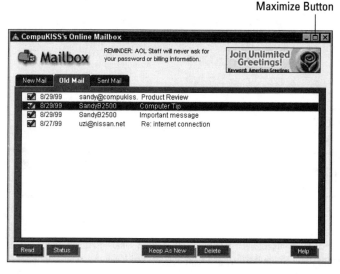

Tip

To increase the size of your mailbox on the screen, use the maximize button on the right side of the title bar, or double-click anywhere on the empty part of the title bar. Your mailbox will fill the screen, making it much easier to read (see Figure 1-4). Click the button again to bring the mailbox back to its original size.

Figure 1-4. The maximize button on the right side of the title bar increases your mailbox to fill the screen, making it much easier to read.

Cross-Reference

More information on maximizing and minimizing the screen can be found in the Jump Start section at the beginning of this book.

When you open a piece of mail, it fills the mailbox screen, as shown in Figure 1-5. You see the Subject, Date, From, and To information for that message, as well as the message itself. Use the scroll bar (refer to the Jump Start for instructions on how to use scroll bars) to see the bottom half of the message if it is not shown on your screen.

Windows users can use the arrow-shaped Prev and Next buttons to read the rest of the mail one e-mail at a time (see Figure 1-5). If you have only one piece of mail, the Prev and Next buttons will be grayed out or will not be visible. (This feature is not available on the Mac.)

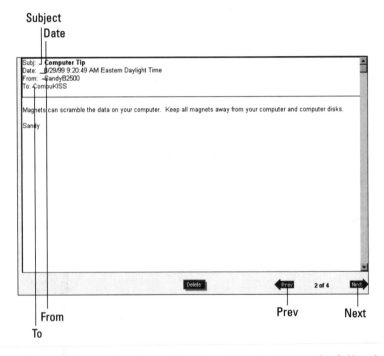

Figure 1-5. An open piece of e-mail shows the Subject, Date, From, and To fields and the message itself. Notice the Prev and Next buttons, which will show you other pieces of received e-mail.

You can also close each piece of mail by using the X button on the title bar. After you read each piece of mail, the envelope icon for that piece of mail will have a red check mark on it. The next time you open your mailbox, the mail you have read previously will be under the Old Mail tab. If you want to keep an item in your New Mail box, after you have read it, simply click the Keep As New button on the bottom of the page (refer to Figure 1-4). It is best to keep your New Mail box as clean as possible, so that you can easily identify the new mail when it arrives. However, sometimes you'll want to keep a piece of mail in your New Mail box so that you'll be reminded to take action on it.

Understanding Headers

A *header* is a section of the e-mail that contains information about the mail, such as the subject of the e-mail message, the sender, the recipient, and so on. AOL has its own header, which you will see at the top of the screen when you receive an e-mail (see Figure 1-6).

Header

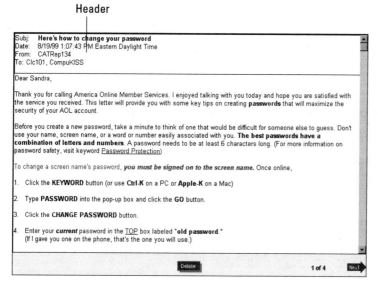

Figure 1-6. The AOL header is at the top of the screen on received e-mail.

In most everyday e-mail situations, you won't have to understand or concern yourself with any of this information, but this information can be valuable if a problem occurs with some mail. For those of you who are the inquisitive type, go ahead and look at the contents of a header.

If you receive mail from the Internet, you will see that it contains a different type of header section. As if the computer world isn't confusing enough, this header section will be at the bottom of your AOL mail rather than at the top, where you might expect a header to be (see Figure 1-7). This header contains information about how and when the e-mail was transmitted over the Internet. It tracks the journey of the e-mail from computer to computer.

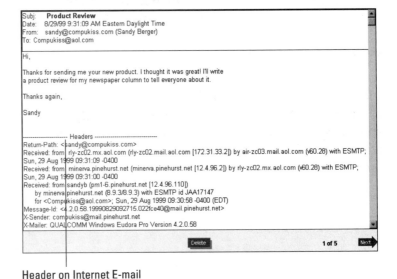

Header on Internet E-mail

Figure 1-7. The header section of an e-mail from the Internet is located at the bottom of the page.

Deleting Mail

Any time a piece of mail is highlighted or open, you can click the Delete button at the bottom of the screen to delete that piece of mail. Deleting the mail will remove it completely, and you will not be able to get it back.

Forwarding Mail

If you receive a piece of e-mail that you would like to forward to another person, just open that piece of mail and click the Forward button. The screen that opens will have the subject and a copy of the original message already filled in. Just fill in the address of the person, add your comments, and click Send Now. The e-mail will be automatically forwarded.

Tip

Every piece of e-mail that you send automatically includes your return e-mail address.

Basic Features of AOL E-Mail

▶ AOL pledges that your e-mail content is kept totally private.

▶ Most mail between AOL members does not use the Internet; it is more like interoffice mail that uses only AOL computers.

▶ Your AOL service includes unlimited use of e-mail at no extra charge.

▶ When you send mail to addresses outside of AOL, the message sent is automatically converted to Internet mailing standards.

Writing E-Mail

After you become accustomed to writing e-mail, you will find that using it is quicker and easier than most other types of correspondence. No playing telephone tag, no stamps, and no bother. No wonder e-mail has become so popular. This section outlines the few basic things that you should know about writing e-mail.

Addressing Your Mail

What you put in the subject header of your e-mail messages will either entice your recipients to read your messages or deter them from doing so. Be sure your subject is clear, meaningful, and indicative of the contents of the e-mail.

To write an e-mail message, click the Write Mail icon on the toolbar. A blank e-mail form will appear on the screen. Fill in the Send To box by typing in the address of your intended recipient. If that person is also using AOL, you need only to fill in his or her screen name. If the person you are writing to is not on AOL, you must fill in his or her Internet address.

You can keep all of your contacts and their online addresses in the your address book. This will allow you to send mail to frequently used addresses without having to retype the address each time. To add a contact to your address book, simply click on the address book icon, which is seen on the right side of the screen when you start to write an e-mail message. When the address book window pops up, click New Person and fill in your contact's name and screen name or Internet address. After you have entered names and addresses into your address book, you can click on the address book icon, highlight the name of the person you want to write to and click on Sent To.

Inserting the Subject

The *subject* is an important part of any e-mail. The recipient will look at the subject line of the e-mail message before he or she sees what you have said in the body of the message. The subject will either entice the receiver to read the e-mail or draw his or her finger to the Delete button. Be sure that your subject is meaningful and indicative of the contents of the e-mail. Your subject should also be as short and clear as possible.

Writing the Main Message

After you enter the subject, press the Tab key
or position the cursor over the large box and click
your mouse. You can now type the main text of
your message. If you need a dictionary or thesaurus
to help you write your text, just click the word Edit
at the top of the screen and choose the appropriate
tool from the pull-down menu.

Just above the main box in the Write Mail screen, you
will see a small toolbar displaying several different
icons (see Figure 1-8). Each of these icons controls
some attribute of the text in your e-mail message.
Click any of these icons and then start typing to see
its effect. Another method is to type your text first
and then highlight any or all of it by clicking your
mouse at a chosen point and dragging it across any
portion of the main message. After you highlight
some text, you can click the various icons to see
the effect that they have on the highlighted text.
You can use these icons to change the color, size,
alignment, and style of the text.

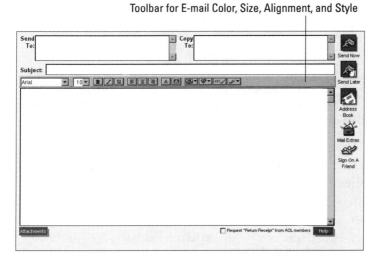

Figure 1-8. The toolbar just above the main box in the Write Mail screen contains several
different icons that let you change the color, size, alignment, and style of the text.

This fancy formatting that you do will be seen by any other AOL member who receives your e-mail. However, it may or may not be sent to a non-AOL member/Internet recipient, depending on his or her software.

When you click the Write button on the AOL toolbar and a blank e-mail template appears, you will also see a button on the right side of your screen marked Mail Extras. By clicking this button, you can add photos, smileys, colors, style, and *hyperlink*s to your e-mail. You can also use this button to send online greeting cards and create your own personalized stationery (see Figure 1-9).

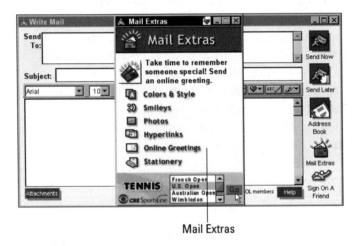

Mail Extras

Figure 1-9. The Mail Extras screen offers you the chance to add photos, smileys, colors, style, and hyperlinks to your e-mail, as well as send online greeting cards and create personalized stationary.

AOL's e-mail feature is quite powerful. Click File on the top of the screen and choose Open Picture Gallery to insert any graphic or photo or even a complete picture gallery into your e-mail. If you have a scanner or digital camera, you can click Edit and then choose Capture Picture to easily insert a picture into your e-mail.

To use the Picture Gallery to send pictures in e-mail, follow these steps:

1. Click Open Picture Gallery from the File menu.
2. Navigate to a folder on your disk that contains image files.
3. Click Open Gallery. The Picture Gallery window will appear, with the first six images in the folder.
4. If you have more than six image files in the folder, click the right arrow to move to the next set of six images.
5. Click the picture you want to use.
6. Click Insert in E-mail.

 **Cross-Reference**

For more information on using the red heart or Favorites features, see Chapter 5.

Adding a Hyperlink to E-mail Messages

If you have found a new auction site that your sister would just love, or an investment site that your brother would be interested in, you can easily insert a hyperlink to that site into an e-mail message to them. When they receive your message, they can simply click on your hyperlink and be immediately transported to the site you recommended.

There are several ways to do this, but one of the easiest is to navigate to the Web site that you want to recommend. Click the red heart on the title bar of that Web site. When the pop up window appears choose Insert in Mail. The Write Mail box will appear with a hyperlink already inserted. You can then address the e-mail, write a message, and send it on its way.

Tip

Most computer programs have an Undo feature. In AOL, Undo is found under the Edit menu. If you make a mistake, choose Edit from the menu bar at the top of the screen and choose Undo from the drop-down menu. Your last action will be undone.

Checking It Twice

After you write your e-mail message, you may want to reread it to make sure that it doesn't contain mistakes.

First, reconfirm that you really want to convey the message that you wrote. Don't ever write an e-mail when you are very angry or upset. After you click the Send button, you can't always get your mail back. It may be permanent, so be certain that your message is appropriate.

Spelling Check

AOL comes to your aid with a built-in spelling checker for your e-mail. Just click the Spell Check button, as shown in Figure 1-10, to have your spelling checked for errors. The spelling checker pops up a box and highlights words that it suspects may be misspelled. Suggestions are also offered for the correct spelling.

To accept the spelling checker's correction, highlight the correct spelling and click Replace. Or, type your own correction into the Replace With box. Other options include Skip, which leaves the word as you have spelled it, and Learn (Windows) or Add (Mac), which adds the word to the custom spelling dictionary so that it will not be brought up as a misspelling in the future. This is helpful for proper names that you use often.

It's a good idea to work with the spelling checker a little if you have never tried it before. AOL's spelling checker is a powerful tool that can make your e-mail look and read better.

Remember that e-mail is a reflection of you. You want to look your best, so check your punctuation and capitalization. Typing in all uppercase letters is considered SHOUTING in the e-mail world. Typing in all lowercase letters can be faster for a nontypist, but it will make you look unprofessional.

1

Spell checker

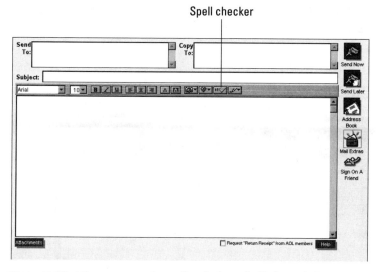

Figure 1-10. AOL equips you with a spelling checker to highlight words that it suspects may be misspelled and to offer suggestions for the correct spelling.

Tip

AOL screen names, also used as e-mail addresses, are neither case-sensitive nor space-sensitive. However, Internet e-mail addresses are more particular. Generally, Internet addresses are written in all lowercase letters with no spaces. The rule to remember is that you should always type the Internet address *exactly* as it was given to you.

Sending E-Mail on Its Way

Before you send your e-mail, double-check the address to make sure that it is correct. After you double-check your e-mail, you send it on its way by clicking the Send Now button. It's quick and it's easy.

Determining Whether Your E-Mail Was Sent

So, now you've found out how simple it is to send your first e-mail message. In fact, it's so easy that most folks are not really sure whether or not their e-mail has been sent. As a matter of fact, many newbies have sent me the same e-mail message twice, because they were not sure whether their first message was actually sent.

If you want to make sure that your message was sent, you can easily check by double-clicking the Read mailbox on the toolbar. Select the Sent Mail tab from the e-mail screen that appears (see Figure 1-11). If you see your message listed here with the date, recipient's name, and subject, you can be confident that it has been properly sent.

Sent Mail

Figure 1-11. If you want to be certain that your message was sent, you can check the Sent Mail section of your e-mail program, which shows each e-mail that you have sent, complete with its date, recipient's name, and subject.

Understanding the Language of E-Mail

After you start communicating by e-mail, you will need to understand some of the popular online jargon. Because e-mail is so abbreviated, it has spawned a whole new list of acronyms. Here are a few of those that are widely used:

CYA	See ya
IMHO	In my humble opinion
TIA	Thanks in advance
BTW	By the way
B4N	Bye for now

E-mail is usually short and to the point, so including any emotional sentiment in e-mail messages
is hard. Therefore, a new way to denote emotions
has also developed. Many e-mail users include small
symbols called *emoticons* in their messages. The
most common emoticon is a smiley :-). This indicates a happy state. If you turn your head to the
left while you view the smiley, you will see why.
Other common emoticons are as follows:

Cross-Reference

More acronyms and
emoticons are listed
in Chapter 2.

    :-(Sad

    ;-)   Wink

    :-D   Laughing

    (-:   Happy left-hander

Emoticons are also used for fun. Here are a few
examples:

    8-(Unhappy person who wears glasses

    :-{) Happy person who has a mustache

    :-3   User who has a double chin

AOL has a fun list of smileys and shorthands. If you
want to know how to type and use these emoticons,
just type the Keyword: **Smiley** (see Figure 1-12).

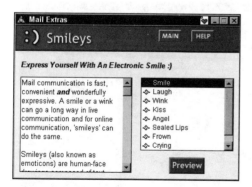

Figure 1-12. The Keyword: *Smiley* will give you a brief introduction to smileys.

Emoticon is a keyboard character used within e-mail to convey emotion. Tilting your head to the left helps to read emoticons. :-)

Although using abbreviations and emoticons may seem a little foreign at first, try it. You'll catch on quickly and find that it really can be fun.

Keeping Your E-Mail

As part of the AOL system, your e-mail is received and kept on AOL computers. AOL retains for several days the e-mail that you've received and read (except, of course, if you have deleted it). Although read e-mail is deleted from AOL's computers after a few days, any unread e-mail in your New Mail list is retained for about four weeks.

If you want to keep both your read and sent e-mail longer, AOL offers an easy way to do this. Click the Mail Center icon on the toolbar and choose Mail Preferences from the drop-down menu (see Figure 1-13). Then, click the up arrow next to the number of days you want to keep your old mail online. You can keep it for up to seven days.

Mail Preferences

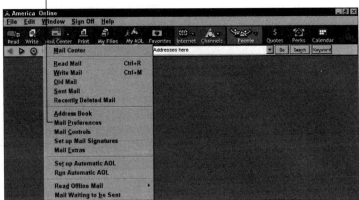

Figure 1-13. The Mail Center icon on the toolbar lets you pick Mail Preferences from the drop-down menu.

Communicating Through E-Mail

Windows Users

Place a checkmark in the box labeled Retain all mail
I send in my Personal Filing Cabinet. Do the same for
Retain all mail I read in my Personal Filing Cabinet
(see Figure 1-14). The Personal Filing Cabinet (PFC)
is AOL's built-in system for saving, organizing, and
searching e-mail you've read or sent. It's part of the
Offline Mail system. To reach it, click My Files on the
toolbar and select Personal Filing Cabinet. Messages
saved in the PFC will remain there until you delete
them. You can reread them or delete them when
working offline.

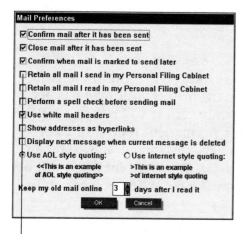

To keep e-mail longer, check this box.

Figure 1-14. To keep your sent e-mail longer than a few days, place a checkmark in
the box labeled Retain all mail I send in my Personal Filing Cabinet.

Mac Users

Click the empty box next to Save the mail I send,
to place an X in that box. Do the same for Save
the mail I read (see Figure 1-15).

While you are setting up your Mail Preferences, click the box next to Perform a spell check before sending mail (Mac Users: Spell check before sending). When you click Send, the spelling checker automatically checks your spelling for you every time you send an e-mail.

Using your Personal Filing Cabinet to keep your e-mail is beneficial to most users. However, it does take up hard disk space. If you have an older computer with limited hard disk space, be aware of the space constraints when you save your mail in the Personal Filing Cabinet.

Save mail box

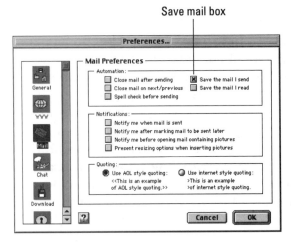

Figure 1-15. Mac users can save the mail they send by placing an X in the Save the mail I send box.

Now, your e-mail will be saved in your Personal Filing Cabinet, which is located on your own hard drive. That means that even after your mail has been deleted from AOL's computers, it will remain on your own computer to be a permanent record of all of your e-mail. After you have instructed AOL to retain your mail in your Personal Filing Cabinet, you will be able to access your e-mail even when you are off-line (not connected to AOL).

Using E-Mail When You're on the Road

If you are on the road, you can access AOL from any computer.

If the computer you are using has AOL installed, just sign in as a guest at the Welcome screen. Click the down arrow under Select Screen Name and choose Guest from the drop-down menu. The computer will then prompt you to fill in your screen name and your password.

If the computer doesn't have AOL installed, you can access your mail from any computer that has Internet access. Just log on to the Internet, and go to www.aol.com. Or, type the address http://aolmail.aol.com/. Fill in your screen name and password. You will see a Security Alert, telling you that you are entering a secure area. Click Yes to enter the secure area. At the Welcome screen that appears, click "Please click here to complete the sign-in process." Another Security Alert appears, warning that you are leaving the secure area. Click Yes, and you will arrive at your AOL mailbox.

Some advanced features of e-mail will not be available when accessing e-mail as a guest or from the Internet, but you will be able to send and receive e-mail just as you can at home.

Keeping Your E-Mail Organized

Just like a closet, your e-mail will be easier to manage and use if you keep it organized. The use of e-mail as a means of corresponding is growing every day. After you start using e-mail, you can expect that it will become an integral part of your life. So, keeping your e-mail organized is important — and is very easy when using the tools provided by America Online.

Your Personal Filing Cabinet

Your Personal Filing Cabinet (PFC) will also help you organize your e-mail. You can create new folders in the PFC to help you arrange your mail according to different categories.

Tip

For Windows users, double-clicking a closed folder will open it and display its contents. Mac users can click the right-facing arrow to display the contents of the folder.

To access your PFC and create a new folder, follow the steps provided next for your particular operating system.

Windows Users

1. Click the My Files button on the AOL toolbar and then select Personal Filing Cabinet from the drop-down menu (see Figure 1-16).

2. Highlight the folder named Mail by clicking it.

3. Click the Add Folder button (see Figure 1-17).

4. Give the folder a name and click OK. A new folder with the given name will appear inside the Mail folder.

Personal Filing Cabinet

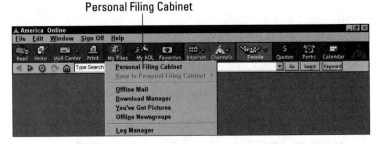

Figure 1-16. For Windows users, your PFC will help you organize your e-mail. From My Files, select Personal Filing Cabinet from the drop-down menu.

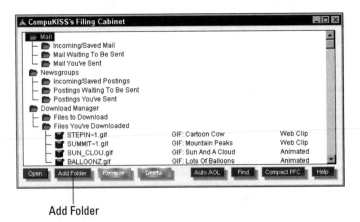

Add Folder

Figure 1-17. To finalize adding a folder to your PFC, click Mail and click Add Folder. Give your new folder a name, and then click OK to make it official.

Mac Users

1. Click the My Files button on the AOL toolbar and then select Personal Filing Cabinet from the drop-down menu.

2. Double-click Offline Mail.

3. Click the New Folder button (see Figure 1-18).

4. Type a name for the folder and press the Return key. Your new folder will appear in alphabetical order.

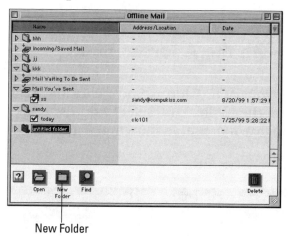

New Folder

Figure 1-18. For Mac Users, after you select PFC from the drop-down menu, double-click Offline Mail and then click the New Folder button. Name your folder and press the Return key. Now you have a new folder.

When you create a new folder, it will be created inside whichever folder you have highlighted at the time. This can be a bit tricky at first. Don't worry. If you create a folder in the wrong place, simply drag it to wherever you want it. If you need to delete a folder, highlight it and press the Delete button.

Once you have created a new folder, you can save your mail in that folder by choosing File from the menu bar. From the drop-down menu that appears, choose Save to Personal File Cabinet. Then select the folder that you want to use to save the e-mail.

Caution

If you delete a folder that contains a document, that document will also be deleted. However, if you try to delete a folder that is not empty, the computer will give you a warning and offer you a chance to change your mind.

You will notice that the PFC also keeps track of all the files that you download or the newsgroup postings that you send or receive. It keeps the contents of the files for the amount of time you specify, but it keeps a record of the type and title of the file indefinitely. The PFC also has a very helpful Find feature, so you can search through your mail for anything written by a certain person or on a given subject, provided you have either saved it or chosen to save all mail in your PFC.

Working with the Address Book

To start using your AOL Address Book, click the Mail Center icon on the toolbar and select Address Book from the drop-down menu, as shown in Figure 1-19.

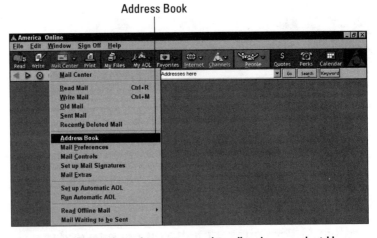

Figure 1-19. Clicking the Mail Center icon on the toolbar shows you the Address Book choice on the drop-down menu.

To add a name to your Address Book, click the New Person button. Fill in the person's real name under first name and last name. Put the person's screen name or Internet address under e-mail address. You also can add a note, if you like. Then, click OK.

Communicating Through E-Mail

To write an e-mail to anyone in your Address Book, simply double-click the chosen person's name, and the now-familiar e-mail composition window opens automatically. At any time while writing the message, you can choose to send the same e-mail simultaneously to another person, by clicking the Address Book icon, choosing another name from the Address Book, and clicking Send To.

AOL gives you an even easier way to enter e-mail addresses. You can add the address of anyone who sends you e-mail without having to retype it. Simply open a piece of mail from the person you would like to add to your Address Book. Click the Add Address button (for Window users), as shown in Figure 1-20, or the Remember Address icon (for Mac users). The New Person screen will open with the e-mail address already in place. Type a name, and you're done. It couldn't be easier.

Tip

To fill out the form for adding a New Person to your Address Book, press the Tab key to move between the fields. For example, type the person's first name and press Tab. Your cursor moves to the next field, in which you can type the last name.

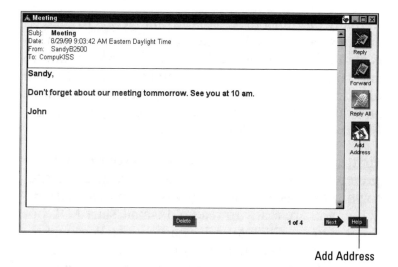

Add Address

Figure 1-20. With an e-mail open that you have received, click the Add Address button, and the New Person screen opens with the e-mail address already in place.

Definition

Offline is the state of being disconnected from AOL, the Internet, or another online service or computer network. A member can have the AOL program running and yet not be signed on to AOL. Some AOL functions are still available under this scenario.

Definition

Online is the state of being connected or signed on to AOL, the Internet, or another online service or computer network.

Often, you may want to send e-mail to the same group of people on a regular basis. For example, you may want to send the same e-mail to all of your children or grandchildren. To form such a group, open your Address Book and click the New Group button. Give the group a name that is meaningful to you. Then, enter the addresses of all the recipients who you want in the group. Press the Enter or Return key after each address. Click OK when you're done. You will see that a group in your Address Book has a picture of two people next to it, so you can differentiate it from a singular-person entry. When you want to send an e-mail to your group, just choose it from the Address Book, and the e-mail will automatically be addressed to each of the group names you included.

Working Offline

In many circumstances, it is advantageous to read and compose e-mail offline. Perhaps your modem is attached to the only telephone line in your home and you don't want to tie up the line. Or, maybe you just want to be a considerate member and free up an AOL line when you are writing a lengthy e-mail. In either case, working offline is easy.

First, make sure that you have set up your e-mail preferences to retain all the mail you read and write to your PFC, as explained previously in this chapter. When you are ready to read old e-mail, start AOL, but don't sign on. Click My Files and choose Personal File Cabinet from the drop-down menu. You can now read e-mail, just as though you were online. You can also click the Mail Center icon on the AOL toolbar and select Offline Mail from the drop-down menu choices (see Figure 1-21). To write mail offline, select Write Mail from the Mail Center drop-down list and choose Send Later.

Personal File Cabinet

Figure 1-21. Clicking the My Files icon on the toolbar lets you select Personal File Cabinet from the drop-down menu.

After you complete the e-mail you are writing offline, instead of clicking Send Now, click Send Later. You can then concentrate on other tasks. Did you know you can even turn off your computer and the mail will be saved? The next time you sign on to AOL, a notice will appear on your screen telling you that you have mail waiting to be sent.

Running Automatic AOL

Automatic AOL is a nifty feature that enables your computer to access AOL, send unsent mail, and get all of your new mail without requiring you to do anything, other than leave your computer on.

To set up Automatic AOL, click the Mail Center icon on the AOL toolbar and select Set up Automatic AOL (see Figure 1-22). Follow the instructions on the screen. During the setup process, you will have the option of choosing whether or not to let Automatic AOL download any attached files. For security reasons that I will discuss shortly, you may want to prevent Automatic AOL from downloading attachments. When you set up Automatic AOL, you can choose when and how often you want the computer to check for mail.

Windows users do not have to be signed on to set up Automatic AOL, but Mac users must be online to use the Automatic AOL setup.

Caution

Automatic AOL is a great feature, but it poses some security risk. Your password is stored in your computer in order for Automatic AOL to work. Unless you have initiated some other password protection on your computer, anyone having access to your computer will also have access to your e-mail.

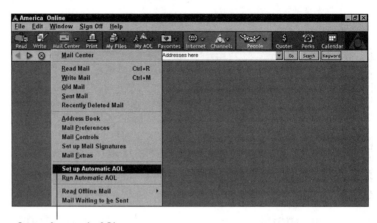

Set up Automatic AOL

Figure 1-22. To set up Automatic AOL, click the Mail Center icon on the toolbar and select Set up Automatic AOL.

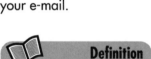

Definition

Attachments are files (documents, images, programs, and so on) that are connected to and sent along with messages that you are distributing online.

Working with E-Mail Attachments

After you start working with e-mail, you'll find that it is a very powerful tool. You not only can write your message, but also use e-mail to send entire documents, photographs, and files. You do this by attaching the photo or file to an e-mail. With America Online, the process is really quite easy.

Sending Attachments

E-mail attachments are very useful. Right now, you may think that you'll never want to attach a file to an e-mail, but you probably will someday. For instance, you have just used your word processor to help revise the by-laws for your local church group and want to run your ideas by other members of the group. You regularly correspond with the other group members through e-mail, so the easiest way to get others' opinions is to attach your word processing document to an e-mail message to them.

Because this process is different for Windows and Mac users, two separate sets of instructions are provided next.

Windows Users

1. Click the Write icon on the toolbar.
2. When the mail composition screen opens, write your e-mail as usual.
3. Click the Attachments button at the bottom of the screen.
4. Click Attach from the next screen.
5. Choose the file you want to attach. You must remember where you saved the file and what you named it.
6. Once you have found the file, click Open.
7. Click Okay.
8. A small floppy disk icon appears on the bottom of the Write Mail screen; the name of the file is next to it. This means the file is attached and will automatically be sent with the document (see Figure 1-23).

I wish I could say that this process is very easy, but it is not. It isn't difficult after you become accustomed to it, but for the uninitiated, it has one daunting step: Step 5. The Choose the File to Attach screen can be confusing. Near the top of the screen is a box labeled Look in (see Figure 1-24). That box will contain the name of a folder whose contents are shown under the box.

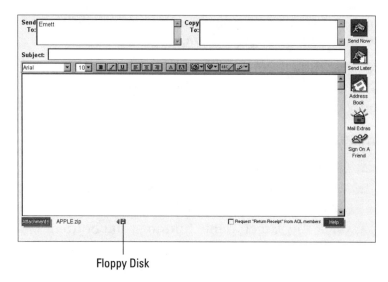

Floppy Disk

Figure 1-23. Make sure that the small floppy disk icon shows up on the bottom of the Write Mail screen next to the name of the file; this confirms that the file is attached and will automatically be sent with the e-mail.

You may see the name of the file you want to attach in the lower box. If you do, simply use your mouse to highlight the specific file. When you do that, the name of the file you have highlighted will appear in the box labeled *File name.* After you have the proper filename in that box, you can proceed to Step 6.

If you do not see the specific name of the file in the box, you will have to find it. Click the down arrow next to the name in the Look in box. Choose My Computer from the drop-down box. Your file is most likely in the My Documents folder, if that is where you normally save your work. If you have created a special folder for a project, your file might be there. Look through the various folders until you find the file you want. You may use the up arrow, also shown in Figure 1-24, to help you move around.

Down Arrow

Look In Box   Up Arrow

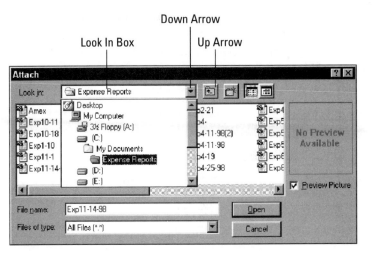

When you create a file, you should always remember to make a note of where you saved the file. This will make it much easier when you want to use the file later.

Figure 1-24. The down arrow next to the name of the folder in the Look in box enables you to look through the contents of that folder.

See Chapter 13 for more information on downloading files.

Mac Users

1. Click the Write icon on the toolbar.

2. When the mail composition screen opens, write your e-mail as usual.

3. Click the Attachments tab at the top of the screen.

4. Click the Attach File button from the next screen.

5. Choose the file you want to attach.

6. Click Attach.

You will see a small floppy disk icon on the top of the Write Mail screen. The name of the file will be listed in the attachment box. This means that the file is attached and will automatically be sent with the document.

Step 5 can be a little confusing for a Mac user, although it is easier than in the Windows scenario. You will see a box in which you can click the up or down arrow to select the Macintosh HD, for *hard drive* (see Figure 1-25). Then, scroll through

Tip

Depending on where you are calling from, the nearest AOL access phone number listed may or may not be a local phone call. You should confirm this with your phone company.

Caution

If you receive an e-mail from AOL requesting your password or credit card information, do not respond. No one from AOL will ever ask for your password or financial information via e-mail.

the folders you see listed. Use the scroll bar to search through the folders and files that are listed. Click the Open button to see the contents of any folder. When you find the file you want, select it with the mouse and click Attach.

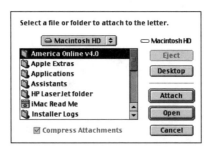

Figure 1-25. Mac users can scroll through the contents of folders in search of a particular file by clicking the up or down arrow to select the Macintosh HD. Click the Open button to see the contents of any folder.

AOL's e-mail is a powerful tool that has even more functions than I have been able to cover here. After you conquer the basics, don't be afraid to try other features by clicking any icon on the AOL toolbar and fully exploring all the drop-down menus.

Whether you use e-mail for business, pleasure, or both, it is sure to become a useful part of your everyday life. Welcome to the online world of instant communication!

Coming Up Next

Next, we look at how to use AOL and the Internet to chat with others in real time. We also look at how to read and post messages to message boards and newsgroups. In this chapter, we discussed how to communicate through e-mail, covering the following information:

▶ Electronic mail, or *e-mail,* is quickly becoming a standard method of communication because it is fast, fun, easy, and inexpensive.

▶ Your AOL service includes unlimited use of e-mail at no extra charge.

▶ AOL gives you a powerful tool to make your e-mails look better — a built-in spelling checker.

▶ Even after your e-mail has been deleted from AOL's computers, you can keep a permanent record of it on your own computer in your Personal Filing Cabinet.

▶ The Address Book feature provided by AOL is an easy way to index the addresses of your e-mail correspondents, family, friends, business acquaintances, and so forth.

▶ Automatic AOL is a nifty feature that enables your computer to access AOL, send all unsent mail, and get all of your new mail without requiring you to do a thing, other than leave your computer on.

CHAPTER

2

CHATTING AND POSTING

MESSAGES

Quick Look

▶ **AOL Live** **page 78**

At Keyword: **AOL Live**, you will find more chats on AOL! Here, you will find regularly scheduled chats in the AOL Live area, in which large groups get together to discuss important issues of the day or communicate with special guests of AOL. Some of the notable past guests on AOL Live include Rosie O'Donnell, Barbara Streisand, Rod Stewart, Michael Jordan, Dean Ornich, and Edmund Morris.

▶ **Hot Chats and Top Picks** **page 78**

Be sure to check out AOL's featured chats of the day (Keyword: **Hot Chats**) as well as the top picks of the week (Keyword: **Top Picks**) for even more chatting options.

▶ **Personalized Signature** **page 84**

In cyberspace, a personalized signature is called a *sig* or *sig file*. This is a short text message normally seen at the end of every message you write. Your personalized signature might include your name, e-mail address, favorite quotation, pastime, hobby, and so on. If you are inspired, create a sig file so that you have an interesting signature to use with message postings. The easiest way to create a sig file is to use the new-style message boards with the colorful push-pin background. These message boards will save your signature and automatically include it with every message that you post.

Chapter 2

Chatting and Posting Messages

Are you starting to feel a little more comfortable with America Online? I certainly hope so. AOL and the AOL Welcome screen will soon become your cozy stepping-off point to the online world.

Let's look at the Welcome screen again. See those excited and friendly looking people waving to us from the bottom of the blue America Online stripe? Look at Figure 2-1. They are inviting us to come and chat. But what is chatting? How does it work?

Interested? Let's check it out.

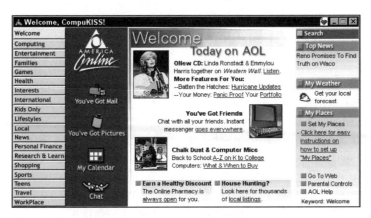

Figure 2-1. Chatting is one of America Online's most popular features, and the invitation to chat is prominently displayed on the Welcome screen.

Chatting involves friendly, light talk online in an informal or familiar way. How can you do that on the computer? It is like the reverse of the yellow pages: you let your fingers do the talking instead of the walking. Simply put, you type a message, and someone else types a response. Almost no lag time occurs between sending a message and receiving a response.

Chatting online is one of AOL's most popular features. As such, AOL could be called "the Great Introducer." AOL is the largest online community, made up of millions of members who often communicate by chatting in either a personal private chat, a member chat room, or one of the many chat rooms organized by AOL. Chatting is a great way to share common interests, meet new people, learn new ideas, and get more involved with your AOL online world.

Online chatting is not just for teenagers. Today's widespread families are using private chat rooms to keep up with family happenings or plan special events like family reunions, weddings, and other celebrations. People of all ages are coming together in chat rooms to discuss problems, share information,

Definition

Chatting is a live, interactive online dialogue between two or more people. When one chat participant sends a message, other people in the chat can see the message on their screens.

2

Chatting and Posting Messages

and make important decisions. Grown-ups are using chats to get information and to exchange ideas.

Chat rooms are also wonderful places to find others who are understanding and supportive. If you have a rare disease or an unusual problem, you may not be able to find anyone in you neighborhood or your town who has encountered the same situation. But it is often possible to find someone who shares your dilemma among the millions of AOL users. For many, chatting is a way to use high tech instruments to find the good old-fashioned camaraderie that is sometimes lacking in our fast-paced world.

The People Connection

Chatting is fun and it's easy with AOL. The People Connection is where it all starts. The People Connection screen is your gateway to AOL's chat rooms. This screen serves as home base for the many AOL chat areas where members can talk interactively. The label "People Connection" is most appropriate, because connecting people is an activity that AOL is famous for. The three different ways to get to the People Connection are the following:

▶ The Chat icon is waving to you on the Welcome screen (see Figure 2-1). Just click it to begin.

▶ The same friendly group waving to you from the toolbar is labeled People (see Figure 2-2). Click the People icon and then click People Connection on the drop-down menu that appears.

▶ Click the keyword box on the Navigation bar, type **People Connection**, and then click the Go button (see Figure 2-3).

People Icon

Figure 2-2. Clicking the People icon on the toolbar will bring you a drop-down menu. Click the People Connection and, presto, AOL takes you straight to the People Connection.

Figure 2-3. Type the Keyword: *People Connection* in AOL's keyword box and then click Go, and you will find yourself at the People Connection.

Meeting People and Getting Started

Now that we are at the People Connection, let's meet some of those friendly looking people. What do we do now? To join in the chatting fun, we have to have someone to talk to. In striking up a conversation, it is always helpful to have a topic you are interested in that can serve as a common denominator between people. How do you find people with the same interests? How can you meet them? AOL has some clever tools for introducing its members. They are the Member Directory and the Member Profile.

Member Directory

The Member Directory is an important feature of the People Connection. It is a way for meeting or finding people online, a way to locate family and friends and people who share similar interests and hobbies. Searching the directory is a fast and easy way for meeting or finding people online.

2

Chatting and Posting Messages

To search the Member Directory for friends-to-be, start with, you guessed it . . . the People icon.

1. From the People drop-down menu, instead of the People Connection, this time pick Search AOL Member Directory (which brings up the search dialog box).

2. Enter a keyword that describes the people you would like find. For example, enter a city, an occupation, a hobby, a game, to find people who match certain criteria.

3. Click Search.

4. From the results, double-click the name of anyone who looks interesting.

All that is left to do is to note the screen name or add it to your address book. Why not write an email message introducing yourself with a little bit of information and send it on its way?

Member Profile

The Member Directory is great. I can look for people interested in golf or search for an alumni from my college. I like this. I want to get involved myself. How does that work?

AOL has an easy system for gathering individual information on each user called a *Member Profile*. Using a Member Profile is totally elective and your personal profile will contain whatever you want other AOL subscribers to know about you. List as much or as little as you want to share about yourself. Some members fill out detailed profiles, some members forget to create profiles, some fill out limited profiles, and some choose not to do so at all. Of course, you will meet more new online acquaintances if you participate, so here is how to join in:

1. Make sure that you are signed on to AOL with your correct screen name.

2. Choose My AOL from the toolbar.

3. Select My Member Profile from the drop-down list. The Edit Your Online Profile dialog box appears.

4. Create a profile or change a profile.

When you are finished creating your profile, AOL advises you that your profile has been updated.

Definition

An *online community* is a group of people connected by a common interest and able to communicate via AOL, the Internet, or any other computer network.

Online Community

From People Connection you can click an online community. Wonder what that is? An *online community* is an AOL program that you can create based on your interests, beliefs, lifestyle, and the way you connect with the people around you. AOL makes it easy and fun to find and build relationships with people who share your interests. Community is about belonging to something unique, something special. You can build your own online community on AOL or find one already established that is just right for you.

A quick way to find online communities is through the Keyword: **Top Picks**. From the Top Picks screen, click What are online communities? (See Figure 2-4.) You will be able to join chats, participate in message board communications, share pictures, and so on. AOL will help you start your online community so that you can gather people around you with the same interests (see Figure 2-5).

2

Chatting and Posting Messages

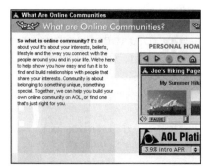

Figure 2-4. An online community can be created around your interests, beliefs, lifestyle, and the way you connect with the people around you and in your life.

Figure 2-5. AOL will walk you through the steps of creating your own online community so that you can meet people with the same interests.

Newcomer's Quick Guide to Chatting

This is your AOL cheat-sheet. AOL has put together a "New 2 Chat" guide at the Keyword: **New 2 Chat** (see Figure 2-6). This guide will help you learn to avoid spam and learn chat-room lingo.

Don't be shy. If you are new to AOL, use the Member Directory, an Online Community, or even another feature we are going to explain — the Find a Chat feature — to find a chat room to match your interests, and then jump right in.

Figure 2-6. Just follow these four easy steps offered by AOL, and you can enjoy the popular online activity of chatting.

Spam is a message posted to dozens, even hundreds or thousands of unrelated chats, message boards, newsgroups, or e-mail recipients. It is similar to real-world junk mail.

Entering a Chat

To find out how to chat and how to join a chat that interests you, just click Find a Chat on the People Connection screen (see Figure 2-7).

Figure 2-7. To find out how to chat and how to join a chat that interests you, click Find a Chat on the People Connection screen.

Each chat on AOL discusses a certain subject. Chat topics are organized into two main areas, based on how they are created. One area contains chats

Definition

A *chat room* is a virtual "place" or online area where two or more members gather to send messages and receive responses from other members for real-time communication.

created by AOL's People Connection; the other area includes chats created by AOL members.

The first area, the People Connection chats, reflects a broad range of interests, such as arts, entertainment, and romance. These featured *chat rooms* created by AOL are hosted by volunteers who greet members and make sure the conversations flow smoothly.

In the second area, individual AOL members can create chats on topics they personally want to initiate, and can invite all AOL members as well.

To enter a chat, follow these easy steps:

1. At the Find a Chat screen, pick either the tab "created by People Connection" or the tab "created by AOL Members" to see the topics under each chat area (see Figure 2-8).

Figure 2-8. The Find a Chat screen offers a choice of two categories of chats: chats created by AOL or chats created by AOL Members.

2. Highlight a category from the chat area list and click the View Chat button. The chats shown in the list box on the right will change to those within your selected category.

3. Highlight your selected chat in the list box and click the Go Chat button. Now you are ready to start chatting.

You'll find that the chat room you are visiting has a large window in the middle, called a *discussion box,* displaying the topic in the title bar and the conversation as it is taking place.

When you first arrive, you will see a notation from your Online Host telling you where you are. Moments later, you will see the conversation scrolling by, like the dialogue of a play whose characters are the current members of the chat room. If you want to join in, simply type what you want to say into the box at the bottom of the window and click Send (see Figure 2-9).

Definition

The *discussion box* is the window in a chat room where you can read the messages that are posted by the participants.

2

Chatting and Posting Messages

Figure 2-9. In a chat room, you see the conversation scrolling by, and can join in by typing what you want to say in the box at the bottom of the window and clicking Send.

As soon as you send your text, it appears in the conversation window with your screen name in front of it. In a regular chat room, everyone present in your room will be able to see what you have typed, and they will be able to respond. (Some auditoriums and staged chats work differently — more on that later in this chapter.)

Cross-Reference

See Chapter 3 for more on AOL's Instant Messenger feature and how to send an Instant Message to an AOL member.

A finite number of seats, or positions, are available in a chat room. If the chat room is full, hopefully a spot will open in a few minutes. Or, you can go to another chat room while you are waiting. If your first choice of chat rooms is full, you get a notice saying that it is full and asking whether you would like to go to a chat like it (see Figure 2-10).

Figure 2-10. If the chat room of your choice is full, you get a notice saying it is full and asking whether you would like to go to a chat like it.

To the right, the chat room screen shows a smaller box listing the screen names of all the participants in the chat room. Double-click any name, and AOL offers you the choice of the following:

> ▶ **Get Profile:** Enables you to read about that particular person's background (if they have created one).

> ▶ **Send Message:** Enables you to send a message to that person via a private Instant Message note.

> ▶ **Ignore a member:** Enables you to prevent that person's comments from appearing on your screen.

Starting Your Own Chat

Two types of chat rooms exist in the AOL Members' chat room area: Open and Private.

Members' Open Chat Rooms

AOL has many chat rooms going at the same time, but you still might not find what you want. If that's the case, why not initiate a chat on a topic that you like? From the People drop-down menu, select Start Your Own Chat, and you will be prompted with instructions for doing just that.

Members' Private Chat Rooms

We have seen open chat rooms that any member can initiate and be joined by other members. However, another, more personal, chat room option is available for AOL members.

AOL members can create *private* chat rooms that only members who know the name of the chat room can join. Private chat rooms allow AOL members to have business or personal conversations in private. This kind of chat is ideal for having private, long-distance discussions with colleagues or family members.

Starting or Entering a Private Chat

To start a private chat or to enter a private chat already created, follow these steps:

1. Go to the People Connection.
2. Click Find a Chat and, magically, the Find a Chat screen appears (or from the People drop-down menu, choose Find a Chat).
3. Click Enter a Private Chat.
4. The Enter or Start a Private Chat window appears.
5. Type the name of the private chat room you want to create or enter (see Figure 2-11).
6. Click Go Chat to go to your private chat room.

Tip

A private chat is unlisted and cannot be joined unless you type the name of the private chat room *exactly*. AOL has no list of private chat rooms.

Figure 2-11. Type the name of the private chat room you want to create or enter, and then click Go Chat to find your way to that private chat location.

7. The chat window appears.

8. Send and view comments as you would in any other chat room.

Setting Chat Preferences

AOL lets you set up your preferences regarding chats. Start at the People icon on the toolbar and follow these steps:

1. Select Chat Now (or from the People Connection, click Chat Now).

2. Click Chat Preference in the lower-right portion of the Chat screen.

3. On the Chat Preference screen, select the preference you would like to enable. To enable a preference, click the checkbox associated with it. To disable the preference, click the box again to remove the check.

The following are your choices of chat preferences:

▶ **Notify me when members arrive:** Notifies you when AOL members join the chat you are in.

- ▶ **Notify me when members leave:** Notifies you when AOL members leave the chat you are in.

- ▶ **Double-space incoming messages:** Double-spaces the text of your incoming messages to make them easier to read.

- ▶ **Alphabetize the member list:** Sorts members' names alphabetically to make locating friends and family easier.

- ▶ **Enable chat room sounds:** Allows you to hear chat room sounds, so you know when someone sends you a message, without looking at the screen (see Figure 2-12).

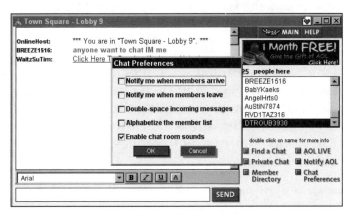

Figure 2-12. AOL lets you set up your preferences regarding chats.

Golden Guidance

With over 16 million members of AOL, many of them skillful in the gift of gab, some basic ground rules for chatting are in order. These rules of etiquette really follow the Golden Rule: do unto others . . .

These commonsense rules ask you to be civil and respectful of others when you are online. As a matter of a fact, AOL members must agree to these rules

Note

To review the AOL Terms of Service agreement, go to Keyword: **TOS**.

as part of the Terms of Service when joining this great online community. To view your complete Terms of Service agreement, go to Keyword: **TOS**.

Here is a general review of the basic rules:

▶ Be safe; don't give out your password.

▶ Be respectful of others. Treat others with civility, kindness, and consideration. Keep in mind that vulgarity and disruptive behavior are inappropriate and unacceptable online. Do not use offensive language; people of all ages and backgrounds join chat rooms.

▶ Report problems when they occur. If anyone online asks for your password or credit card information, report it immediately at Keyword: **Notify AOL**.

If you encounter a troublesome member in a chat area, try first to manage your own chat experience by either leaving the chat or using the Ignore feature. If you encounter Terms of Service violations, click the Notify AOL button to request assistance or report the violation.

To notify AOL of disruptive behavior that violates Terms of Service, follow these steps:

1. Go to Keyword: **Notify AOL**.
2. Click the Chat button to the left.
3. Select the category of the chat room you were in.
4. Note the Date and Time of the violation.
5. Type the Room Name and the Person You Are Reporting.
6. Click Send.

How to Use the Ignore Feature

If you come across someone in a chat who is annoying you in some way, you might want to consider using the Ignore feature. You can censor a specific member so that you don't have to see what he or she is typing. To activate your Ignore feature, follow these steps:

1. In the People Here list box in the chat window, double-click the screen name of the person whose comments you no longer want to see.

2. A window appears. Click the box beside Ignore Member. A check appears in the box.

3. Click X to close the window.

If you no longer want to ignore a member, perform Steps 1 and 2. This reverses your notation to ignore that member in Step 2.

Chat Room Etiquette

A whole new language and new rules of etiquette (called *netiquette*) have developed as a result of chatting. First, check your chat comments for spelling, grammar, and clarity. Do not type comments in all CAPITAL LETTERS. This is seen as shouting and will annoy and distract others.

Although you shouldn't type in all caps, AOL gives you other enhancement tools for your type — bold, italics, and underline. Change the font and font color to emphasize your words. Insert links into a chat so that you can point people to places you recommend on the AOL service or the Internet.

Your comments are limited to 92 characters when typing in the box at the bottom of the page under the dialog box. With a limit on the number of characters in a comment, it is no surprise that abbreviations have become popular, because they save both space and time.

Here are a few of the more popular acronyms and abbreviations that are used in chat rooms:

AFK	Away from keyboard
BRB	Be right back
BTW	By the way
CUL	See you later
GMTA	Great minds think alike
HTH	Hope this helps
IAC	In any case
IMHO	In my humble opinion
LOL	Laughing out loud
ROFL	Rolling on the floor laughing
TIA	Thanks in advance
TTFN	Ta-ta for now
WTGP	Want to go private?
WYSIWYG	What you see is what you get

Emoticons

The secret to good online chats is to get the feel of a real live dialogue — with real people. A smile or a wink can often express so much more than words. You won't find a shortage of this expression of feelings online; you can use *emoticons,* or smileys. Emoticons are human-face drawings or icons composed of text characters that express emotions online. (For you first-time emoticoners, it helps to tilt your head to the left when getting acquainted with these figures.)

:-)	Smile
;-)	Wink
:-(	Frown
;-(	Cry
[]	Hug
:-x	Kiss

Emoticons can be a lot of fun. As usual, many folks have applied their creativity to come up with some very unusual variations. Here are just a few:

#:-)	Bad hair day
d:-)	Baseball fan
(:-)	Bald
*:o)	Clown
<:-)	Dunce
%-\	Hung over
:~)	Needs a nose job

Emoticons, or *smileys,* are special characters that express emotions in online communication.

Excessive sound playing goes against good chat room etiquette, because playing too many sounds in a chat room can annoy other members.

Sounds

Can you believe that you can even play sounds with your chat conversations? You can play sounds that everyone in a chat room will hear. These sound files come with AOL and are stored in the AOL folder on your computer. You can play these sound files and others can hear them if you and the others have a sound card. The different sounds you can add are Buddyin, Buddyout, Drop, Filedone, Goodbye, Gotmail, Gotpics, IM (for Instant Messages), Inactive, and Welcome.

Meeting People Through Chatting

Making friends is easy through chatting with AOL's help. When you are in a chat room, you can view

2

Chatting and Posting Messages

Cross-Reference

More information can be found earlier in this chapter on Member Profile or in the Member Directory section of Chapter 3.

information about another member, such as his name, location, hobbies, and occupation, by accessing that member's profile information. To access someone's AOL profile, follow these steps:

1. In the People Here list box, double-click the screen name of the person whose profile you want to see.
2. When a window appears, click Get Profile.
3. The Member Profile window appears, displaying information about the member. A dialog box appears if no profile exists for the member.
4. Click OK to close the dialog box.
5. When you finish viewing the information, click X to close the window.

Finding a Chat

At the Find a Chat screen, you will find some handy search and locate features to help you find a specific chat or see who is chatting in the room you've selected. The Search All People Connection Chats button will list all the chats on the service that are created by the People Connection. Conversely, the Search All AOL Member Chats button will list all the chats on the service that AOL members have created. (Remember to change the tab at the top to switch back and forth between these two areas.)

Planning for a Chat

At the Find a Chat screen, you will also find the AOL Chat Schedule. This list gives a complete schedule of all People Connection Chats, by 24-hour periods for the next week. Click the day of the week you want to view, and then select the tab for the time slot during which you are available that day. Scroll through the list and take a look at all the chats that are scheduled for your convenient day and time (see Figure 2-13).

Figure 2-13. The AOL Chat Schedule gives you a list of the chat topics to be discussed by 24-hour periods for the next week.

Finding Out Who's Chatting

Want to get a preview of who is opinionating at a certain chat? Just click the Who's Chatting button located right under the scrollable box on the right side of the Find a Chat window. After you click this button, you can see a list of all members chatting in the chat you have just selected (see Figure 2-14), by clicking the List More button, which expands the list of available chats.

Figure 2-14. A list of all members chatting in a particular chat is available by clicking the Who's Chatting button. The screen that lists the screen names of all members involved in that chat also lets you get a member profile on each person and send them an Instant Message.

More Chats: AOL Live and Hot Chats

How about AOL Live? More chats, can you believe it? AOL offers daily chats, regularly scheduled events in the AOL Live area, where large groups get together to discuss important issues of the day or communicate with special guests of AOL. Some of the notable past guests on AOL Live include Rosie O'Donnell, Barbara Streisand, Rod Stewart, Michael Jordan, Dean Ornich, and Edmund Morris.

Find this location at the Keyword: **AOL Live** (see Figure 2-15). In addition to previews of events coming soon, and a search area to enter a date, name, or topic to search for incoming chats, you can read event transcripts of earlier chats.

Figure 2-15. At AOL Live, large groups get together to discuss important issues of the day and communicate with special guests, such as Michael Jordan and Rosie O'Donnell.

More Chats? Yes, don't forget Featured Chats, where you can find changing current topics. Today's Hottest Chats, at Keyword: **Hot Chats**, is always very popular (see Figure 2-16). Top Picks at Keyword: **Top Picks** invites you to spend time chatting, not searching. Select Top 7 and have the option of picking a chat from the Top Seven of the Week or looking through the previous weekly lists. Top Picks will also whisk you away to an online community.

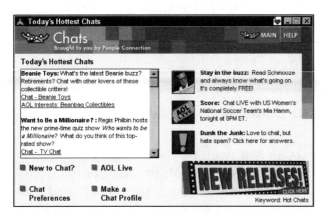

Figure 2-16. Today's Hottest Chats is always a very popular chat spot and is usually filled to capacity.

Most of the celebrity chats on AOL Live are held in large chat rooms called *auditoriums*. In these chats, you are assigned to sit in a row with 3 to 15 other members. The discussion box is called the *stage,* where you will see the guests chatting and answering questions. You are encouraged to chat among other members of your row; however, you will only see the celebrity's comments, your own comments, and those of others in your row.

You may also encounter chat rooms that have two discussion boxes. The guest's comments are shown in the upper box, and everyone else's comments are shown in the lower box.

As you get more comfortable with chatting, you will find that these different types of chat platforms help everyone to follow the chat comments and help to keep the chats orderly. You may find that you would like to document the chats you are participating in to keep a log of interesting resources or comments. AOL makes it possible to keep a record of chats. You then can re-read the text file of the chat or Instant

Tip

If you want to read a transcript of an AOL Live Chat that you participated in or missed, you can access a text copy of what was discussed by typing **Transcript** in the keyword box. Then, click a hyperlink for the topic of your specific chat or use the Search feature to find it for you. After you find your chat, you can read the text onscreen, print it, or save it on your computer.

2

Chatting and Posting Messages

Definition

A *message board* is a non-dialogue form of communication. You post your query or statement, and others can read and respond if they have information to share or comments to offer.

Message conversation and print it out if you like. Also, if your best buddy let you know you missed the greatest AOL Live Chat yet, you can catch up by reading a transcript because AOL keeps logs of previous chats you can access.

Message Boards

Sometimes, you just want to get an answer to your question and don't want to sift through unnecessary conversation. If that's the case, a message board may be your answer. A *message board* is an area where you can post your questions, and other members will respond to them.

Message boards were the first version of online communication. They represent the generation prior to chatting when communicating became almost interactive (as it is now with Instant Messenger; see Chapter 3), but they remain popular today as a question-and-answer type of communicating.

Online message boards have been called *discussion boards* and even *forums* or *discussion groups*. Today's message boards are the second- or third-generation descendants of the old bulletin boards that cluttered classrooms and hallways in old academic settings. Message boards are found all over AOL, in every nook and cranny; nearly every area has its own topic-specific message boards. Explore the various channels and areas of AOL to find the many message board icons. These icons picture a message being held up by a pushpin. Click the icon to be transported to the forum's message board.

Using Message Boards

Message boards offer a variety of helpful uses, such as gathering information, collecting insights, and learning from other members' experience and advice. You can use message boards to collect travel tips from other members, get recommendations for a quality discount broker, get help for a computer problem, or share computer shortcuts.

Message boards, like chat rooms, can also put you in touch with people with similar interests, such as gardening, golf, and so on. They are a way to share your opinions.

Basic Rules

Some of the same basic rules apply to messages posted on a message board as those that apply in chat room communication. AOL emphasizes two key points with message boards: Be kind, honest, and respectful, and don't propagate chain letters or advertisements.

Reading Message Boards

You will find message boards organized something like a family tree. Branching is the dominant activity. The board starts with a main topic but then branches down into smaller subjects, and each subject branches down into individual messages. You will find a path to follow, according to your interest, when you read a message board. You can select the first topic and then a subject within that topic. Keep selecting, and eventually you will pick messages, also called *posts,* within that subject (see Figure 2-17).

To read a posting within a message board, follow these steps:

1. With the message board open, click a topic.

Often, companies and manufacturers have message boards available for their customers. Just post a question to get help directly from the manufacturer.

AOL organizes a few message boards strictly for advertisements. You can find them at Keyword: **Classifieds**.

2

Chatting and Posting Messages

Use the buttons to move to the previous or next post in the same subject or to the previous or next subject within a given topic.

A subject may have hundreds of posts. Reading them all could be impossible. Often, message boards have a Search option that can help you find what you are looking for.

2. Click List All to see the subjects of the topic.

3. Double-click the subject or post that looks interesting.

Figure 2-17. A forum's message board contains the topics that fall under the broad category of the forum. The number of subjects under each topic is listed to the right of the topic.

4. Click the Previous Post and Next Post or the < and > buttons to proceed to another post (see Figure 2-18).

Each message shows the subject, the date it was posted, who it's from, and then the actual message.

Posting Messages

Two ways are available to post a message of your own on a message board. You can initiate a new subject or you can reply to an existing message.

Reply to a Message Board Post

To reply to a message board post, follow these steps:

1. Click the Reply button at the bottom of the window. A form will appear with Author and Subject fields already filled in.

2. Type your message just as you would an e-mail message.

3. Click the Send button. AOL adds your message
to the list of posts for that specific subject
(see Figure 2-19).

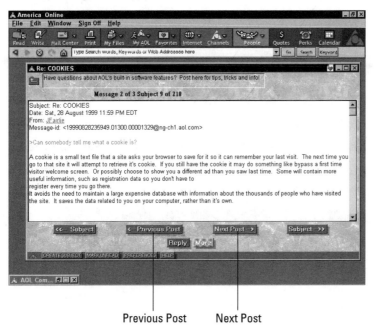

Previous Post   Next Post

Figure 2-18. Click the Previous Post and Next Post or the < and > buttons to
proceed to another post.

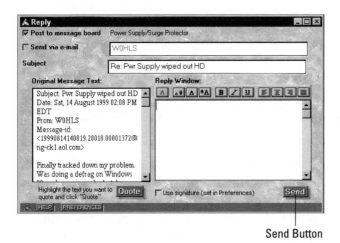

Send Button

Figure 2-19. Fill in the Reply Window with your reply to a message board post and
click the Send button to have your message added to the list of posts for that specific
subject.

Create a New Message Board Post

To create a new message board post, follow these steps:

1. Click the Create Subject button. A message form will appear with the Send To box already filled in with the topic title.
2. Type the title of the new subject you are creating in the Subject box.
3. Type your post just as you would a regular e-mail.
4. Click Send, and AOL adds your message to the list of posts for the subject you have selected (see Figure 2-20).

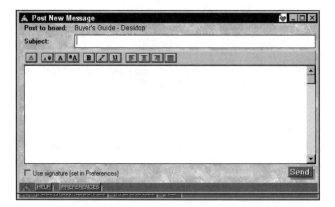

Figure 2-20. When creating a new message board post, type your comment in the Post New Message window just as you would a regular e-mail.

Personalized Signature

In cyberspace, a personalized signature is called a *sig* or *sig file*. This is a short text message normally seen at the end of every message you write. Your personalized signature might include your name, e-mail address, favorite quotation, pastime, hobby, and so on. If you are inspired, create a sig file so that you have an interesting signature to use with message postings.

The easiest way to create a sig file is to use the new-style message boards with the colorful push-pin background. These message boards will save your signature and automatically include it with every message you post.

To create an automatic signature, follow these steps:

1. Click the Preferences button at the bottom of the message board window.

2. Type you signature message in the box provided.

3. Click OK.

When you post a message, click the Use Signature box at the bottom of the window, and your personal signature will be added to your post.

If you want to create your own personalized signature for a message board that does not have an automatic signature option:

1. From the File menu, click New.

2. Type your signature.

3. From the File menu, click Save. (You will be prompted to name the file and select its location on your computer. Write down where you saved it and the filename for easy future reference.)

4. When you want to include your signature at the end of a message, select File ➪ Open. Go to the location of your signature file, highlight the filename, and click Open.

5. Highlight all the text to select it.

6. From the Edit menu, click Copy.

Continued

 Cross-Reference

After you find a message board topic that you like, you should return to it later to see what is new and check up on any replies to your personal post. Use the Favorite Places heart icon in the upper-right corner of the message board. Click this heart and then click the Add to Favorites button on the dialog box that appears. More information on creating Favorites is presented in Chapter 5.

2

Chatting and Posting Messages

Definition

A *newsgroup* is a specialized form of message board or discussion group where you can discuss just about any subject. Like online forums, newsgroups cover a wide variety of topics, both general and specific.

Tip

After you are in a newsgroup, you can post questions and get a variety of answers. Be careful. The information that you receive here can be invaluable, or it can be grossly inaccurate. Join these groups and enjoy the company. You will probably learn some new things. Just remember that you will be dealing with many different people with a variety of different opinions.

Personalized Signature *(continued)*

7. Switch back to the message board, position your cursor where you want to sign the e-mail, and select Edit ⇨ Paste. Your personalized sig will be inserted into your message.

Newsgroups

Newsgroups are forums, similar to public bulletin boards, where people post messages that are read by others; replies can appear either as new posts or in e-mail.

More than 25,000 topics are available in newsgroups, so you will certainly be able to find an interesting subject. When you visit a newsgroup, you can read the messages that were written by all the others who have accessed that group. If you respond to a message, everyone else will be able to read your response. Some of the newsgroups generate a lot of activity, so get out those reading glasses; you are in for a lot of armchair action.

By typing the Keyword: **Newsgroups**, you can find AOL's many options for learning about and using newsgroups. You can filter and manage junk posts, specifying newsgroup messages that you would like to filter out of your list of unread messages (see Figure 2-21). A new option is available to include your real name in parentheses after your e-mail address. If you want your real name to appear in parentheses after your e-mail address on all of your newsgroup posts, click Set Preferences on the Newsgroup screen, found by typing the Keyword: **Newsgroups**, and select the Posting tab to enter your real name.

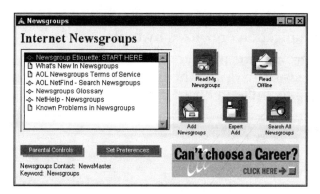

Figure 2-21. By typing the Keyword: *Newsgroups*, the AOL Newsgroups screen appears, which gives you a choice of several options for learning about and using newsgroups.

Coming Up Next

In the chapter that follows, we look at how to use AOL's Buddy List and Instant Messenger features to keep up with friends and family as well as to meet new people on the Internet. In this chapter, we saw how to use and take advantage of chats, message boards, and newsgroups, including the following:

▶ The People Connection organizes chats to reflect the broad range of interests of AOL members.

▶ Netiquette has developed as an informal code of behavior that should be followed during communication on AOL or the Web.

▶ Acronyms and emoticons save time and space and convey meaningful messages.

▶ Background information found in the Member Directory's Profile Information can serve as a good introduction and point out similar interests and hobbies when AOL members are meeting each other.

Caution

Newsgroup discussions are varied, but always down-to-earth. Many of these discussions often include language that may be offensive to some. For that reason, you may not find newsgroups to your liking. You may also want to consider blocking access to newsgroups for children (Keyword: **Parental Controls**).

2

Chatting and Posting Messages

▶ A message board is a non-dialogue form of communication organized by topic.

▶ Newsgroups are another means of sharing messages on AOL and the Internet that work like public bulletin boards.

CHAPTER

3

CREATING YOUR OWN
ONLINE NETWORK

Quick Look

▶ **Buddy List Window** **page 93**

With the Buddy List window, you can easily note which of your friends and family have just signed on to AOL or left AOL. You can also see how many of the buddies in each Buddy List Group are online. To view the Buddy List window (if it isn't already showing), click View Buddy List from the People drop-down menu on the AOL toolbar.

▶ **Buddy List Locate Button** **page 99**

If one of your buddies comes online, you will know it when his name appears in your Buddy List. You can check whether he is in a public chat room and, if he is, join him in that particular room. Use the Locate button in the Buddy List window to find and join him.

▶ **Member Directory** **page 106**

Register your Member Profile in the AOL Member Directory if you'd like other AOL members to know a little bit about you and your interests. You can also search the Member Directory for profiles of other AOL members to find people with similar interests. Select Get Member Profile from the People menu on the AOL toolbar to start.

▶ **Instant Messenger** **page 109**

Because e-mail is not interactive, Instant Messenger was developed to blend the speed of e-mail with the interactivity of a phone call by letting you type back and forth with someone else on the system. Instant Messenger is a way to have a quick conversation with someone regardless of what else either of you is doing on the computer at the time. These messages are private: only you and your correspondent know what's passing between you, as opposed to a chat room conversation, where two or more — sometimes many more — take part in the conversation.

▶ **Sharing Favorite Online Areas** **page 115**

You can share your favorite online areas with your buddy by including hyperlinks to those areas in an Instant Message. AOL gives you two convenient ways to do this, each of which depends on whether or not you are in the process of conversing with your buddy by Instant Messenger.

Chapter 3

Creating Your Own Online Network

More kudos to the computer. This time the compliments are for the way the computer has provided an opportunity to reestablish contact with old friends, enhance our links to family and special friends, and find new friends who share common interests.

And, as a tool for keeping up with friends and meeting new people, America Online is second to none. AOL has a wonderful system — called the Buddy List — of keeping track of screen names of family, friends, and people you meet online. After you meet new friends in cyberspace or are joined online by old friends and relatives, it is time for AOL's help. The Buddy List organizes friends in a list that makes online contact easy.

Your Buddy List

You know *who* your buddy is, but do you know *where* he is? Your Buddy List can tell which of your friends are online at any time, day or night. The Buddy feature posts your Buddy List window in the upper-right corner of your screen every time you sign on to America Online, and updates the list as your friends sign on and off the system. That way, you know who is online, enabling you to engage in easy, spontaneous communication. Invite these friends to a chat room, start Instant Message conversations, or locate your friends online.

Setting Up Your Buddy List

The Buddy List is easy to use, simple, and accommodating. AOL offers you three separate ways to get to your Buddy List and start the setup activities. Let's take the first step and meet the Buddy List window. The following are the three ways to get to the Buddy List window and begin your setup:

▶ Sign on to AOL, and the Buddy List window appears by default in the upper-right corner of your screen. Labeled Buddies Online, it can become your constant companion. To start the Buddy List setup, just click the Setup button on this screen, as shown in Figure 3-1. At the Buddy List Setup screen, click Create, as shown in Figure 3-2.

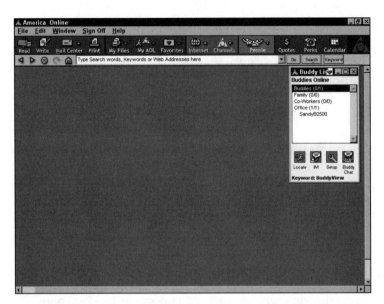

Figure 3-1. By default, your Buddy List window appears in the upper-right corner of the screen after you sign on to AOL.

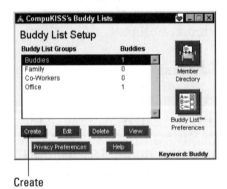

Create

Figure 3-2. To add friends, family, and coworkers to a Buddy List, click Create on the Buddy List Setup screen.

▶ Click View Buddy List in the People drop-down menu on your toolbar, as shown in Figure 3-3. To start the Buddy List setup, just click the Setup button on this screen. At the Buddy List Setup screen (shown in Figure 3-2), click Create.

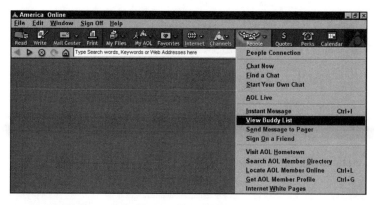

Figure 3-3. Clicking View Buddy List in the drop-down box under People on the toolbar also brings up your Buddy List window.

▶ Use the Keyword: **Buddy** to dive directly into the Buddy List window. To start the Buddy List setup, just click the Setup button on this screen. At the Buddy List Setup screen, click Create (shown in Figure 3-2).

Now that we are all at the same location, no matter which of the preceding three roads we followed, we are ready to add names to our Buddy List.

Adding Entries to Your Buddy List

AOL organizes Buddy List people by groups. The program's default Buddy List categories are Buddies, Family, and Co-Workers. You will be able to use these categories for the first entries you make to your Buddy List.

The Create a Buddy List Group window, shown in Figure 3-4, is ready to help organize your buddies into groups. Use any of the three default categories or customize categories by giving your Buddy List Group a label, such as College Alumni, Golfing Partners, or Friends.

Tip

If you plan to use one of the predefined AOL Buddy List Groups, highlight your choice with the cursor and double-click the group name. You can also high-light your group choice and click the Edit button to add names. If you want to define a new group of your own, click the Create button to label the new group and add names.

Tip

Clicking the Cancel button (or the X in the upper-right corner of the screen) closes the window. If you click this button prior to clicking Save, any changes made to your Buddy Lists during that session will not be remembered.

Tip

Limit the labels of your Buddy List Groups to 16 characters or less. List names can include letters, numbers, and nonal-phanumeric characters, such as & and $.

Customize A Label

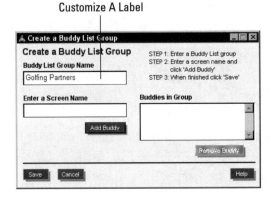

Figure 3-4. To organize your Buddy List Groups, use any of the three default cate-gories: Co-Workers, Family, and Buddies. Or, customize a category by giving it a label, such as College Alumni or Golfing Partners.

Now, type the AOL screen name or the AOL Instant Messenger screen name of the person you want to add in the Enter a Screen Name field (more informa-tion on Instant Messenger appears further in this chapter). Click Add Buddy or press Enter. Add all the names that fall into this particular group, and click Save to save your Buddy List Group.

You will receive confirmation that your Buddy List Group was saved. After you receive that confirma-tion, you can safely click Cancel (or X in the upper-right corner of the screen) to close the Buddy List Setup window.

You can have as many screen names in each Buddy List Group as you want; however, you are limited to a maximum of approximately 100 total screen names within your entire Buddy List.

Keeping Your Buddy List in Good Order

Any time you are online, you can delete or modify the people who appear in your Buddy List Groups.

Adding New Names

To add new names to an existing Buddy List Group, follow these steps:

1. From the People drop-down menu, click View Buddy List.
2. Click the Setup button on the Buddy List window. The Buddy List Setup window appears.
3. Double-click the group that you want to modify. The Edit List Buddies window appears, as shown in Figure 3-5.

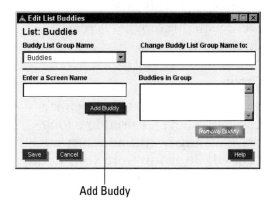

Add Buddy

Figure 3-5. When adding new names to an existing Buddy List Group, double-click the group at the Buddy List Setup window; when the Edit List Buddies window appears, click Add Buddy.

4. Click Add Buddy.
5. Repeat Steps 3 and 4 for all the screen names you want to add to this group.
6. When you are finished adding screen names to the list, click Save.

Removing Names

If you no longer need to communicate quickly with a specific person on your Buddy List, you may want

Tip

You can easily note which of your friends and family have just signed on to AOL or left AOL with the Buddy List window. You can also see how many of the buddies in each Buddy List Group are online. For instance, if you see Family (3/7), you know that three of your seven family-member buddies are signed on to AOL.

Tip

To bring your Buddy List window onscreen when you need it, type the Keyword: **Buddy**.

to delete that name from your list. To remove a name from your Buddy List, follow these steps:

1. From the People drop-down menu, click View Buddy List.
2. Click the Setup button on the Buddy List window; the Buddy List Setup window appears.
3. In the Buddies in Group box, click to highlight the screen name you want to remove.
4. Click Remove Buddy.
5. Repeat Steps 3 and 4 for all the screen names you want to remove from this group.
6. When you have finished removing screen names from the list, click Save.

Deleting a Whole Group

Sometimes, you may have occasion to reorganize and remove addresses you haven't used in a long time; maybe you are cleaning house, administratively speaking. To delete a whole group from your Buddy List, follow these steps:

1. From the People drop-down menu, click View Buddy List.
2. Click the Setup button on the Buddy List window; the Buddy List Setup window appears.
3. Click to select the group you want to delete.
4. Click Delete, as shown in Figure 3-6. Click OK on the next screen that appears.

Renaming a Group

Changing the name or label of a Buddy List Group is easy. Just follow these steps:

1. Go to the People drop-down menu and click View Buddy List.
2. Click the Setup button on the Buddy List window; the Buddy List Setup window appears.

Delete

Figure 3-6. To delete an entire group, select the group by clicking it once, click Delete, and then click OK.

Take a moment to recon-firm that you really want to delete an entire Buddy List Group before you click OK to delete the list. If you delete the Buddy List Group by mistake, you will have to reenter it from scratch, one entry at a time.

3. Click the Edit button; the Edit List window appears.

4. Select the name of the group you want to change from the Buddy List Group Name drop-down list.

5. Click inside the Change Buddy List Group Name to box and type the new name.

6. Click Save. A small dialog box appears, letting you know that your Buddy List has been updated.

7. Click OK and you will see the new name on the Buddy List window.

Locating a Friend Online

If one of your buddies comes online, you will know it when his name appears in your Buddy List. You can check whether he is in a public chat room and, if he is, join him in that particular room. Use the Locate button in the Buddy List window to find and join him, as follows:

1. Click the buddy's screen name in the Buddy List window to select it.

2. Click the Locate button. A small window appears (see Figure 3-7), letting you know whether he is in a public or private chat room, or online but not in a chat room.

Figure 3-7. After you click the Locate button, a small window appears letting you know whether your buddy is in a public or private chat room, or online but not in a chat room.

3. You now you have three options:

a. Click Go to join your buddy in the public chat room.

b. If you buddy is online (or in a private chat room) but not in a public chat room, click Send IM to send him an Instant Message that will immediately pop up on his screen (more information on Instant Messenger appears later in this chapter).

c. Click Cancel to close the window.

Setting Your Preferences

Now that you are more familiar with your Buddy List, you are ready to decide how and when your Buddy List appears. The Buddy List Setup screen has a Buddy List Preferences button that you can click to customize your Buddy List functions.

To set your Buddy List Preferences, follow these steps:

1. From the People drop-down menu, click View Buddy List. In the Buddy List window that appears, click Setup to get to the Buddy List Setup window. On the right side of the screen, click Buddy List Preferences to open the Preferences dialog box.

2. Make your choices in the boxes next to each of your preferences (see Figure 3-8).

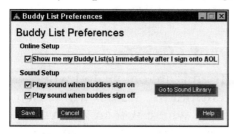

Figure 3-8. Make choices regarding how and when your Buddy List appears in the Buddy List Preferences screen.

3. After you set your Buddy List Preferences, click Save.

4. You will see the Preferences Updated dialog box. Click OK.

5. Click the Cancel (X) button in the upper-right corner of the Buddy List Preferences window if you are satisfied and do not want to make more changes.

View Options. In the Buddy List Preferences window, if you check the box labeled Show me my Buddy List(s) immediately after I sign onto AOL, you will see the Buddy List in the upper-right corner of your screen each time you sign on to AOL.

Sound Options. If you want to make sure that none of your buddies arrives online unnoticed, you could have your computer notify you of your friend's arrival with an audio signal. To hear sounds when your buddies arrive, click Setup from the Buddy List window; then, click Buddy List Preferences. Click the box next to Play sound when buddies sign on. To hear sounds when they leave, click the box next to Play sound when buddies sign off.

The default sounds for buddies coming and going are opening and closing doors. If you are adventure-some, you can also enable customized sounds. To do

The option labeled Show me my Buddy List(s) is checked by default. If you change it, you can use the Keyword: **Buddy View** to see your Buddy List whenever you want to.

If you do not change the default action of having the Buddy List appear automatically, you can easily close it by clicking the X in the upper-right corner of the Buddy List window.

Sounds won't be played unless you have your Buddy List window open. To open your Buddy List window, go to Keyword: **Buddy View**.

3

Creating Your Own Online Network

Tip

If your Buddy List Groups are large and your friends are extremely busy on their computers, the noises from all this activity may be distracting. If so, use the Buddy List Preferences dialog box to uncheck the sound options.

Note

If you enable the sound options and don't hear the opening and closing doors when your buddies come and go, click the Go to Sound Library button of your Buddy List Preferences window. At the next window, click Download Buddy Sound Installer "Door Theme" button. Next, click Download Now to begin the download.

so, you need to download a Buddy Sound Installer from AOL. Directions appear when you click the Go to Sound Library button on the Preferences screen.

Protecting Your Online Privacy

Knowing when your friends are online and where they are can be a benefit, but the system works two ways. *They* can also know where *you* are! Do you have days when you don't want to talk to anyone because you have the urge to be alone? I thought so. That is why AOL's messaging system has an entire collection of privacy choices.

This Buddy List feature enables you to protect your online privacy by selecting who can and cannot add your screen name to their Buddy List Groups, send you Instant Messages, or locate you online. You have the capability to block all AOL screen names or screen only the names that you specify.

Setting Privacy Options

To set your privacy options, follow these steps:

1. From the People drop-down menu, click View Buddy List. The Buddy List window appears.

2. Click Setup; when the Buddy List Setup window appears, click the Privacy Preferences button.

3. The Buddy List Privacy Preferences window appears (see Figure 3-9). This window is well laid out. The left side shows two sections: Choose Your Privacy Preferences, and Apply Preferences to the Following Features. Clicking one of the radio buttons in each section deactivates all the others.

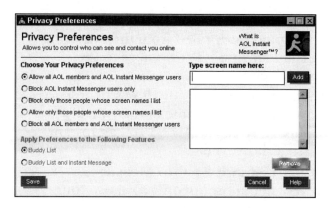

Figure 3-9. The privacy preferences offered by AOL allow you to control who can see and contact you online.

4. Choose Your Privacy Preferences from the following options:

- **Allow all AOL members and AOL Instant Messenger users:** If this default choice is not what you want, click the radio button next to another option.

- **Block AOL Instant Messenger users only:** Check the box to select this option.

- **Block only those people whose screen names I list:** You can block certain members by clicking this option and typing the screen names where indicated and then clicking the Add button.

- **Allow only those people whose screen names I list:** Click this option and indicate which screen names you wish to allow by typing them in the space provided and then clicking the Add button.

- **Block all AOL members and AOL Instant Messenger users:** Click this option to prevent all members from having you as a correspondent or locating you online.

Tip

The default setting in AOL is Allow all AOL members and AOL Instant Messenger users. Everybody with a Buddy List can add your name to it.

5. After you choose a level of privacy, indicate how it should be applied from the following options under Apply Preferences to the Following Features:

   ▪ **Buddy List:** Prevents or allows people to show your screen name in their Buddy List Group. They can still send you an Instant Message, however.

   ▪ **Buddy List and Instant Message:** Prevents or allows people to show your screen name in this Buddy List Group or send you an Instant Message.

6. Click Save.

Creating a Private Chat

Are you ready to be an online host? Want to organize a Buddy Chat by inviting your buddies in the group to enter a private chat room or meet you at a Favorite Place? Here is how to start a Buddy Chat:

1. Click the buddy's screen name in your Buddy List window, or click a Buddy List Group name in your Buddy List window to select the entire group.

2. Click the Buddy Chat Button, and a Buddy Chat window appears, showing you who will be invited (see Figure 3-10).

3. Make additions or changes to the Screen Names to Invite list if you want to add or remove people from that list. You can alter the list by erasing some names and adding others. You can invite only one person for a private encounter or as many as you can fit into a chat room and still have a good conversation.

By keeping your Buddy List window open, you will always have an up-to-the-minute list of your friends and coworkers who are online.

Figure 3-10. Organize a Buddy Chat by inviting your buddies in a group to enter a private chat room or meet you at a Favorite Place.

4. Select the Location: a Private Chat Room or a Keyword/Favorite Place. Normally, Private Chat Room is checked in the Location part of the window. Leave it as it is to organize a Buddy Chat.

5. In the Message To Send box, type a reason for getting together. AOL starts your message with "You are invited to"; complete that phrase or replace it with a phrase of your own. Make it sound inviting, to interest your friends in attending the chat.

6. Click Send to send them the message. An invitation window pops up on both your monitor and theirs. Everyone invited has the option to go to the area specified in your invitation, to send you an Instant Message, or to cancel your message.

AOL chats offer larger text areas for scrolling messages and the ability to talk to more than one person at one time. The Buddy Chat system quickly creates a private chat room and invites the screen names you specify.

3

Creating Your Own Online Network

Buddy List Symbols

- ▶ **Asterisk (*):** Appears next to the screen name of the person who has most recently signed on. The asterisk disappears the next time your Buddy List window is updated.

- ▶ **Parentheses ( ):** Placed around the screen name of a person who has just signed off AOL or the Instant Messenger service. You cannot locate, send an Instant Message to, or invite a member to a Buddy Chat if the screen name is enclosed by parentheses.

- ▶ **Group Count (3/5):** Tells you how many people on that list are online out of the total number of screen names on the list. For example, (3/5) means that three of the five people in a Buddy List Group are currently online.

- ▶ **Plus sign (+):** Indicates that a Buddy List Group has been *minimized*: the entire list of names in that group has been temporarily hidden to save screen space. Double-click the Buddy List Group name and all the screen names listed underneath will appear. Double-click the Buddy List Group name again to hide the names.

Using the Member Directory

We have used the Buddy List Setup window for many activities. The Member Directory button is the one button on this screen that we have not yet explored. All the other features were used to contact and categorize people we know. This last feature, the Member Directory, can introduce us to people we do not know — new potential friends with similar interests.

If you want other AOL members to know about you, you need to register in the AOL Member Directory. A collection of information about the owner of a screen name found in the directory is a *Member Profile.* Your personal Member Profile is supposed to be a brief description of yourself and your interests that can be viewed by other AOL members who want to know more about you. The information you share for your profile can include as little or as much as you would like to disclose. Your information is shared with other AOL users as they search the Member Directory or select Get Member Profile from the People menu. Profiles are a great way for old friends, relatives, or business associates to find out about you. Profiles are also good networking tools.

To create or edit your Member Profile, click View Buddy List on the People drop-down list, and then click Setup to take you to the Buddy List Setup window. Click the Member Directory button.

The Member Directory screen appears, as shown in Figure 3-11. Click the Create or Modify My Profile button. You can fill out a questionnaire about yourself to create a profile for the first time, or revise the profile you have already created if, say, you have recently changed screen names (see Figure 3-12).

The *Member Profile* is a collection of information about the owner of an AOL screen name that gives a brief description of that member and his or her interests. Other AOL members can view profiles to learn more about their fellow AOL members.

Profiles can serve as good networking tools.

3

Creating Your Own Online Network

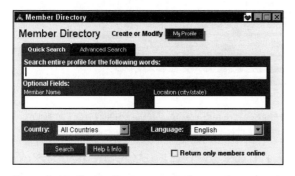

Figure 3-11. The Member Directory can be a catalyst in introducing AOL members to each other.

Edit Your Online Profile

To edit your profile, modify the category you would like to change and select "Update." To continue without making any changes to your profile, select "Cancel."

Your Name:

City, State, Country:

Birthday:

Sex: ○ Male   ○ Female   ● No Response

Marital Status:

Hobbies:

Computers Used:

Occupation:

Personal Quote:

Update   Delete   Cancel   My AOL   Help & Info

Figure 3-12. The information that AOL members share in their profiles can include as little or as much as they choose to disclose.

From the Member Directory screen, you can also do a search of the AOL Member Directory to see the profiles of other members. Simply type something to search for, such as another member's name, a city, or a hobby (see Figure 3-13). Then, click the Search button and you will see a list of members who matched your search. If any are online at that moment, they are indicated with a red arrowhead.

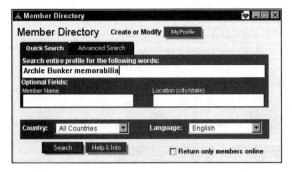

Figure 3-13. To do a search of the AOL Member Directory, simply type a topic to search for, such as another member's name, a city, or a hobby, and then click Search.

Suppose you have discovered an AOL member listed in the directory who shares your passion for collecting Archie Bunker memorabilia. (And you thought you were the only person in the whole world who

collected Archie Bunker mementos!) I bet you'd
want to talk to this person to trade notes. Instant
Messenger to the rescue! It's finally time to introduce you to America Online's convenient and flexible communication tool.

Instant Messenger

Communications continue to be the cornerstone
of the Internet, and AOL's Instant Messenger is a
wonderful way for people to communicate. Instant
Messenger is a buddy-chat program that lets users
communicate through their keyboards in real time
by sending messages that recipients see instantly,
without having to go through e-mail. Unlike regular
e-mail, Instant Messages pop up immediately on the
screen of the recipients, and their responses can be
back to you instantly. Because e-mail is not interactive, Instant Messenger was developed to blend the
speed of e-mail with the interactivity of a phone call
by letting you type back and forth with someone
else on the system.

Instant Messenger is a way to have a quick conversation with someone regardless of what else either of
you is doing on the computer at the time. These messages are private: only you and your correspondent
know what's passing between you, as opposed to a
chat room conversation, where two or more — sometimes many more — take part in the conversation.

Until recently, Instant Messenger territory was limited to those inside the fence of AOL. In 1997, however, AOL extended Instant Messenger to Internet
users by offering them a free download program.
AOL Instant Messenger allows AOL members to
communicate instantly via private, personalized

Tip

Two of AOL's popular fea-
tures are chats and e-mail.
But, chats are not private
and e-mail is not instant,
so, being the enterprising
entity it is, AOL incorporated the best features of
chats and e-mail, combin-
ing privacy and interactivity, and produced Instant
Messenger.

3

Creating Your Own Online Network

Tip

Although the Internet user must download and install the Instant Messenger program, the AOL user doesn't need to install any additional software to use Instant Messenger.

messages with non-AOL members, after an Internet user has downloaded the program and registered a screen name for AOL. If you have a non-AOL friend who has set up Instant Messenger software on their computer, you can send Instant Messages back and forth just as you would with AOL users. You can also add your friend to your AOL Buddy List, if you know his or her registered screen name.

AOL is by far the market leader in this popular Instant Messenger program. For example, Saul Hansell, in an article about instant messaging distributed by the news service of the *New York Times* (July 23, 1999), shares these statistics:

▶ More than 80 million AOL and Internet users communicate by Instant Messenger.

▶ Instant messages are outpacing postal mail.

▶ AOL says that its networks carry some 780 million messages a day, which is more than all the mail handled by the U.S. Postal Service in a day.

AOL reinforced benefits to its membership with the *Knock-Knock* feature. Only AOL members can select and choose which incoming messages to accept from Internet users. Knock-Knock announces that an Instant Messenger user is sending you a message from the Internet. You can accept or decline the message.

Using Instant Messenger

Instant Messenger is wildly popular. AOL and Internet users find it helpful to do the following:

▶ Have a private "aside" with someone in a chat room.

▶ Get a friend's attention and let him know you are also online.

▶ Introduce yourself to someone you've never met before.

Okay, suppose you want to locate an AOL member that you discovered in the Member Directory who has the same interest in collecting Archie Bunker memorabilia that you have. What do you do?

Locating Your Recipient

First, you have to make sure the recipient of your Instant Message is online. To check whether someone is online, you can use either the Locate button on the Buddy List window or the Locate command (Ctrl+L for Windows users; Apple+L for Mac users). When the Locate Buddy window appears, as shown in Figure 3-14, follow these steps:

Tip

If you are sending an Instant Message to someone you have already registered as your buddy, you can check your Buddy List. Go to your Buddy List window and click your buddy's name to find out whether he or she is online. If he or she is, click the Send Instant Message button in the Buddy List window.

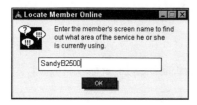

Figure 3-14. To send an Instant Message to someone, first make sure the recipient is online. Use the Locate Member Online screen to do this.

1. Type an AOL member's screen name or the Internet user's screen name in the blank and click OK.
2. The Locate window appears, telling you whether that person is online and, if applicable, which chat room he or she is in (see Figure 3-15).

Figure 3-15. The Locate window lets you know whether a buddy is online and, if applicable, which chat room he or she is in.

Tip

It is best to keep your Instant Messages short; 10 to 12 words is about right. Instant Messages are limited to 512 characters. If you have a longer message, you might want to send a few sentences at a time or use e-mail.

Sending an Instant Message

To start a one-on-one conversation with your buddy or someone on the Internet, follow these steps:

1. Click the screen name of your buddy in the Buddy List window.
2. Click the Instant Messenger button. The Send Instant Message window will appear (see Figure 3-16).
3. Type your message into the bottom, larger box.

Type your message here.

Figure 3-16. Type your message into the bottom, larger box of the Send Instant Message window.

4. Click Send and the message appears almost immediately on your buddy's screen. A similar window pops up on your monitor with your message. He or she can respond or cancel your message (see Figure 3-17).

Figure 3-17. After you send an Instant Message, a window pops up on your monitor with your message, similar to the window that pops up on your buddy's screen.

The following are two other ways of getting to the Instant Messenger screen:

▶ From the People drop-down menu on the toolbar, click Instant Message.

▶ Use the Ctrl+I key combination to quickly open the Instant Message window.

Then, type the screen name of the person you want to send a message to, type your message, and click Send.

Receiving and Responding to an Instant Message

When an AOL member (or someone on the Internet with Instant Messenger installed on their computer) sends you an Instant Message, the message immediately appears on your screen. The top bar displays the screen name of the person who sent the message. To respond to an Instant Message, follow these steps:

1. A small window pops onto your screen when someone sends you an Instant Message.

2. Click the Respond button to reply. (Click Cancel if you do not want to reply to the message.) The window will expand to give you a place to type your reply.

3. Type your response in the large box at the bottom of the window.

4. Click Send to send the reply.

The author of the original message may respond to you, and you may reply again. When you finish exchanging messages, click Cancel to close the window.

Sending an Instant Message While Chatting

While you are online participating in a chat and have an opinion to share, but only with your best buddy,

If the recipient of your Instant Message is signed on and accepting Instant Messages, your Instant Messenger window disappears from your screen after you send your Instant Message, but it reappears shortly thereafter.

Use the Buddy List window to invite your buddies to join a group chat, share an Instant Message conversation, or locate them online.

AOL staff will never ask you for your password. Don't fall for impersonations of the AOL staff claiming an emergency need for your password or credit card. If this happens, use the Keyword: **Notify AOL**.

3

Creating Your Own Online Network

Note

You aren't required to respond to an Instant Message if you don't want to.

Tip

If you hear the Instant Messenger chime but do not see the Instant Messenger window appear, click the Window pull-down menu at the top of your AOL screen and click the bottom list of windows: Instant Message from screen name. This brings the Instant Message to the front of your screen.

you can send an Instant Message to exchange private messages with your buddy. Messages that you send appear immediately on the other person's screen. Best of all, only that person sees the message.

To send an Instant Message while chatting, follow these steps:

1. From the area displaying the screen name of each person in the chat room, double-click the name of the person you want to send an Instant Message to.

2. Click Send Message from the window that appears to send that person an Instant Message.

3. The Send Instant Message window appears. The AOL program automatically enters the screen name of the other member for you.

4. Type the message you want to send.

5. Click Send to send the message.

Turning Off Instant Messages

Sometimes, you might not want to be disturbed or might not want strangers to be able to contact you, your children, or grandchildren via Instant Messenger. AOL lets you disable Instant Messages as needed:

1. Open an Instant Message window (from the Buddy List window or from the People drop-down list).

2. In the To box, type the peculiar command **$im_off**.

3. Type an **X** (or anything you like) in the message area of the bottom box (see Figure 3-18).

4. Click Send. Instant Messages will now be ignored.

Any person attempting to send you an Instant Message will be advised that you are not accepting Instant Messengers.

Figure 3-18. To turn off Instant Messages, type *$im_off* in the To box and an X (or anything you like) in the message area of the bottom box.

Turning On Instant Messages

To turn on Instant Message after you have turned it off, follow the same steps just described, but type **$im_on** in the To box. You can now receive Instant Messengers.

Using Parental Controls to Block Instant Message Notes

To set Parental Controls to block Instant Messages, follow these steps:

1. Click the My AOL icon and then click Parental Controls on the drop-down menu.
2. Click Set Parental Controls.
3. Click IM Control (a dialog box appears explaining Parental Controls).
4. Click the Block Instant Message Notes checkbox.

Sharing Favorite Online Areas in Instant Message Conversations

Recall from the Jump Start that Web surfing is all about hyperlinks. A *hyperlink* is a picture, icon, or portion of text within a Web site that you can click with your mouse to take you to another portion of the Web site or to another Web site altogether. Both America Online and the Internet are constantly using these amazing shortcuts.

Tip

The Instant Messenger feature is turned on, by default, every time you sign onto AOL. If you prefer to turn it off permanently, you can use Parental Controls or Buddy List Privacy Preferences.

Note

To use Parental Controls, you must sign on to your master account — that is, the first screen name you created when you installed AOL.

Cross-Reference

More information on Favorite Places such as using and organizing Your Favorites will be given in Chapter 5.

3

Creating Your Own Online Network

You can share your favorite online areas with your buddies by including hyperlinks in an Instant Message. AOL gives you two convenient ways to do this, each of which depends on whether or not you are in the process of conversing with your buddy by Instant Messenger.

Suppose that you are *not* conversing with your buddy at the moment and want to initiate a new Instant Message contact in which you include your favorite hyperlink. To send a hyperlink in an Instant Message, follow these steps:

1. If you find an area online that you like, click the heart icon on its title bar. A dialog box with three buttons appears.

2. Click Insert in Instant Message, as shown in Figure 3-19. Now, the Instant Message appears with the link already inserted.

Figure 3-19. Click Insert in Instant Message to have the online area that you like inserted into an Instant Message.

3. Add an explanation about the link, if you wish, and click the To box to fill in your friend's screen name.

4. Click Send.

Suppose you are in the middle of an Instant Message conversation and want your buddy to look at a site you think is great. To add a hyperlink to an Instant Message, follow these steps:

1. Click the Favorites icon on the toolbar, and click Favorite Places on the drop-down menu. Your Favorite Places list appears. If the item you want to share is inside a folder, double-click to open the folder.
2. Click and drag any area with a heart icon into the bottom box of your Instant Message window. A blue underlined link appears.
3. Click Send.

You can drag the Favorite Places heart from the title bar of any area into your Instant Message, regardless of whether you have added it to your Favorite Places folder.

Coming Up Next

The next part of the book delves into how to navigate through AOL and the Internet to find what you are looking for quickly and easily. In this chapter, we learned how to extend AOL's online communication tools to create our own online network. We learned:

▶ The Buddy List is AOL's convenient system of keeping track of screen names of family, friends, and people you meet online.

▶ At any time you are online, you can delete or modify the people who appear in your Buddy List Groups.

▶ AOL protects your online privacy by letting you select who can and cannot add your screen name to their Buddy List Groups, send you Instant Messages, or locate you online.

▶ The Member Directory can introduce you to people you haven't met yet, potential new friends with similar interests.

▶ Communications continue to be the cornerstone of the Internet, and instant messaging is becoming a more prevalent way for people to communicate.

3

Creating Your Own Online Network

CHAPTER

4

GETTING AROUND

Quick Look

▶ **Today on AOL**   **page 123**

AOL highlights the top headlines of the day, as well as the interesting programs and happenings offered on AOL, in the Today on AOL section of the Welcome screen. Updated daily, these teasers are links to the areas on AOL where you will find more information on the topic that caught your eye.

▶ **My Places**   **page 125**

Have AOL remember your favorite places and highlight them on the Welcome screen each time you sign on. Just click the Set My Places button on the Welcome screen to set them up.

▶ **AOL's Travel Channel**   **page 130**

Want to take a trip? Make your first trip the AOL Travel Channel. This channel offers a wealth of information on travel and includes a message board and chat area to let travelers share recommendations and information.

▶ **Keyword: Parental Controls**   **page 136**

AOL has control over its own content but does not have control over the content of the Internet. Go to Keyword: **Parental Controls** to find full instructions on how to set up AOL to protect children from content on the Internet that may not be suitable for their age group.

Chapter 4

Getting Around

One of the reasons that millions of people use AOL is that it provides a quick and easy way to navigate the online world. Like sailing a ship on the sea, it is easy to get lost on the Internet, so America Online gives you navigational tools to make your online life easier and more carefree.

Starting at the Welcome Screen

The AOL Welcome screen is the first thing that you see when you sign on to America Online. It is a well-organized screen that helps you to navigate through AOL's wealth of information. The Welcome screen, shown in Figure 4-1, contains a list of the available channels, the You've Got Mail and the You've Got Pictures notifications, a link to My Calendar (which enables you to develop a personal calendar), and a link to AOL's Chat area. The Welcome screen also contains information on the day's highlights, exciting new features, current news, weather, and other important information. The Welcome screen will become an important first stop in your online experience.

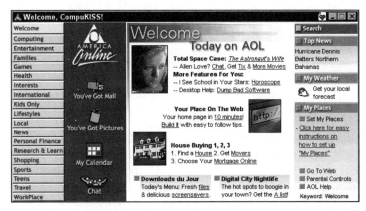

Figure 4-1. The Welcome screen is the first screen you see after signing on to AOL.

AOL 5.0 Welcome Screen

The Welcome screen seen in Figure 4-1 is an AOL 5.0 screen. If you are using an earlier version of AOL, your screen may be slightly different than this illustration. Upgrading to AOL's 5.0 version is easy. To upgrade, go to the Keyword: **Upgrade** and follow the directions. After you have upgraded you can take advantage of the new 5.0 features: seven screen names, expanded search capabilities, My Places, and You've Got Pictures.

Before you upgrade, the system requirements will be given. If your computer does not meet the system requirements, you can still follow the instructions in this book allowing for slight variations. If your computer can handle the upgrade, download the program and start enjoying 5.0 and all the new features today. It is a great change.

Today on AOL

When the Welcome screen appears, you will see many hot topics of the day listed in the Today on AOL section of the screen. AOL often highlights the top headlines of the day as well as the interesting programs and happenings offered on AOL. The headlines and teaser topic lines in this area are linked to take you directly to the area for more information on the topic that caught your eye. For example, click the Find a House link (shown in Figure 4-1) and AOL takes you straight to house-buying information.

The pictures on the Welcome screen are also linked to the articles and topic areas, so be sure to run your mouse across them, too.

You've Got Pictures

Version 5.0 of AOL introduced several new exciting features that appear on the Welcome screen. The first is You've Got Pictures, which enables you to create digital photos without first having to buy a digital camera or scanner. This is an easy way to get your photographs into the computer and ready for digital use.

My Calendar

The My Calendar feature enables you to add appointments to your calendar and access them from any computer with your screen name. With the Fun Events directory, you can click any event and automatically save it to your calendar.

My Weather

Planning a picnic? Need to know what to wear today? The My Weather button on the AOL Welcome screen will come to your aid. Type your area code, ZIP code, or city and state to get the weather for your area.

My Places

Click the Set My Places button on the Welcome screen to have AOL remember your favorite AOL places and include links to them on the Welcome screen. After you click Set My Places, click Choose New Place and then select a link from the list that appears. Repeat this for each of the five My Places shortcuts. After you make your selections, click Save My Changes, and your favorite places will appear on the Welcome screen every time you start America Online.

Note

The Today on AOL section of the Welcome screen changes daily to reflect each day's headlines and topics of interest.

Cross-Reference

Learn more about having fun with You've Got Pictures in Chapter 14.

Tip

Be sure to check the My Weather section of the Welcome screen when you travel, to be prepared for the weather of your destination.

4

Getting Around

Navigating with AOL Channels

Definition

Channels are the navigational feature provided by America Online to help you locate information and to guide you to your destination on AOL and the Internet quickly and easily.

Tip

AOL is constantly updating and changing information offered on its various channels, so it is a good idea to visit your favorite channel often.

Tip

You can easily return to the Channels list, no matter where you are within AOL. Just click the Channels button on the AOL toolbar at the top of the screen and pick your channel from the drop-down list.

Channels are the navigational feature provided by America Online to guide you to your destination within AOL and the Internet. This feature helps you locate the information that you want quickly and easily by grouping topics together under one main heading.

America Online Channels are a great place to find useful information on exciting subjects, and choosing a channel can be the first step in your search process. Click the channel of your choice from the Welcome screen (refer to Figure 4-1) or click the AOL Channels icon on the toolbar to see a drop-down menu of channel choices (see Figure 4-2).

Channels icon

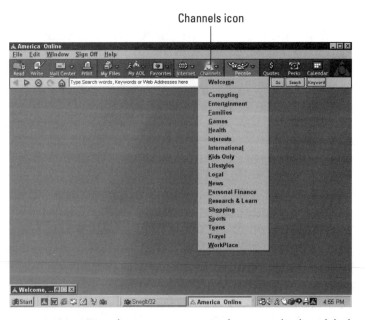

Figure 4-2. No matter where you are, you can easily return to the Channels list by clicking the Channels icon on the toolbar.

Each of the 19 AOL Channels is devoted to a particular subject. The content of each channel is frequently updated, and users are welcome to participate by means of chat rooms, games, suggestion boxes, and message boards. Each of the channels contains explicit information on the topic listed, but each channel takes on its own personality. User participation helps to create unique channels. Although there is plenty of information on the Internet, the America Online Channels are a unique way to access great places, meet new people, and add to your knowledge and online enjoyment.

Each of the following 19 AOL Channels contains some very useful information:

Note

One of the benefits of using the AOL Channels is that an enormous amount of information is available to you in an organized manner.

▶ **Welcome**: The Welcome screen will quickly become your stepping-off point to an online world of adventure. See quickly what's happening in the world today by enjoying Today on AOL. Get the top news stories and other featured information at this location.

▶ **Computing**: Visit this channel to get the most from your computer. Download software, research companies, read hardware and software reviews, join an online classroom, and review popular computer magazines. Computing tips of the day can be very timesaving.

▶ **Entertainment**: Entertainment is your ticket to the cinema, TV, comedy, music, and stars. This channel offers information on TV shows, movies, books, and music.

▶ **Families**: Come to this location for information and advice on modern parenting, family activities, timesaving tips, and ideas for improving your home. Just the place for helping you make your dwelling more comfortable.

4

Getting Around

▶ **Games**: This channel provides nonstop fun for everyone by offering access to many of the popular computer and video games available today. Read reviews of new games, play games, and find tips on how to improve your skills and talents. This channel offers information on the basics of games as well as current highlights.

▶ **Health**: This channel offers information on illnesses and treatments, support groups, and healthy living. It also has a complete medical reference section.

▶ **Interests**: This site incorporates the pieces that make up your daily life: your home, car, pets, hobbies, and meals. The scope of this channel is broad. Explore your passions and pastimes by checking out a wide variety of interests and hobbies, such as pets, home improvement, photography, food, cars, and more.

▶ **International**: Bring the world closer. This channel gives you access to current news as well as business and cultural information on places around the globe.

▶ **Kids Only**: Targeted for grade-school-aged kids (with some areas of interest to teens), this site says "keep out" to grown-ups. Children can find information on sports, games, TV shows, the Web, and clubs, and can even get help with their homework. It's a great resource for entertaining youngsters of any age.

▶ **Lifestyles**: Browse topics such as teens, self-improvement, ethnicity, ages and stages, beliefs, women's issues, and romance on this channel. Find yourself and others like you.

▶ **Local**: This channel provides local news, movie listings, restaurants, classifieds, and real estate information. It will help you find facts about your own area, and is also a great resource when you're on the road.

- ▶ **News**: This channel features the hour's headlines and top news stories on various topics, such as U.S. and world news, business, sports, and weather. News you want, when you want it.

- ▶ **Personal Finance**: If you want to control your financial future, this channel provides information on topics such as stocks, business news, investment research, tax planning, and online banking. Current market quotes are up to date, and guidance is available on mutual funds and insurance, as well. You can enter your portfolio, track it in real-time online and get up to date news articles about your investments.

- ▶ **Research & Learn**: Ever had to write a research paper? Want to expand your knowledge? This channel is the gateway to knowledge. Find information on history, science, health, and geography, as well as a reference section with online encyclopedias.

- ▶ **Shopping**: Do you like the convenience of shopping from home? Browse and shop around the clock. Get information and savings on a wide variety of products and services. Stroll through various departments, such as jewelry, electronics, flowers, home office, sports, and toys.

- ▶ **Sports**: Sports fans can find in-depth infor-ma-tion on a wide variety of sports, such as base-ball, basketball, football, golf, hockey, and tennis. Check out scoreboards, top stories, and the Grandstand section.

4

Getting Around

Place your cursor over any of the channel names on the Welcome screen, and a list of the topics in that channel will pop up on your screen.

▸ **Teens**: AOL features current articles to interest the teen generation, as well as teen-oriented sections on life, friends, style, and fun. The chat and message board areas are popular with today's young people. Youngsters can plug in to some really cool people at Teen People on Line.

▸ **Travel**: Want to take a trip? Make your first stop the AOL Travel Channel. This channel offers information on travel, such as bargain airfares, destinations, and an online reservation center for air, car, hotel, and so on. The message and chat sections let travelers share recommendations and information.

▸ **Workplace**: Need help with your business and career? Check out this channel, which offers business news, classifieds, and discussions about various professions. Here you find professional forums, business services, and business research, which are sure to serve as valuable resources.

When you click a channel, you are presented with that channel's main screen (see Figures 4-3 and 4-4). From that screen, you can jump to a plethora of related information.

How Channels Work

Suppose that you want to know how your favorite sports team fared in last night's game. Just use AOL Channels to find out. Here's how:

1. If you are at the AOL Welcome screen, click the Sports button.

Figure 4-3. When you click a channel, the main screen of that location appears.

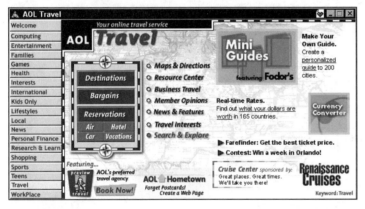

Figure 4-4. From a channel's main screen, you can jump to a plethora of related information.

2. If you are anywhere else in AOL, click the Channels icon on the toolbar at the top of the AOL screen, as shown in Figure 4-5, and choose Sports from the drop-down list.

3. Under Scoreboard, choose the listing that you would like to see. You'll find everything from the National Basketball Association to Major League Soccer.

4. Keep your fingers crossed and look for your team. Maybe it won — you'll know in a minute.

Definition

Keywords are shortcuts that AOL uses to take you instantly to a specific area of information.

Tip

To enter a keyword, press the Ctrl key and the letter K at the same time (Mac users press Control+K). A box will pop up in which you can enter the keyword.

Note

Keywords are not particular about capitalization or spacing. SPORTS, sports, sPorts, or sp orts will all get you to the same place.

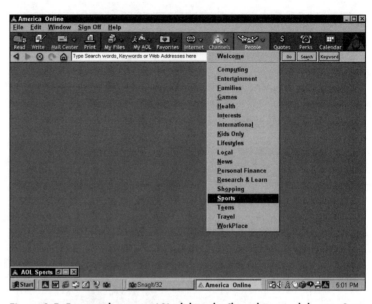

Figure 4-5. From any location in AOL, clicking the Channels icon and choosing Sports from the drop-down menu will take you to the Sports Channel.

Using Keywords as Shortcuts

Another great navigational tool that AOL uses is a keyword feature that takes you instantly to a specific area of information. In most cases, a keyword will exactly or closely match the name of the AOL area, company, forum, Web site, or other destination.

Keywords are among the quickest ways to get from place to place on AOL. Keywords exist for almost every AOL area.

Next time you go to an area on AOL, look for the keyword shown in the bottom-right corner of the window (for example, the keyword for the Shopping Channel is *Shopping*). Use the keyword the next time you want to visit that particular AOL area (see Figure 4-6).

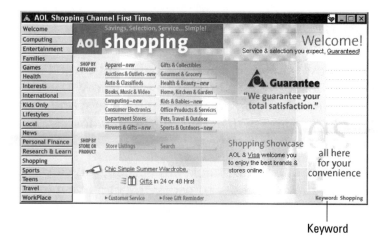

Keyword

Figure 4-6. The Shopping Channel's keyword, *Shopping*, is shown in the bottom-right corner of the window.

Get in the habit of using keywords. They will become shortcuts to your favorite places online.

In the middle of the AOL Navigation bar at the top of the screen is a white box that says "Type Search words, Keywords or Web Addresses here." Place the cursor over that box and click (see Figure 4-7). When you click, the words in the box are darkened. When you type the keyword, the darkened words disappear, and the text that you type appears instead. After you type the keyword, either click the word Go or press Enter (or Return, if you are on a Mac), and you will see the new AOL content page.

Type Keyword Here   Click GO (or press enter)

Figure 4-7. After you type the keyword, click Go or press Enter, and you will see the new AOL content page.

Tip

To display a complete list of keywords on AOL, type **Keyword**. Keywords are listed both alphabetically and by channel.

Definition

The *Navigation bar* is the bar below the toolbar, provided by AOL for finding your way around the Web.

4

Getting Around

Getting Help

Tip

After you enter a keyword or URL, you can either click the word Go or press the Enter key on your keyboard.

Okay, now you understand the basics, but you'll still get lost or need a little help every now and then. When you do, just type the Keyword: **Quickstart**, and AOL's QuickStart Guide for new members will appear.

When you are at the QuickStart screen, you can watch a movie on how to use AOL, get a five-minute tour, or look at the best of what AOL has to offer. Don't miss AOL's Tips, which give tips on everything from using AOL on the road to how to print a file.

Definition

Spam is unwanted e-mail. Like junk mail, it includes unsolicited advertising and often contains unwelcome material.

Type the Keyword: **Help**, and AOL will come to your aid with guidance and help topics on almost every subject. This is the place to come for billing or other account information. You will also find help on connecting to AOL, installing a new version of AOL, and using screen names and passwords. You will also find information here about such things as setting up parental controls and how to deal with spam (unwanted e-mail).

Tip

Type **?** instead of a keyword to get to the QuickStart Guide for new members.

This section has so much information that you may want to visit and sift through the many informative articles even if you don't need help with a specific problem. Checking out the Help files will give you a feeling for the many facets and benefits of AOL.

Identifying How AOL and the Internet Differ

America Online gives you a broad range of topics and so much information that you could be happy just surfing through AOL forever. But AOL offers more. It offers you a seamless integration with the Internet. In fact, the integration is so seamless that you often don't even know whether you are in AOL or on the Internet. And because Internet access is free with your AOL account, you don't have to worry about it. Just go with the flow and enjoy your surfing.

But what is the Internet and how is it different from AOL?

AOL: Your Guide to the Internet

One way to think of America Online is as your guide to the Internet. The Internet is a vast, awesome, and often overpowering resource. As such, the Internet can be chaotic, confusing, and sometimes lonely unless you have a pathfinder, such as America Online. AOL is an easy-to-use, well-organized online service that offers a wide range of information and features. With millions of members, it is the largest online service on the Internet, known and loved for its ease of use.

Definition

The *Internet* is a global network of computers connecting millions of people in countries around the world, providing a quick and easy exchange of information.

Definition

Technically speaking, America Online (AOL) is an *Internet portal*; that is, it's just one especially content-rich location on the Internet.

4

Getting Around

Children and the Internet

AOL has control over its own content but does not have control over the content of the Internet. The Internet mirrors the real world: It has a lot of dark alleys with sexually explicit content and unacceptable characters for your youngsters. For this reason, AOL provides built-in controls for the parent or grandparent who is worried about the information their children or grandchildren can access on the Internet. You can set up these restrictions by age group. Just type the Keyword: **Parental Controls** to get full instructions on how to use and set up these helpful tools.

The Internet: A Global Network of Computers

The Internet is a global network of computers connecting more than 50 million people in countries around the world. The Internet provides a quick and easy exchange of information and has become recognized as the central information tool in this Information Age. Unlike AOL, no central source owns, runs, or is responsible for the Internet. It is a system of many different computers in many different places all linked together through no central facility.

What Is the Web?

The World Wide Web (WWW), commonly referred to as *the Web,* is the popular multimedia branch of the Internet. The Web enables users to view not just text but also graphics and video, as well as hear sound, and also allows hyperlinking to other content or documents, just as you find in AOL.

As with the rest of the Internet, users can access the Web to locate, read, and download documents stored on computer systems around the world. On the Web, however, the documents are presented as a series of pages (commonly known as *Web pages*) that are linked together to form a Web site.

What Is a Web Page?

The basic unit of every Web site, or a document on the Web, is a *page.* A Web page can be an article, an ordering page, or a single photograph. It is usually a combination of text and graphics. An entire Web page may not be fully visible on your computer screen. You may have to click the arrows on the scrollbar on the right side of the screen to scroll up or down to see the full page.

What Is a Web Site?

A *Web site* is a collection of related Web pages. Any government agency, college, university, company, or individual can create and maintain a Web site. The Web is a dynamically moving and changing entity. Many Web sites change on a daily or hourly basis. Some news-related sites change every few minutes. So, if you find a Web site that you like, be sure to visit often to see the changes that are made.

What Is an Internet Browser?

Viewing Web pages on the Internet is accomplished through a Web browser. A *browser* is a software program that enables you to view Web pages on your computer. AOL has incorporated a browser into its own system by building Microsoft Internet Explorer (MSIE) right into the AOL software.

Definition

The *World Wide Web (WWW)*, commonly referred to as *the Web*, is the popular multimedia branch of the Internet that consists of huge collections of documents stored on hundreds of thousands of computers.

Definition

A *browser* is a software program that enables you to view Web pages on your computer.

Using Links and URLs

Definition

A *link*, or *hyperlink*, is text, an icon, a picture, or a button that moves a user from one Web page or Web site to another.

Tip

Move your cursor around the page onscreen by moving your mouse. Whenever the cursor turns into a pointing finger, you have encountered a hot link. Click the link, and you will be transported to the Web page indicated by the pointing finger.

You've seen surfers riding the waves. They weave in and out, enjoying the ride and traveling wherever the waves take them. Using the Internet is something like that. You travel easily and smoothly from one place to another, kind of weaving in and out, reading, learning, and being entertained all at the same time. That's why using the Internet is often called surfing the Web.

Links Take You Where You Want to Go

A *link*, short for *hyperlink*, moves a user from one Web page or Web site to another. Links can be text, icons, pictures, or buttons. Text links are usually underlined and are often a different color than the rest of the text on the page. A hyperlink is clickable. When you click a hyperlink, you instantly jump from one place to another. Using hyperlinks, often called *hot links*, is a wonderful way to browse. You get to explore any subject by clicking the things that interest you. Click a few links and see what happens. You can't hurt anything.

If you do click something and then decide that you want to return to the previous page, just click the backward arrow (also called the Back button) on the left side of the Navigation bar on the top of the AOL screen (see Figure 4-8).

Back Button

Figure 4-8. The Back button on the left side of the AOL Navigation bar will return you to the previous Web page.

URLs or Internet Addresses

Each Web page has a unique address, called a Uniform Resource Locator (URL). A typical Web site address usually looks like `http://www.whatever.com`, where *whatever* represents an actual name.

The first part of the address, before the colon, is the access method. Most of the time you will see `http`, which stands for *Hypertext Transport Protocol (HTTP)*. This means that you are accessing a page on the Internet by using the HTTP protocol. Don't worry; the computer understands this, so you don't have to.

The colon and the slashes are special separators that the computer uses to translate the address. They are a UNIX type of code. (*UNIX* is an operating system used on many of the computers on the Internet.) If you used computers in the DOS days, you will find that DOS uses the backslash (\), while UNIX and Internet applications both use the forward slash (/).

The last part of the URL is the *domain name* where the resource is located. It is often, but not always, preceded by www, for World Wide Web. The domain name often indicates the network where the user is located. This can be considered the place where the user's mail is received. The domain name is followed by an extension (a period and three letters) that indicates the type of organization to which the network belongs. Some common extensions are the following:

Definition

The *Uniform Resource Locator*, or *URL*, is the specific address of a Web page.

4

Getting Around

Tip

Unlike AOL keywords, URLs are very particular about spacing and somewhat particular about capitalization. Be sure to type the URL exactly as it was given to you.

Extension	Used For
.com	Commercial business or company
.edu	Educational institution
.gov	Government agency
.int	International
.mil	Military
.net	Network organization
.org	Organization (nonprofit)

You might also see foreign addresses that add a country code as the last several digits of the address, such as the following examples:

Extension	Country
.au	Australia
.ca	Canada
.fr	France
.it	Italy
.th	Thailand
.us	United States

When You Know the Address

Most of us feel like we are being inundated with Web addresses. Everywhere you go you hear or see www.*whatever*.com. The ad in the newspaper gave you an Internet address to go to for more information. The television program has the transcripts for you to see at its Web site. Even your local bank invites you to its Web site for rate information. Jot down all those Internet addresses, because after you have the URL or Internet address, finding the information you want is easy.

As discussed earlier in the chapter, in the middle of the AOL Navigation bar is a white box that says

"Type Search words, Keywords or Web Addresses here." Earlier, you highlighted this text and replaced it with an AOL keyword. Now, you are going to enter a Web address.

Place the cursor over that box and click (see Figure 4-9), which darkens the words in the box. When you type the Web address, the darkened words disappear and the text that you type appears. After you type the address, either click the word Go or press Enter, and you will see the new Web page appear.

Figure 4-9. After you type a Web address in the text box and click Go or press Enter, a new Web page appears.

In many cases, you can get to the proper Web address by typing **www.,** followed by the name of a particular business or organization, and ending with **.com** or **.org**, and so on, as you often see URLs listed (for example, www.whatever.com). If the Web site doesn't appear, try including http:// at the beginning of the address, which will help to ensure the accuracy of the address.

Don't fret about long Internet addresses, because after you find a page that you like, you can put it on your Favorites list, enabling you to retrieve it later without having to reenter the address. (The next chapter explains Favorites in much more detail.)

When You Don't Know the Address

When you don't know a Web address, you can often guess. We'll talk a little more about finding things on the Internet in the next chapter, but a simple guess will often get you to the right place.

If you are looking for the *USA Today* Web site, for example, try www.usatoday.com. If you are looking for a baseball team to stand behind regardless of whether it wins, try www.chicagocubs.com. If you are looking for me, try www.sandyberger.com.

Remember that you might be looking for a company name, a personal name, or a trademark name. For instance, my personal domain name is www.sandyberger.com. My company's domain name is www.computerliving.com. My main Web site is www.compukiss.com, which is my trademark — Compu-Kiss for The Computer World — Keeping It Short and Simple. Each of these sites will take you to a different place with different information, but all will lead you to information about me.

Try whatever name you associate with the product or company that you are trying to find. Often, the company has acquired domain names for several representative identifiers. For instance, www.cocacola.com and www.coke.com both take you to the official Coca Cola Web site.

Sites with Both Keyword and URL Addresses

A keyword takes you to an area within America Online. A URL, or Web site address, takes you to an Internet site. Sometimes, you will find that the company or organization that you are trying to find has both an area in AOL and an Internet site. For instance, type the Keyword: **AARP** and you will be transported to the AARP/AOL site. Type **www.aarp.org** and you will be taken to AARP's Internet Web site. These sites are similar, but each has a different interface. Sometimes, AOL has special content that is not available on the Internet. For instance, AARP and other organizations may have chat rooms on AOL that are not open to the general Internet public.

If you find a group or organization that has both a keyword and an Internet site, look at both to see which content and which interface you like better.

Navigating Both AOL and the Web

The AOL browser controls are located on the Navigation bar, the area right below the colorful toolbar icons (see Figure 4-10). The browser controls are simple. They consist of five buttons and one text entry box. Whenever these buttons are available to you, you'll see them in color. If the buttons are a pale-gray color, often referred to as being *grayed out,* it means that they are not available to you at that particular moment. As you move around into different screens and different areas of AOL and the Internet, different buttons may become available at different times.

AOL Browser Controls

Figure 4-10. The AOL browser controls are the five buttons located on the Navigation bar.

The five buttons on the Navigation bar help you to move around AOL and the Internet. Starting at the left side, the buttons are as follows (with a description of the icon in parentheses):

▶ **Back (backward arrow):** Takes you to the previous page you viewed in this session. (A *session* takes place from the time you open a browser to the time you close it.)

Interface is the connection and interaction between hardware, software, and the user. What you see on your computer screen and the manner in which you interact with what you see on the screen is generally referred to as the interface.

Holding your mouse over a button or icon for a second or two brings up a balloon explaining the button's purpose.

When you go to the Web, your current Web address (the page you are now viewing) is displayed in the text box on the Navigation bar.

▸ **Forward (forward arrow):** If you've back-tracked to a particular page by using the Back button, this button takes you to the page you viewed after that page.

▸ **Stop (circle with an x in it):** Stops the page you've selected from downloading. Click this button if the page is taking too long to download and you want to turn off the graphics, you change your mind about viewing the page, or you selected the wrong link.

▸ **Reload (curved arrow):** Causes the browser to download the current page again. Click this button if the page has content that changes periodically or if the page is downloading too slowly or not at all. To *refresh* a Web page is to update the displayed information. A fresh copy of the Web page will transfer to your computer.

▸ **Home (house):** Takes you to the page that you have set as your browser's home page.

If you want to go back to a Web site that you've visited this online session, click the small arrow on the right edge of the text box (see Figure 4-11). A drop-down menu will display the titles of the last 25 places you've visited. This is called your *History List.* It lists the pertinent pages whether they were within AOL or on the Web. Just highlight your choice and click, and you will go back to the previously visited page.

At the bottom of the browser window, you will see a blue bar that indicates that the site has been contacted and the page has been retrieved by AOL.

From there, you still have to wait for the page to be transferred to your computer. As it is being transferred, you'll notice the spinning AOL logo (located in the upper-right corner of AOL); when the spinning stops, the page has been downloaded or some problem has occurred. Use the bar to determine how much of the page has downloaded to your machine; for example, when half of the bar is filled in, 50 percent of the page has loaded. The spinning logo indicates that your Web browser is still retrieving parts of a requested Web page. The page is completely retrieved when the logo stops spinning.

Click here to go back to a site you've viewed this session

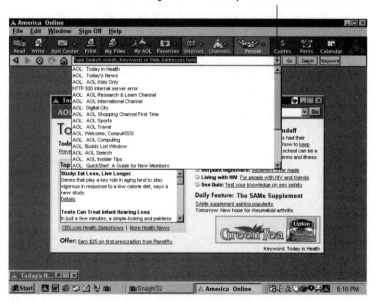

Figure 4-11. To return to a Web site you visited this online session, click the small arrow on the right edge of the text box and choose a previously visited page from the drop-down menu.

Coming Up Next

The next chapter looks at how to use AOL's tools to help you find information within AOL and on the Internet quickly and easily. In this chapter, you learned the following:

- ▶ AOL provides channels to guide you to your destination.
- ▶ Nineteen AOL Channels serve as the first step in the search process.
- ▶ Keywords take you instantly to a specific area of information.
- ▶ Typing the Keywords: **QuickStart** and **Help** bring instant rescue if you are lost.
- ▶ Navigating the Internet is better known as *surfing the Web*.
- ▶ Links and URLs are indispensable tools for navigating the Internet.

FINDING AND
ORGANIZING THINGS

Quick Look

▶ **AOL Search** page 151

AOL Search is a type of search engine created by AOL that uses a database of related words to locate information you want to find. To use AOL Search, click the Search button on the Welcome screen. Or, you can click the Search button on the Navigation bar.

▶ **Search Hotlinks** page 155

When you want to search for information quickly, go to AOL's Search dialog box and click one of the underlined hot links. These links appear at the bottom of the dialog box and will take you directly to several areas where you can search for specific topics. Using these search areas narrows your search and often helps you find what you are looking for more quickly.

▶ **Wildcard Characters** page 161

Wildcard characters are symbols (such as the asterisk and tilde) that enable you to perform a more advanced search. The asterisk (*) represents any number of characters in a search (including none). For example, searching for *bird** will find "birdhouse," "birdie," and so on. The tilde (~) enables you to perform a *fuzzy search,* which is a search for articles containing words with spellings similar to any word in your search. (This works like a spelling checker on a word processor.) Every letter after the ~ in your topic word is considered to be possibly incorrect or misplaced, thereby making sure that successful search results are not ignored because of a minor error. For example, typing *~content* will search for topic words "constant," "contact," and "contents."

▶ **Favorites** page 162

Favorites is a customized list of links to your most frequently used and popular online areas or Web sites. To instantly add a Web page to your list of Favorites, go to the title bar of the page that you want to save and then click and drag the heart icon onto the Favorites icon.

Chapter 5

Finding and Organizing Things

We live in the Information Age. With America Online and the Internet, you could literally spend the rest of your life just reading and absorbing all the information that is available online. However, most of us don't want to partake in all of that knowledge. We are interested in finding the information that we need at a particular moment, so that we can go on with the rest of our day. We may want to get more information about the sports team that we love, about the disease that plagues our family, about the new processes that can make our work lives easier, or about our favorite hobby. AOL gives us the search tools to help us find all the information we'll ever need.

Finding Things on AOL with AOL Search

Several ways exist to find information on AOL (or, in tech-speak, *initiate a search* for information). You can click the Search button on the Welcome screen (see Figure 5-1). Or, you can click the Search button on the Navigation bar (see Figure 5-2). If the Welcome screen is in front of you, using its Search button probably is easier. However, when you are looking at another screen, you will want to use the Search button on the Navigation bar, because it is always available, no matter which screen you are viewing.

Search Button

Figure 5-1. Click the Search button on the Welcome screen to begin a search.

Search

Definition

AOL Search is a type of search engine created by AOL that uses a database of related words to find matches to the overall subject or concept that you are searching for.

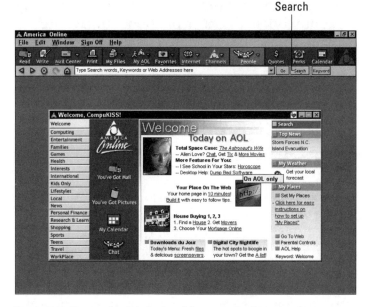

Figure 5-2. You can also click the Search button on the Navigation bar to initiate a search.

Both of these methods take you to the AOL Search dialog box, shown in Figure 5-3.

Figure 5-3. AOL Search is one of AOL's most valuable features.

You can also initiate a search by typing the Keyword: **Find** in the Keyword dialog box (see Figure 5-4).

Figure 5-4. Typing the Keyword: *Find* also initiates a search.

Doing the Same Thing in Different Ways

On the computer, several ways often are available to do the same thing. For instance, to find current news stories on AOL, you can do any of the following:

▶ Click the News Channel button on the left side of the Welcome screen.

▶ Click the Top News button on the right side of the Welcome screen.

▶ Click the Channels icon on the toolbar and choose News.

▶ Click the Keyword button on the Navigation bar and then type **news**.

▶ Click the words "Type Search words, Keywords or Web Addresses here" and type **news**.

▶ Press the Ctrl key (the apple key for Mac users) and the K key simultaneously and then type **news**.

I've just listed six different ways to get to AOL's News screen. To a computer neophyte, this might be confusing, but having all of these various options is actually quite useful. After you become familiar with the way things are done, you'll likely use several different methods to perform a task, based on what's on your computer screen at that particular moment and whether it is easier to click the mouse or to type a letter or key combination.

Continued

Tip

When using AOL Search, capitalization doesn't matter.

Doing the Same Thing in Different Ways
(continued)

If you are just starting out on the computer, when you are faced with several methods for completing the same task, just choose the way that seems easiest to you. You don't have to worry about learning all the various methods for doing things. As you use the computer more and more, you will learn alternative methods quite easily.

As you read this book and other instructional material, just remember that you usually have various ways available to accomplish the same task. Someday, when you are ready, you may want to try a different approach. Alternative ways to do things can also come in handy in a pinch, when, for whatever the reason, the method that you usually use doesn't work.

AOL offers a lot of areas to explore. Just type the subject that you want to search for in the AOL Search dialog box, and AOL Search will scour all of AOL to locate the topic you want to know more about.

To search all AOL online areas from the AOL Search window, follow these steps:

1. Type the words or phrases you want to search for in the Enter word(s) text field of the AOL Search dialog box.

2. Click Search. A list of areas matching the terms you typed will appear.

3. Double-click an item to see its description.

This will call up a list of all the areas on AOL that might have the information you are looking for.

Targeting Your Search

At the bottom of the AOL Search dialog box, you will see underlined hot links that will take you directly to several areas where you can search for specific topics. Using these search areas narrows your search and often helps you find what you are looking for more quickly. Many frequently searched-for topics are listed, including:

- ▶ AOL Yellow Pages
- ▶ AOL Classifieds
- ▶ White Pages
- ▶ People
- ▶ Online Events
- ▶ Message Boards
- ▶ Software
- ▶ Books
- ▶ AOL Hometown
- ▶ Shopping

All of these are self-explanatory except for Hometown AOL, the area where you can search for other AOL members' home pages. Don't forget to investigate each of these categories — you may be surprised at what you find. For instance, try the Online Events to talk to celebrities, such as author Stephen King, actress Sandra Bullock, and musician Sting, to name just a few.

Finding Things on the Internet

Sometimes, you may want to search for things that aren't found on AOL but likely are on the Internet. Maybe you want to find the home page of your college alma mater or a hometown radio station. You can use AOL Search to find things on the Internet, as well. Just click the Search button, as you did previously. When you enter a word or phrase that is not located on AOL, AOL's Search button will automatically give you the Internet links that you are searching for.

Click the Search button on the toolbar. Then, type **Compukiss**. Compu-Kiss is a Web site located on the Internet that isn't part of AOL. You are immediately presented with a results window with several tabs on the top of the window. Links to Compu-Kiss are automatically presented on the tab marked Found on the Web, as shown in Figure 5-5.

Found on the Web Tab

Figure 5-5. Web sites that are found on the Internet are listed on a tab marked Found on the Web.

AOL extends its search capabilities to the Internet. What happens if you click the Search button and type a word or title that appears both on America Online and on the Internet? Let's try it. Type **AARP**. Because AARP has a content area on AOL, as well as a Web site on the Internet, you will see information under two different tabs. One tab is marked On AOL, and the other is marked Rest of the Web, as shown in Figure 5-6.

Tabs

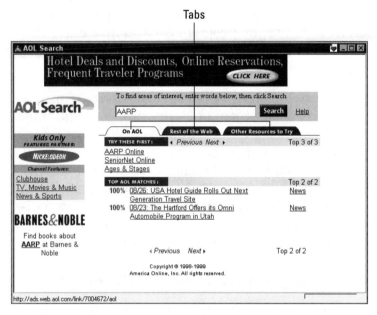

Figure 5-6. The titles on the tabs give information about where the links were found.

If you look at Figures 5-5 and 5-6, you will see that a third tab appears on the Search screen, labeled Other Resources to Try. This tab contains links that will help you locate AOL members, find a business address, find software, and more.

Search Engines

AOL Search is a type of *search engine*. A search engine is simply a program that searches a particular area of content for documents that contain certain keywords. Typically, a search engine uses a program called a *spider* or *Web crawler,* so named

Definition

A *search engine* is a program that searches a particular area of content for documents that contain certain keywords.

because it "crawls" through various Web pages, documenting and indexing the information that it finds. Each search engine uses different timing, methodology, identifiers, and patterns to create its indexes. The search engine returns a list of documents that match the criteria that were entered, based entirely on its own unique program. So, you may enter the same criteria in two different search engines and receive completely different results.

Search engines require no special software or programs to install or run on your computer, and most search engines are free. Some Web sites that use a different search method are categorized as *Web directories.* Many search engines are also called *portals,* because they use their site as your entry to the Internet. While each of these may have its own distinctive terminology, in common everyday use, they are all referred to as *search engines.*

Identifying the Types of Search Engines

AOL Search is an excellent search engine, but certainly it is not your only choice for accessing the Web. Search engines come in a variety of offerings and online locations. Some search engines are very general, and others are targeted toward a specific type of search. Here are a few of the most frequently used search engines:

> AltaVista (`www.altavista.com`)
>
> Excite (`www.excite.com`)
>
> HotBot (`www.hotbot.com`)
>
> Infoseek (`www.infoseek.go.com`)
>
> Lycos (`www.lycos.com`)
>
> Magellan (`www.mckinley.com`)
>
> WebCrawler (`www.webcrawler.com`)
>
> Yahoo! (`www.yahoo.com`)

Several new search engines called *metasearchers* are also available. Metasearchers enable you to enter one query that they submit simultaneously to several search engines. Some of the more popular metasearchers are the following:

Ask Jeeves (www.askjeeves.com)

Dogpile (www.dogpile.com)

SavvySearch (www.savvysearch.com)

Learning to Work with Search Engines

Each search engine is slightly different and may have different rules that apply to its use. Although you may be tempted to jump from one search engine to another, it's actually best to choose one and stick with it until you have learned all the ins and outs. Read the online help that will assist you in customizing your searches. After you master your first search engine, you may want to try others, or you may be happy to stay with the first one.

The instructions given here explain how to use AOL Search to its fullest capability; however, you will find that these instructions are applicable to most other search engines, as well.

Be Specific

The more descriptive you can be, the better your results. Typing *apple* is better than just *fruit*; *Porsche* is better than *sports car*.

Use Phrases

Don't use one-word searches. Instead, type multiple words or phrases. AOL Search searches by concept and automatically looks for related ideas. The search results are sorted by relevance, so the one nearest the top will most accurately match your topic.

AND Means Including

Use **AND** (all in capital letters, as printed here) when you want to find articles that contain all the words you enter. This is a powerful feature when used properly. To find articles on rock-and-roll music, try typing *rock AND roll AND music*. If you don't add the AND, you will get all the documents that contain *any* of these three words rather than those containing *all* three words.

Cut It Out

Use **AND NOT** (all in capital letters, as printed here) to limit your results to documents with only the words you want. For example, if you want articles about pets, but aren't interested in dogs, try typing *pets AND NOT dogs*.

Narrowing Your Search

In most search engines, using quotation marks instructs the search engine to look for everything inside the quotation marks in the same exact order. For instance, a recent search for the word *Jefferson* came up with 159,000 links. Searching for *Thomas Jefferson* yielded 986,000 links, because the search engine looked for any documents with either the name *Thomas* or the name *Jefferson*. Searching for *"Thomas Jefferson"* with quotation marks narrowed the search to 13,000 links, because the search engine returned only the documents that had the name *Thomas Jefferson* in them.

Tips for Searching

Following are some tips to help you find what you want on the Internet with ease:

▶ Capitalization usually doesn't matter. In other words, *Jefferson* is the same as *jefferson*. But, some search engines, such as AltaVista, are case-sensitive. This is true even if you're looking for a proper name.

5

Finding and Organizing Things

▶ Compound words do not count as words with suffixes. For example, although *race* will find *racing,* it will not find *racetrack, racecar,* or *raceway.*

▶ AOL Search does not ignore prefixes, so the words *employment* and *unemployment* are different.

▶ You can type as many topic words as you want. Be careful not to use too many, however, or your search will end up being too specific and you won't find anything.

▶ Thin is in; narrowing your search is always beneficial.

Definition

Wildcard characters are symbols (such as the asterisk, *, and the tilde, ~) that enable you to perform an advanced search.

Advanced Searching with Wildcard Characters

Wildcard characters are symbols (such as the asterisk and tilde) that enable you to perform a more advanced search. Following are the wildcard characters you may wish to use:

▶ **Asterisk (*):** Represents any number of characters in a search (including none). As an example, searching for *bird** will find "birdhouse," "birdie," and so on. Note: A search term using an asterisk must include at least two characters in addition to the asterisk.

▶ **Tilde (~):** Enables you to perform a *fuzzy search,* which is a search for articles containing words with spellings similar to any word in your search. This works like a spelling checker on a word processor. Every letter after the ~ in your topic word is considered to be possibly incorrect or misplaced, thereby making sure that successful search results are not ignored because of a minor error. For example, typing *~content* will search for topic words "constant," "contact," and "contents."

Tip

Mac users can download an excellent Sherlock Plug-In at www.aol.com that will make the AOL Search work seamlessly with their operating system.

Definition

Favorites (also called *Favorite Places*) is a customized list of links to your most frequently used and popular online areas or Web sites.

Note that all letters before the ~ are treated as normal characters. For example, whereas *con~tent* would still find the three words just listed, *cont~ent* would not look for "constant." (The "cont" is assumed to be correct.)

Favorites

Favorites is a customized list of links to your most frequently used and popular online areas or Web sites. After you find your Favorite Places in AOL or on the Web and add them to your Favorites list, returning to visit again is easy.

You can easily create a customized list of links to your favorite online areas or Web sites. The AOL symbol for Favorites is the red heart icon on a yellow folder, which is found on the toolbar (see Figure 5-7). After you save a site to your list of Favorites, you can access it again from your list with a simple click of your mouse.

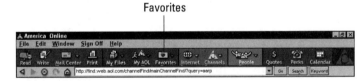

Figure 5-7. The AOL symbol for Favorites is the red heart on a yellow folder icon, located on the toolbar.

Adding Favorites

When you find an area online that you'd like to save, whether it is in AOL or on the Internet, just click the red heart icon on the yellow folder, located on the toolbar. When the choice box appears, click Add Top Window to Favorites. Click Add to Favorites at the next window (see Figure 5-8), and the area will be added to your Favorites list.

Figure 5-8. Adding Favorites is easy: click Add to Favorites, and the area is added to your Favorites list.

To save a Favorite Place even faster, simply go to the title bar of the page that you want to save and then click and drag the heart icon onto the Favorites icon (the folder with the heart on it) on the toolbar. The area will instantly be added to your list of Favorites (see Figure 5-9).

Favorites Folder with Heart Icon   Heart Icon on Title Bar

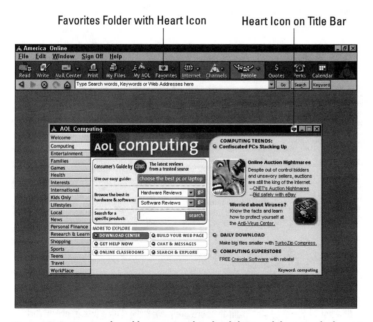

Figure 5-9. You can also add a Favorite Place by clicking and dragging the heart icon on the title bar onto the Favorites folder icon (the folder with the heart on it).

Cross-Reference

See Chapter 3 for more information about AOL's Instant Messenger feature.

To visit your Favorite Places or to go back to a Web page or place on AOL that you saved in your Favorites list, follow these steps:

1. Click the Favorites icon on your AOL toolbar and click Favorite Places.

2. Double-click the place name you want to visit (or click to highlight it and then click the Go button). The online area or Web site appears.

Sharing Favorites

You can share your Favorite Places with your family and friends by adding a Favorite Place hyperlink to either an e-mail or an Instant Message note. When you find a page that you want to share with another AOL member who is currently online, click the heart icon on the title bar (see Figure 5-10). When the dialog box appears, click Insert in Instant Message. An Instant Message note appears with the link already inserted. You can add a note to the link, if you wish.

Heart Icon

Figure 5-10. Share your Favorite Place with a friend by clicking the heart icon on the title bar of the page you want to share and, when the dialog box appears, click Insert in Instant Message.

If you want to e-mail a Favorite Place to anyone on AOL or the Internet, first find the page you want to share and click the heart icon on the title bar. When the dialog box appears, click Insert in Mail. An e-mail form appears with the link already inserted and a subject filled in. Add an explanation about the link, if you wish. Then, type your friend's e-mail address into the Send To box and click Send.

Organizing Favorites

You can organize your Favorite Places by creating folders in your list and then grouping your Favorites into those folders (see Figure 5-11). You can also modify your Favorites, as needed.

Figure 5-11. Organize your Favorite Places by creating folders and grouping your Favorites into these folders.

To create a new folder in your Favorites list, follow these steps:

1. Click the Favorites icon (the folder with a heart) on the toolbar and click Favorite Places in the drop-down menu. Your Favorite Places list opens.
2. Click the New button.
3. Click the New Folder button.

Tip

To provide quick access to locations you may find interesting, AOL automatically adds four items to your list of Favorite Places: About AOL, Member Exclusives, Meeting People and Staying in Touch, and AOL's Top Picks.

4. Type a name for the folder and click OK. The new folder is created.

5. Click each item and drag it into the desired folder.

To modify your Favorite Places, follow these steps:

1. Click the Favorites icon (the folder with a heart) on the toolbar and click Favorite Places in the drop-down menu. Your Favorite Places list opens.

2. Click to highlight the item or folder that you want to change.

3. Click the Edit button.

4. Type the new name or address. Be careful with addresses; they are very exacting, and it's easy to make an error.

5. Click OK.

Tips for Working with Favorites

The following are quick tips for working with Favorites:

▶ Double-click a folder to display the contents of the folder. Double-click the folder again to hide the folder's contents.

▶ In the drop-down menu from Favorites, menu items displaying an arrow contain Favorite Places that are related.

▶ The order of items in your list of Favorite Places can be adjusted. Click Favorites on the toolbar and choose Favorite Places. Then, drag the item or the folder to a new location on the list.

▶ Delete Favorite Places that you no longer use, to keep your Favorite Places list uncluttered. To remove the Favorite Places icon from the toolbar, right-click the Favorite that you want to remove and choose Delete from the drop-down menu.

5

If you want to add that special Favorite Place to the toolbar complete with its own icon, that is also possible. Then, you can go there simply by clicking the icon.

To add a Favorite Place to the toolbar, follow these steps:

1. Open the window for the Favorite Place you want to add to your toolbar.

2. After you drag the location's heart icon onto the toolbar, the Icon Selector window appears.

3. Select a picture you like by clicking it; this will be your Favorite Place's customized icon.

4. Type a short label (no more than eight characters). Click OK, and the picture and label will appear in the toolbar. (Because of the limited width of the screen that governs the width of the toolbar, you are limited to three custom-selected Favorite Places on your toolbar.)

If you click the area's heart and then click Add to Favorites in the window that appears, the area will be added to the top of the list. If you drag an area's heart icon onto the tool-bar's Favorites icon, the area will be added to the bottom of the list of Favorite Places in the Favorites pop-up menu. To rearrange the order of the items in the list, choose Favorite Places from the Favorites pop-up menu and then drag items to reposition them in the list.

Coming Up Next

A wealth of information can be found within AOL alone, as well as on the Internet. In the next chapter, we begin to discuss the information available in each AOL Channel, starting with the Travel Channel. In this chapter, you learned how to find and organize information, in addition to the following:

▶ Because Internet information is endless, search programs are the tools for finding things quickly and easily.

▶ AOL Search will scour AOL and the Internet to locate the topic you want to know about.

▶ In an effort to target your search, AOL offers hot links to take you to topic-specific search categories.

▸ Favorites are customized links to your most frequently used and popular Web sites.

▸ Share your Favorite Places with friends by adding a Favorite Place hyperlink to an e-mail message.

▸ Organize Favorite Places by creating category folders and then grouping your Favorites into those folders.

PART

III

FAVORITE PURSUITS

CHAPTER

6

TRAVEL

Quick Look

▶ **Custom Mini-Guides**   **page 181**

AOL's Custom Mini-Guides let you build your own customized travel guide to
any featured destination. The program takes you through a series of checklists
to build your customized guide.

▶ **The Bargain Box**   **page 183**

At the Bargain Box, found on the Travel Bargains screen of the Travel Channel,
you can find the best rates on airfares, car rentals, and lodging. This area provides
information on joining travel clubs and on other techniques for keeping your
travel budget under control. Go to the Bargain Box by double-clicking Bargain
Box in the scrollable box on the Travel Bargains screen or type the Keyword:
Bargain Box.

▶ **Preview Travel's FareAlert**   **page 184**

Preview Travel has a feature for AOL members called FareAlert. AOL members
are notified by FareAlert e-mail when their favorite round-trip itineraries reach
the prices they are looking for. Preview Travel's Farefinder tracks the lowest
airfares on popular routes, bolstered by the FareAlert e-mail service. With
Preview Travel's Farefinder and FareAlert, finding the lowest airfares is a
breeze. (Try also Carfinder, which tracks the best car rental rates.)

▶ **AARP Travel Discounts**   **page 188**

AARP offers some wonderful discounts for its members. If you are 50 or older,
for a membership fee of $8 a year, you can participate in AARP's discounts on
airlines, auto rentals, cruise lines, hotels, motels, resorts, and sightseeing. Travel
is an important activity for its members, and AARP dedicates a large section of
its Web site to Trips 'n Travel (www.aarp.org/travel/).

▶ **SeniorsSearch.com**   **page 189**

Visit SeniorsSearch.com and go to its travel site (www.seniorssearch.com/
stravel.htm) for information on a wide range of topics, such as accessible travel,
city guides, travel accessories, tours, cruising, travel guides, group travel, and
travel discounts. It also has a wonderful selection of links on its Web site, including over four pages of interesting links, ranging from "A Gourmet Fly — Discover
another France only known by Anglers, Hunters, and Country Gourmets" to
"Harley-Davidson Tours in the American Southwest." A hyperlink can take you
to the official U.S. State Website Directory, as well as to Worldwide Brochures
listing over 10,000 free travel brochures.

Chapter 6
Travel

IN THIS CHAPTER

Explore America Online's Travel Channel

Choose a destination

Locate and compare travel bargains

Enjoy senior discounts

See the world from your armchair

Travel is a great form of entertainment and relaxation. You can visit new places, examine new cultures, or just soak up some sun on the beach. The travel industry has catered to a multitude of different people and different destination choices for years, but recent advances in the Internet and online resources have completely revamped the travel industry.

The Internet has brought travel information and the ability to book reservations to any traveler. In the past, travel agencies and airlines had a lock on ticket purchases. But thanks to online communications, anyone who has access to AOL or the Internet and has a credit card can shop for flights, hotel rooms, and rental cars and — after making travel decisions — make reservations online without any of the middlemen. Whether you are looking for a holiday cruise or a bed-and-breakfast in a quaint little town, all of your travel needs are just a few mouse clicks away.

Older Americans are hitting the highways, the rails, and the skies more than ever before. During the last five years, travel in the U.S. has increased by 23 percent. Also during the last five years, the Travel Industry Association of America has determined that travelers age 55 and over have increased their travel by almost 40 percent. Today, many people are retiring in their early 60s. Armed with a lot of wanderlust, more leisure time, and a longer life span, they are smitten with a spirit of adventure and the desire to travel.

With its sights set on this growing, more mobile group, AOL offers a plethora of resources. Wherever your dream vacation may carry you, from a round-the-world swanky cruise to an RV campsite 50 miles away, the America Online Travel Channel has extensive information, help, and forums available. The Travel Channel will help you with your travel needs, whether you are looking for high-priced accommodations or focusing on the great American word, "HOWMUCHISIT?" So, let's get some travel practice and cruise through the Travel Channel.

AOL's Travel Channel

The magic carpet ride through AOL's Travel Channel begins either by clicking the Travel button on the Channels list of the Welcome screen or by entering the Keyword: **Travel**. This brings you to the main

Note

The Internet is radically changing the leisure travel business. By 2003, online leisure travel bookings will exceed $29 billion, generating 12 percent of the total industry online revenue, according to Forrester Research, Inc. Travel Industry Association of America reports that within a one-year period a 19 percent increase has occurred in the share of Americans who prefer to use the Internet rather than a travel agent to book travel reservations. After they book reservations online once, they continue to book online in the future, according to PhoCusWright, Inc. Online travel buyers are almost unanimous in their opinion that they are satisfied with the online purchasing process. Of the respondents who bought airline tickets online, 99 percent were satisfied or very satisfied with the online purchasing experience.

6

Travel

Tip

Information in AOL's Travel Channel is extensive. To see what I mean, check out the keywords listed by channel under Travel. Go to Keyword: **Keyword**, pick Travel from the categories listed, and have a look. You are sure to be amazed.

Travel screen, as shown in Figure 6-1. The left side of the Travel screen has a list of departments. On the right side of the Travel window you will find Fares & Reservations. At the bottom of the window, you are linked to previewtravel.

Figure 6-1. America Online's Travel Channel has extensive information, guides, and forums available to help you with all of your travel needs.

Destination Guides

Click the Explore over 6,000 destinations button and you are transported to AOL's *Destination Guides,* which have detailed information on over 80 featured cities and resorts, as well as coverage on the rest of the world (see Figure 6-2). If you know your destination, you type it in the first box on the left and click Go. You will be given the opportunity to expand your knowledge about your travel destination with information from Fodor's guides and other selections of tourism information from TravelFile. AOL uses TravelFile to serve as your source for destination information, great travel suppliers, and upcoming events. Suppose that we know our destination and want to explore this "Know your destination?" section further.

Figure 6-2. Destination Guides expand your knowledge of travel sites with facts from Fodor's and information from TravelFile.

If You Know Your Destination

I decided to let Berlin be my destination, so I typed the word "Berlin" in the box beneath "Know your destination?" and clicked Go. I highlighted the Fodor's Berlin choice and double-clicked. The screen that popped up, shown in Figure 6-3, gave me more information on Berlin than I could have imagined.

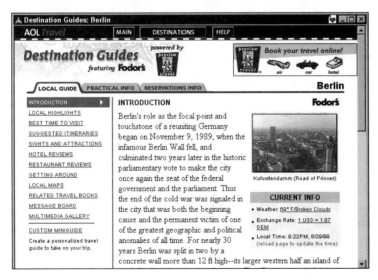

Figure 6-3. Fodor's shared more information on Berlin than one could imagine.

Note

Hunting for travel information is one example in which message boards come in very handy. What better advice can you get than the valuable experience of someone who has already "been there and done that"?

Fodor's provided stories about the reuniting of Germany, the Berlin Wall, and the spirit of the city. I found local highlights, including museums, nightlife, best time to visit, suggested itineraries, and many sights and attractions. Local maps, travel books about Berlin, and extensive hotel and restaurant reviews were also available.

Clicking the Practical Info tab, shown in Figure 6-4, took me to even more information. My screen was filled with helpful facts and valuable weather information, such as current conditions, forecasts, and monthly climate and precipitation averages. The currency converter is a "sure-to-need" section with a feature that allows you to create and print a currency cheat sheet to take on the trip. Also included is specialized information for disabled travelers and for families traveling with children.

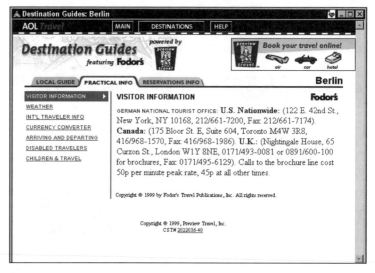

Figure 6-4. The Practical Info tab supplies information on such topics as weather, currency, and traveling with children.

Clicking the Reservations Info tab, shown in Figure 6-5, brought up a complete reservation program powered by a system called Preview Travel. This is AOL's recommended reservation service site to use to reserve airline tickets, hotel rooms, and rental cars.

Well, I'll just put my trip to Berlin on hold for a while, although it does look like a fascinating city. But, if you are ready to take a trip, be sure to explore Preview Travel. It's easy and it can take you where you want to go.

Note

To use Preview Travel to book your reservations, you must first become a member. Signing up is fast and free and can be done from the Reservations Info tab in AOL's Travel Channel.

6

Travel

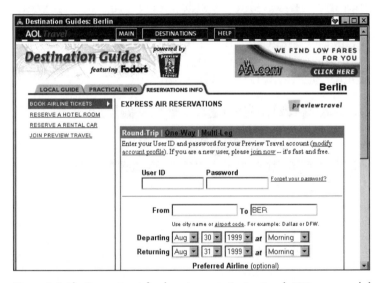

Figure 6-5. The Reservations Info tab carries you to Preview Travel, AOL's recommended reservations service site.

Finding a Destination

For those of you undecided on your destination, you need to retrace your steps to the Destination Guides. For a quick trip back, press Ctrl + K and type **Destinations**. These guides will help you make your decision and find a destination, if you don't have a prepicked one. The Destination Guides also let you explore the entire world, to find just the right spot for you.

Click Parks Guide or Cruise Guide for detailed information on either of these great types of travel. Cruising caught my eye, and why not? Over 50 different cruise lines are represented in AOL's Cruise Guide. Be prepared to browse over 425 cruises, the ship ratings, cost per day, amenities, and an overall opinion.

If you are still undecided, step through the question-and-answer guide to have an ideal cruise list created for you. Maybe you are interested in comparing specific cruises side by side (see Figure 6-6). If you fit into a distinct category, the narrowing down is easier. Categories include anniversary cruise, college student, family trip, mature adult, and single vacationer. See what I mean?

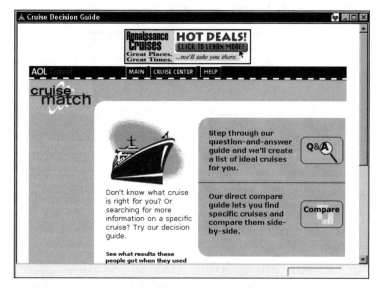

Figure 6-6. The Cruise Guide contains information on 50 different cruise lines and 425 different cruises.

If you happen to be more interested in camping and life in the great outdoors, the Parks Guide is the place for you. It has the same kind of extensive choices as the Cruise Guide — certainly enough to help any park lover find the right destination.

The entire world is at your mousetip and available as a choice under the Want to explore? column on the right side of the Destination Guides screen. Here, you can explore major destinations and get world-wide tourism information. This is one time when the planning can be as much fun as the trip itself. Just looking through all the wonderful places available can be an exciting adventure and a learning experience in itself.

Custom Mini-Guides

So, now you have made your destination decision and are ready to go. What you need is a miniguide to take on your trip with all the "what you have to see and do" information. AOL's Custom Mini-Guides will take you through a series of checklists to build a customized travel guide to your choice of destination. America Online will create a customized miniguide that contains exactly the information you requested (see Figure 6-7). The pink sand and clear azure water of Bermuda's Horseshoe Bay tempted me, so I created a miniguide for Bermuda. I was amazed by the choices to pick from in the checklist, and equally amazed to see the customized miniguide of Bermuda that was created especially for me.

My printer produced 11 pages with current information on the best time to visit, the climate, and Fodor's choice of beaches. I also found recommendations for lodging and accommodations, restaurants (with directions, menus, and price range), and special sites and attractions. I found that out-of-season visits could save about 40 percent off the rather expensive overall prices found in Bermuda, so I noted the off-season dates and put Bermuda on my list of must-see-in-this-lifetime places to visit.

Note

AOL keeps its travel screens current, and often the listings and information change with the season. The Travel Channel is constantly changing and incorporating new information. You will find the travel information is always easy to find, fun to use, and up to date. After you get the feel for how much information is offered on a wide range of travel topics, just keep surfing until you uncover what you are looking for.

Tip

Knapsacks, backpacks, laptops, and shopping bags all count toward your carry-on item limit on most major airlines.

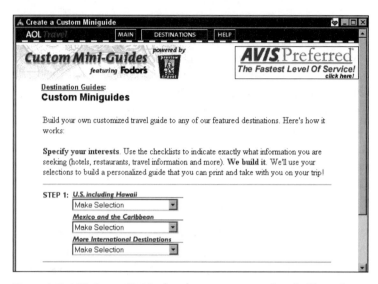

Figure 6-7. AOL's Custom Mini-Guides take your answers to their checklist and create a customized miniguide that contains exactly the information you requested.

Travel Bargains

Who doesn't like a bargain, especially when traveling? Just type the Keyword: **Travel** and click the Go button next to "Find a bargain" on the main Travel screen. You will be presented with the Travel Bargains screen, which is full of bargain choices (see Figure 6-8). This is a great area for the budget-minded traveler. The low fares are offered by Preview Travel, AOL's online reservation booking system. A scroll-down box invites you to check out the best bargains on airfares, car rentals, cruises, family rates, hotels, and so on.

The Travel Bargains screen points out ways to save 15 percent on European car rentals as well as ways to obtain $20 to $40 midweek and weekend discounts at certain hotels. It also lists purchase dates for taking advantage of airline travel discounts. One of the tips I found most valuable was the information on saving money, such as the explanation of how the length of your stay affects the rate. A treasure chest of tips is available to help you get more miles for your travel money.

Figure 6-8. Travel Bargains is the perfect screen for the budget-minded traveler.

Double-clicking the Bargain Box in the scrollable box on the Travel Bargains screen opens a screen that lists the Bargain of the Week, AOL Special Member Offers, and Today's Bargains. Special discounts are offered for Family, Senior, and Student categories, as well as for other categories, located along the left side of the screen. Drift into the Independent Traveler section and you will benefit from the chats, advice, and bargain tips from fellow travelers.

Preview Travel

Okay, you're convinced that you have enough money saved to take a trip to California. The excitement is killing you and you want to book your ticket right now. What do you do? You have to get back to the Travel main screen (Ctrl + K and Travel, remember?). Now, it is time to click Reservations and pick your category: Air, Car, Hotel, or Vacations. Let's check out the airfares; just click Air. With Preview Travel's Farefinder, tracking the lowest airfares is a breeze (see Figure 6-9). To view the best airfares, select

Understand the restrictions and change fee on any airline ticket you are considering. Some bargain fares come with unusually high change fees.

6

Travel

your departure city from a drop-down menu. Sample round-trip airline fares are listed from selected cites and are constantly updated, with the posting day and time given:

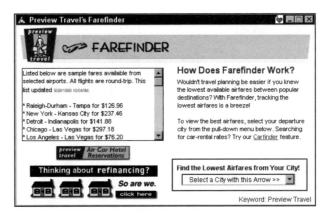

Figure 6-9. To view the best airfares at Farefinder, select your departure city from a drop-down menu.

Try the Carfinder feature for the best rental car rates. These fares should be used as a guide when pricing airfares and car rentals for your itinerary.

Preview Travel guarantees that the transactions of AOL members are safe and that their privacy is protected. The customer service agents of Preview Travel are available via phone or e-mail 7 days a week, 24 hours a day. Preview Travel offers airfares from over 500 airlines, as well as rates from major car rental agencies and thousands of hotels.

Preview Travel has a feature for AOL members called *FareAlert*. AOL members are notified by FareAlert e-mail when their favorite round-trip itineraries reach the prices they are looking for. Preview Travel's Farefinder tracks the lowest airfares on popular routes, bolstered by the FareAlert e-mail service. These services are becoming even more sophisticated: the latest version of Preview's service permits you to set the price at which it will notify you. Other online services have similar alert programs. Travelocity's Fare Watcher will automatically send you an update when prices on your favorite itineraries are discounted. The weekly e-mail and Web specials for individual airlines, which come out every Wednesday, generally cover travel for the same weekend. AOL compiles the best deals on its Weekly Internet Specials page. Plus, you can search for flights departing from your city of choice.

Senior Discounts

Did the mention of special discounts for seniors catch your eye in the Bargain Box? Let's go there. Type the Keyword: **Travel Bargains** and then scroll down the list until you see Senior. Double-click and you're there.

The section called Senior Discounts, as shown in Figure 6-10, will appear with special deals for travelers 50 and older. Use this area to find many bargains on airfares and other travel-related items.

For more choices for senior discounts within AOL's Travel Channel, click the Senior Travel Discounts entry on the Senior Discounts screen.

Tip

Never think it is too late to book a bargain ticket. Sometimes, round-trip t ickets to vacation destinations will be sold for as little as 25 percent of their usual costs, as a means to fill the last remaining seats on the plane.

Find It Online

Many of the special airfares are released by e-mail by the respective airline that is offering the fare. Just sign up at the Web site of the airline, indicate the departure and destination cities that you are interested in, and the airline will e-mail you a listing of fares as they become available. Here are the Web addresses for several prominent airlines: American Airlines (www. aa.com); Delta Airlines (www.delta-air.com); United Airlines (www. ual.com); US Airways (www.usairways.com)

Tip

Go to Keyword: **Travel Bargains** for great travel discounts for travelers 50 and older!

Figure 6-10. Senior Discounts keeps up with special deals for travelers 50 and older.

Again, the choices in the Senior Travel Discounts section are full of valuable information. As they say, you don't need to reinvent the wheel. Learn from another senior's experience — both the things to do and the things to avoid. A wealth of experience also stands behind the Senior Travel Tips. Be sure to incorporate these tips as part of your travel equipment (see Figure 6-11).

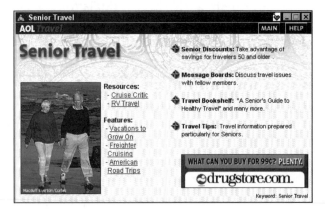

Figure 6-11. A wealth of experience stands behind the Senior Travel Tips and the Senior Travel Message Boards.

The term *seniors* in airline lingo usually applies to travelers age 62 and above. Hundreds of amazing deals seem to be available on domestic fares for senior travel, and often a companion of any age can travel for the same low fare. Seniors don't always have to settle for the small ten percent discount most airlines offer seniors. You can often travel on a much cheaper ticket. The cheapest fares are generally available for Monday through Thursday travel, with a modest surcharge for travel on weekends. Senior airfare coupons provide a popular way to save for travelers age 62 and above. Often, bonuses are given for grandparents flying with grandchildren. Seniors also enjoy special travel programs, such as airline clubs, which require an enrollment fee but more than compensate for it with discounts. Senior coupon booklets are usually valid for one year from purchase and can be used as a one-way ticket in the continental U.S.

Senior fares are hidden fares, typically anywhere from 50 to 70 percent lower than the lowest regular fares, according to Tom Parsons of www.bestfares.com. These senior fares are available in 80 percent of the market. Tom Parsons recommends that you ask your travel agent specifically for the special senior fare instead of the usual ten percent senior discount.

Most major hotel chains have special senior fares offering discounts of up to 50 percent, but you must ask for the rates. Be prepared for the age for senior rates to vary from hotel to hotel. Check whether the current special rates are any cheaper than the senior discount.

Amtrak offers seniors 62 and over 15 percent off its train fares. Certain cruise ships have up to $300 off select cruises for those 55 and over, but again you must ask for the discount.

AARP Discounts

Tip

Make sure you review the safety tips from the American Hotel and Motel Association before you take off on either a short trip or an extended vacation (`www.aarp.org/benefits/msppst.html`).

AARP offers some wonderful discounts for its members. If you are 50 or older, for a membership fee of $8 a year (sign up at `www.aarp.org`), you can participate in AARP's discounts on airlines, auto rentals, cruise lines, hotels, motels, resorts, and sightseeing. Travel is an important activity for its members, and AARP dedicates a large section of its Web site to Trips 'n Travel (`www.aarp.org/travel/`), as shown in Figure 6-12. This AARP travel site has links to "Previous Travel, a Complete Index of Travel Stories" and the interactive travel bulletin board called "Share Your Stories."

Figure 6-12. Trips 'n Travel is an important and extensive portion of AARP's Web site dedicated to travel.

Internet Resources

Finding a reliable travel site on the Internet is easy. Deciding which one to use may be the difficult part. Several excellent Web sites exist that, like AOL's Preview Travel, offer extensive travel services. Microsoft's travel services Web site,

Expedia.com (www.expedia.com), Biztravel.com (www.biztravel.com), and Travelocity.com (www.travelocity.com) are my favorites. Each of these sites allows you to shop for vacations, book flights, reserve rooms, and rent cars. Each of these sites also has special deals and personalized features. You will need to register at all of these sites, but registration is free.

If you have the time, your best bet is to spend some time at each of these sites to look at the features that each location offers. If you are looking for the best fares, you may also want to compare some airfares or hotel rooms and see who comes up with the best deal. Whereas many travel Web sites used to be confusing for consumers to navigate, and unreliable in delivering the best available fares, recent improvements have drastically improved these sites. Online travel services are excellent resources for purchasing simple items, such as airline tickets and car rentals. For more complex travel packages, you may want to seek out extensive advice on where to go, where to stay, and what to do.

Tom Parson's Bestfares.com (www.bestfares.com) is one of the places leading you to the best deals available. This Web site will also give you excellent travel news and tips.

You may also be interested in trying one of the many travel wholesalers, such as Travelscape.com (www.travelscape.com), or reverse-auction sites, such as Priceline.com (www.priceline.com). Likewise, many traditional travel agencies now have Web sites.

The Internet offers other worthy sites for travelers. Visit SeniorsSearch.com and go to its travel site (www.seniorssearch.com/stravel.htm) for information on a wide range of topics, such as

---

Tip

After you complete your registration at any of the travel booking sites, you should print the final page and keep it on file for your records.

6

Travel

Caution

If you are tempted to buy one of those bargain-priced travel packages sold over the telephone or the Internet, be careful. A person's dream vacation can become a misadventure if he or she falls victim of a travel scam. Although many travel opportunities are legitimate, scam operations defraud travelers of millions of dollars each year. Watch out for apparent bargains that require or entice you to purchase more expensive add-ons. Also, check out the services and accommodations in advance to avoid paying for nonexistent services or accommodations in less than desirable locations.

Remember that advertised rates of domestic airfares rarely include the extra tariffs that impact international fares. Often, these extra tariffs add hefty taxes and government fees. Ask about them ahead of time so that you will be fully prepared. Check to see if these fees have to be paid in cash.

Dogs and cats and other furry friends don't get the most accommodating seat selection in air travel. If you are flying with Fido or Fluffy and your pet is in the cargo hold, and should your flight be delayed, ask the flight attendant to make sure the climate control of the cargo hold is functioning.

Often, booking a round-trip flight that requires a Saturday night stay is cheaper than traveling within the workweek.

accessible travel, city guides, travel accessories, tours, cruising, travel guides, group travel, and travel discounts.

SeniorsSearch.com also offers another important area to look at for a dose of caution: travel scams.

SeniorsSearch.com has a wonderful selection of links on its Web site. It has over four pages of interesting links, from "A Gourmet Fly — Discover another France only known by Anglers, Hunters, and Country Gourmets" to "Harley-Davidson Tours in the American Southwest." A hyperlink can take you to the official U.S. State Website Directory, as well as to Worldwide Brochures listing over 10,000 free travel brochures.

Many seasoned travelers have learned most of the ins and outs of travel. If you don't know it all, you will want to surf on over to Travel Secrets (`www.travelsecrets.com`), where you will find tips and tricks for the shrewd traveler. Learn frequent-flyer tactics, how to handle hotels, what to do about lost baggage, and how to prevent Montezuma's revenge. This is truly a site worth visiting before any trip.

Online airline discounts represent the most popular aspects of Internet travel sites. These Internet-available airline discounts are offered through major airlines, low-cost and niche airlines, international carriers, online booking sites (such as Travelocity.com and Biztravel.com), credit card companies, merchants, banks, and other travel vendors. Everyone has joined the online booking game, and the competition is good news for travelers.

Wired Access

If you want to stay wired when you are traveling, you will find that many hotels offer their
guests Internet access. Public access points
to check e-mail and surf the Web are also
becoming commonplace at airports and
in hotel business centers.

You will even find cyber cafés and CyberFlyer
clubs, where you can access the Internet from
special tabletop computers while you eat.

6

Travel

Practical Resources for Travelers

Do you need a passport to travel to the Bahamas?
What if you get sick while you are away from home?
Will your insurance cover you when you are traveling? What should you tip a porter? What kind of
money do they use in Peru? How do you say
"please" in French?

America Online and the Internet have answers to all
of these questions. The first place you should look
for the answers is at the AOL Traveler's Resource
Center (Keyword: **Resource Center**), as shown in
Figure 6-13. This area is a multifaceted site packed
full of useful information. The Getting Started section offers great help on researching destinations, air
travel basics, car travel basics, phone basics, parking
checklist, customs, weather, and so on. This area provides you with links to all the practical things that
you need to know when you travel, including health
and safety, money, insurance, passports, and packing.

Figure 6-13. The AOL Traveler's Resource Center is a multifaceted site packed full of useful information.

Many individual Web sites are also available with good practical advice for the traveler. Whether you are trekking around the country in an RV or traveling around the world by air, you will want to check out some of these excellent online resources.

Travel Health Issues

For online information covering what you need to know about your health while traveling, go to the Travelers' Health area of the Centers for Disease Control and Prevention Web site (`www.cdc.gov/travel`). This site will give you health information for any destination around the world (see Figure 6-14). Also, click Health & Safety from the AOL Traveler's Resource Center (Keyword: **Resource Center**), which takes you to the location where you can find information about drinking water, health care abroad, food safety, and many other general travel health tips (see Figure 6-15).

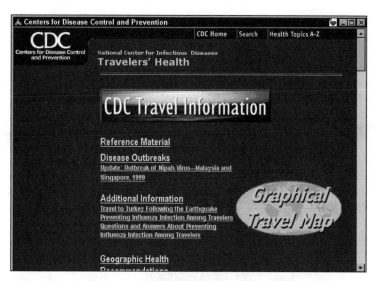

Figure 6-14. The Travelers' Health area of the Centers for Disease Control and Prevention Web site offers online information concerning health.

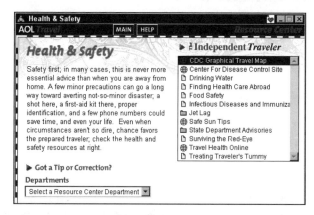

Figure 6-15. AOL's Health & Safety location provides facts on drinking water, finding health care abroad, food safety, and other general travel health tips.

Qualms about traveling? The Independent Traveler button under the Traveler's Resource Center offers you an opportunity to learn about the Fear of Flying, the Air Travel Consumer Report, Advisories from the U.S. State Department, Travel Insurance, Tips for Women Traveling Alone, and many more constantly changing topics.

Tipping

The standard tip for a waiter or waitress in a restaurant is 15 percent. But, how much do you tip a bellhop, airport baggage person, beautician, or barber? In France, the tip usually is included in a restaurant bill; in the United States, it usually is not included. Consult The Original Tipping Page (`www.tipping.org`) to be prepared when you travel. You'll find a tip calculator as well as invaluable information on tipping when traveling abroad (see Figure 6-16).

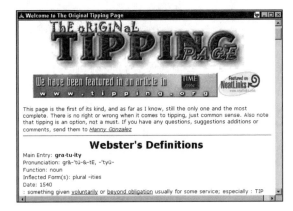

Figure 6-16. The Original Tipping Page supplies you with a tip calculator as well as invaluable information on tipping when traveling abroad.

Language

A crash course in the language you are going to need is just a Web page away. Go to `www.travlang.com` and select from over 70 languages. Select the language that you speak from the drop-down list and then click the icon for the language spoken in the country of your destination. The Foreign Languages for Travelers site can prepare you with basic words and numbers for shopping/dining, travel, directions, places, times, and dates. A pronunciation guide is a mouse click away (see Figure 6-17).

Figure 6-17. Foreign Languages for Travelers can prepare you with basic words (and more) in over 70 languages.

Traveling the Highways and Byways

The automobile is part of the American way of life. Click Car Travel in the Traveler's Resource Center (Keyword: **Resource Center**) to find AOL's travel-related auto information. Whether you are looking for a car rental, a driver to transport your car to a specified location, or options for renting a car overseas, America Online comes to the rescue.

When it comes to driving, some people seem to have an inborn sense of direction; others, like me, are completely devoid of any navigational abilities when traveling more than a mile from home. Those of you who share my lack of directional abilities will be glad to take advantage of AOL's maps and directions. Just type the Keyword: **Mapping**, and then fill in the city, state, or zip code in the origination address or intersection and the destination address or intersection. You will be presented

with a detailed map to help you find your way.
AOL also rises to the challenge of providing state
and even international maps. Need directions to
or from an airport? Simply type the airport code
(if you know it) in the Address or Intersection
field (see Figure 6-18).

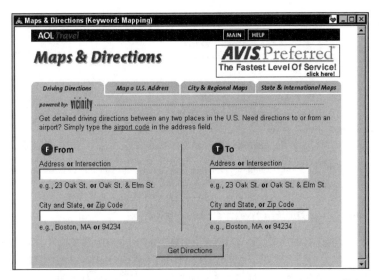

Figure 6-18. Need directions to or from an airport? AOL's mapping location will show
you the way if you type the airport code in the Address or Intersection field.

An exciting way to travel the highways and see
the world is by recreational vehicle (RV). The
America Online RV information can be found
with the Keyword: **RV Travel** (see Figure 6-19).
This is an area where you can find family camp-
sites and frequently asked questions about RV
travel. You can also read the RV Message Boards
for advice from other RV travelers. They say an
RV becomes your home away home, and you'll
find this is true when you visit the interesting
array of members' RV home pages.

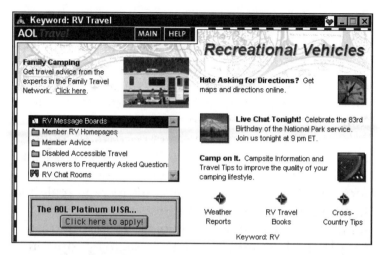

Figure 6-19. A very popular way to travel and see the world is by recreational vehicle. Check out AOL's informative RV Travel site.

Chatting with Others About Travel

What better way is available to get information about a proposed destination than to talk with someone who has already been there? Or, maybe you are just dying to tell someone about your fabulous trip, or to warn him or her about a disastrous one. Chat rooms and message boards are ways to share your travel experiences and adventures.

Most of the travel sites already mentioned have chat rooms in which you can talk with others. America Online also hosts many travel-related chats (Keyword: **Chats**). Expedia.com already hosts 40 chats a week that revolve around different regions. You can chat with other adults about their travel adventures at the Expedia senior forum (`http://expedia.msn.com /forums/senior`).

Armchair Travel

Definition

A *Web cam* is a digital camera that catches live action and transfers it to the Internet.

Would you like to see the world, but either don't want to travel or can't travel? The Internet has the answer for you. Now, you can do more than just look at pictures in travel brochures and magazines. You can take a virtual tour around the world and see actual happenings on street corners, harbors, and other unique venues via Web cam. A Web cam is a digital camera that catches live action and transfers it to the Internet, so that you can view real-time happenings. Knowing that the sun shines at midnight in Sweden in the middle of summer is great for playing Jeopardy, but actually seeing people in Sweden playing basketball in the park at midnight is quite enlightening.

You will find Web cams all over the Internet. One site where you can get a good feel for how it all works is Around the World in 80 Clicks (`www.steveweb.com/80clicks`). The tour starts in New York and continues on to Canada, Ireland, France, Monaco, Denmark, Poland, Finland, Peru, and 71 other great sites around the world. Each stop is unique. You may see a live camera shot showing the activities at the Eiffel Tower, a casino in Monte Carlo, or a street corner in Montreal. Sometimes the information is given in Polish or Norwegian, or whatever the language of the locale is. The pictures are worth a thousand words, so it's never boring. As the multimedia content of the Internet matures, you will find more and more exciting sites like this. If you are unable to travel but long to see the world, perhaps the Web cam and your computer will be your ticket.

Happy Trails!

Today's older generation is blessed with more leisure time, more discretionary income, and a longer life span. Add to these factors the revolution in the travel industry credited to computers and the Internet, and you will find that travel today is more accessible and more affordable than ever before.

So, whether you are collecting real miles in the air or on the highways or just racking up virtual miles in front of your computer, I wish you happy trails.

Coming Up Next

In the next chapter, we take a look at AOL's Personal Finance Channel and explore the options available to the savvy investor as well as to those just starting an investment portfolio. In this chapter, we checked out AOL's Travel Channel and the resources it provides the avid — and armchair — traveler. We learned that:

▶ Online resources can link you to information formerly available only to travel agencies and airlines.

▶ AOL's Travel Channel is the starting point for all phases of your travel plans.

▶ Destination Guides help you determine where to go, what to see, and how to get there.

▶ America Online and the Internet will link you to travel bargains galore — especially for seniors.

▶ Online chatting on travel topics is a great pastime before and after your journey.

▶ With your Internet-connected computer, you can see much of the world without leaving your living room.

Quick Look

▶ **Motley Fool** **page 207**

They say that a fool and his money are soon parted, but The Motley Fool (Keyword: **Fool**), found in the Investing Basics area of the AOL Personal Finance Channel, gives investing tips and tools that will make sure you increase your wealth rather than deplete it. This AOL area has some of the best basic investment advice available. The Motley Fool's format is organized and easy to follow. Best of all, The Motley Fool takes investing seriously, but presents the information in a lighthearted, entertaining manner.

▶ **AOL's MarketDay** **page 212**

Check out AOL's MarketDay (Keyword: **Market Day**) area for live market analysis from Briefing.com, where you can get market commentary, sector reports, Federal Reserve briefings, and other useful information. You can also get to AOL's MarketDay from the Active Trader screen's box labeled More Resources, as well as from My Portfolios. The later is very helpful when you are checking your portfolio and want a quick overview of what's happening in the market at that moment.

▶ **AOL's Banking Center** **page 217**

Online banking, also known as *PC banking* or *home banking,* is now available to millions of consumers. Close to 5 million people already bank online, and by the end of 2001, the number is expected to grow to about 22 million. AOL created the Banking Center, found at Keyword: **Banking**, to provide its members with safe, secure, online banking services. It partners with over 30 financial institutions that you can access by clicking a button. If the bank you're interested in isn't there, another click will call up a complete list of banks.

▶ **Brokerage Center** **page 220**

Several brokerage houses have set up shop on AOL at the Brokerage Center (found at Keyword: **Broker**); among them are DLJdirect, Waterhouse Securities, Ameritrade, and E*TRADE. AOL customers can shop and compare one brokerage to another and decide which best suits their needs. Like the banks, each of the brokerage houses has set up its own procedures for online trading, so you may want to check them all out before you make a decision.

Chapter 7

Investments

IN THIS CHAPTER

Establish your investment goals

Research investments

Create a personal portfolio

Bank and trade online

nvesting, in everyday terms, is putting something of value to work to yield more than its original value. To make itself "more valuable," money is usually invested in some form of a *security,* which, for our purposes here, is anything backed by a secure asset. Stocks, bonds, CDs, and mutual funds are among the most common securities.

However, before you invest in anything, you need to develop a strategy based on what you want to accomplish, how much money you have available to accomplish it, how much risk you can afford to take, and how much time you can dedicate to managing whatever investments you choose.

Investing is a means of satisfying individual financial needs and is a very personal endeavor. As an investor, you will need to decide your goal and determine the method by which you will accomplish that goal. To be a smart investor, you must also make an introspective assessment of the kind of person you are, so that you can be comfortable with your investment strategy.

Definition

Investing, in everyday terms, is putting something of value to work to yield more than its original value.

Definition

A *security* refers to anything that is backed by a secure asset.

Setting Goals and Selecting Strategies

Setting personal investment goals and selecting appropriate strategies to help you reach them is basically a four-step process:

1. *Establish your goals and determine how much money you will need to accomplish them.* Are you saving for retirement? Your child's or grandchild's education? A second home? Income to live on in your golden years? How much yearly income will you need for retirement? Do you have short-term financial needs that must be satisfied first?

2. *Determine realistically how much money you actually have available to invest, before you start.* Knowing what you have to work with, balanced against your need for a certain rate of return, will help you eliminate investments that won't work for you, and identify those that could.

7

Investments

3. *Determine how much risk you want to take.*
   Just as everyone has his or her own unique
   personality, everyone also has his or her own
   unique tolerance for investment risk. What
   percentages of your available investment capital can you comfortably keep in low-risk,
   medium-risk, and high-risk investments? In
   other words, your approach should reflect
   your disposition — more than anything else,
   it must allow you to sleep at night. Some folks
   enjoy taking large risks and would be bored
   with safe, low-risk investment programs.
   Others wouldn't be able to function at all
   if their portfolios were filled with high-risk
   investments. Be honest with yourself. Trying
   to implement a style that is out of sync with
   your personality is like trying to put a round
   peg in a square hole.

4. *Decide how much time you can devote to
   investing.* If you enjoy researching companies
   and poring over financial statements and have
   a lot of free time, you will develop a different
   investment style than someone who wants an
   expert to choose his or her investments and
   wants to check their progress only occasionally.

After you answer the preceding questions, the computer can help you to deal with most of the equally
tough questions about how to invest your money.
Any discussions involving money and investing will
require quite a bit of number crunching. But, you
don't have to do the math yourself. Plenty of online
help is available to assist you in matching your
money needs with appropriate investments.

Using AOL's Personal Finance Channel

Money plays a central role in all of our lives, yet many people don't know where to go for basic money information. America Online provides a form of "one-stop shopping" by linking several investment resources closely together under the Personal Finance Channel.

AOL's Personal Finance Channel, shown in Figure 7-1, comes to your aid with all the financial information needed to make intelligent decisions on both long-term investing and everyday money matters. While the Personal Finance Channel has information suitable for beginners, it is also robust enough for seasoned investors.

Note

AOL's Personal Finance Channel is one of America Online's most popular channels. It boasts over 1 million visitors a day.

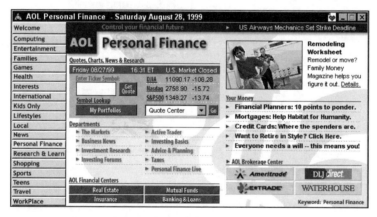

Figure 7-1. AOL's Personal Finance Channel has information for beginner investors, yet is comprehensive enough for the experienced investor.

The Personal Finance Channel can help you get control of your financial future. It is divided into the following money-related departments:

- ▶ The Markets
- ▶ Business News
- ▶ Investment Research
- ▶ Investing Forums

Note

Two other areas you may want to explore are Keyword: **Sage** and Keyword: **TheStreet. com**.

▸ Active Trader

▸ Investing Basics

▸ Advice & Planning

▸ Taxes

▸ Personal Finance Live

Basic Money Issues

If you need to develop a financial plan, start at the Advice & Planning Center, shown in Figure 7-2 (Keyword: **Advice & Planning**). Here, you will find advice on how money issues affect you at various stages in your life, including topics such as Health Care Issues, Retire in Style, and Can't Take It With You.

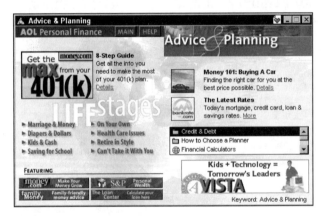

Figure 7-2. The Advice & Planning Center offers insights on how money affects the various stages of your life.

Beginners will also want to visit the department called Investing Basics at Keyword: **Basics** (see Figure 7-3). This is a great place to learn the basic investment concepts before you start on your financial journey. Besides teaching you about stocks, bonds, mutual funds, and other investments, this section illustrates the power of compounding and will help you learn about the common pitfalls that can ruin even a sound investment plan.

They say that a fool and his money are soon parted, but The Motley Fool (Keyword: **Fool**), shown in Figure 7-4, gives investing tips and tools that will help you make sure you increase your wealth rather than deplete it. This AOL area, run by the Gardner brothers in conjunction with AOL, has some of the best basic investment advice available. The Motley Fool's format is organized and easy to follow. Best of all, The Motley Fool takes investing seriously, but presents the information in a lighthearted, entertaining manner.

Cross-Reference

See Chapter 8 for information on how The Motley Fool can also help in researching retirement options.

Figure 7-3. Investing Basics is your starting point for mastering the basic investment concepts before embarking on your financial journey.

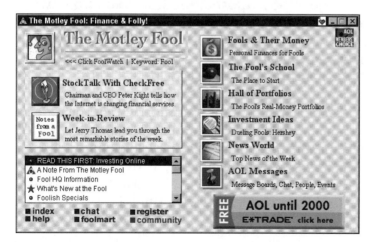

Figure 7-4. Although The Motley Fool is entertaining, investing is a serious subject at this Web site.

7

Investments

Other good advice is shared at theWhiz location (Keyword: **Thewhiz**). Current topics are investing, banking, credit and debt, real estate, insurance, taxes, chats, and messages. One chat focused on "Learning to Budget," a good subject to master.

The inevitable, taxes, also pops up (Keyword: **Taxes**). You can't avoid them, so get prepared with information on preparing and filing your tax return online.

News & Research

You'll find several helpful subjects under this topic of the Personal Finance Channel.

Business News

If you are a serious investor, you will be spending a lot of time at AOL's Business News Center. To be an informed investor, you need the top news about the economy, and you need to stay on top of all the latest financial news.

News from the world's major financial publications is compiled in the Business News Center (see Figure 7-5). Information is sorted into news categories, such as News Summary, Technology, Economy, International, Industry, and Consumer Briefs. Under the Business News Search area, you can search by subject for news on business tips. You can also search by ticker symbol for news, charts, quotes, or a company fund or index. The Business News Center also offers you The Markets, Business Newsstand, and Bloomberg Slideshows. A popular feature is the inside look at Wall Street given by *Business Week,* the world's most widely read business publication.

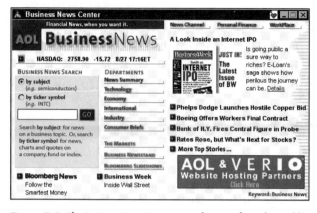

Figure 7-5. The Business News Center compiles news from the world's major financial publications.

Investment Research

Investment Research (Keyword: **Investment Research**) offers a spot where you can read up on a company before you invest. You can get comprehensive stock reports, financial statements, past earnings, Wall Street's estimates of future potential, as well as historical stock quotes for long-term tracking (see Figure 7-6). Links are available to various related resources, message boards, and investment chats.

Figure 7-6. Read up on a company at the Investment Research site before you invest.

You may search for a research report either by ticker symbol or by company name. A daily Industry Snapshot is featured, and help is available on screening for mutual funds and stocks. Tools and Resources covers Quotes and Portfolios, S&P Personal Wealth, Business Research, Stock Splits and Dividends, Historical Charts, and Business News.

Investing Forums

Would you like to hear about other people's investment experiences? Or, would you like to tell others about something you learned the hard way? Investing Forums (see Figure 7-7) is the place to voice your opinions and get the opinions of others. Whether you want to talk about the economy in general or a specific stock, there is always someone to talk to (Keyword: **Investing Forums**).

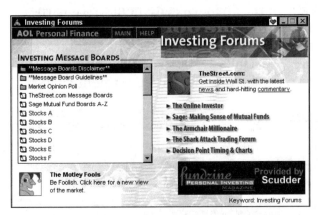

Figure 7-7. Learn about other investors' experiences at Investing Forums.

Another popular chat location is AOL Personal Finance Live (Keyword: **PF Live**). For opportunities to join in the discussion of a wide range of financial topics, chat-style, check out the current schedules of upcoming topics on AOL Personal Finance Live (see Figure 7-8).

Figure 7-8. Join in a wide range of financial topics, chat-style, at AOL's Personal Finance Live.

Getting Quotes

After you start investing, you will want to know how your investments are faring. The main page of AOL's Personal Finance Channel (Keyword: **Personal Finance**) gives you the Dow Jones Industrial Average (DJIA), Nasdaq, and S&P 500. These are hot links, so when you click them, you will see charts and more in-depth information. You can also enter the ticker symbol for a given stock and get a quick quote. The Quotes and Portfolios Web page also offers a lookup service for the symbol if you enter the first few letters of either the symbol or the company name. Whereas this is a good place to visit for a quick overview, AOL provides other areas where you can get more detailed information.

Be cautious about the investment advice that you get in a chat room or a discussion group. You can never be sure of the source. The advice-giver might be a certified financial planner, or he or she might be a 12-year-old child.

The Refresh button keeps you up to date with the latest information, and updates the display when needed. Because financial information can change rapidly, it is a good idea to click the Refresh button often (see Figure 7-9).

7

Investments

Refresh

Figure 7-9. The Refresh button updates a Web page when needed; use the Refresh button often.

Tip

Some Web sites give real-time quotes. Some are slightly delayed quotes. Be sure you know how current the quotes are.

Definition

An act that occurs in *real time* is an act that occurs with little or no delay.

Try the Active Trader area (Keyword: **Active Trader**) for newsletters and feature stories. Then, check out AOL's MarketDay (Keyword: **MarketDay**) for live market analyses from Briefing.com, where you can get market commentary, sector reports, fed briefings, and other useful information. You can also get to AOL's MarketDay from the Active Trader screen's box labeled More Resources. AOL's MarketDay is one of the choices on your selection list. MarketDay's strong point is its information on what is driving the market at the moment. Further information is given on Industry Focus and Economic Update. Of course, bonds and currencies are covered as well.

Portfolios

If you would like to follow any particular stocks, mutual funds, or indexes on an ongoing ba-sis, AOL lets you create a personal portfolio. Enter the Keyword: **Portfolio**. AOL automatically creates a portfolio file for you, called Portfolio #1 (see Figure 7-10). Click the Rename button, give your portfolio a more meaningful name, and add your stocks. You can also click Create to make a new portfolio if you want to track several different groups of investments.

To display your portfolio, just double-click the name of the portfolio. Click the Add button to add an invest-ment (see Figure 7-11). Type the symbol for the invest-ment, the exchange, the number of shares, the price, the date, and the commission paid. Click OK. Repeat this process to add all the investments that you may have. You can add cash to a portfolio simply by click-ing the Cash tab and entering the amount you want to add (see Figure 7-11).

Your Portfolio

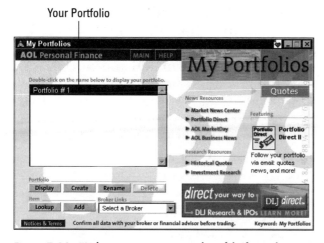

Figure 7-10. AOL lets you create a personal portfolio for tracking your stocks.

Add Button

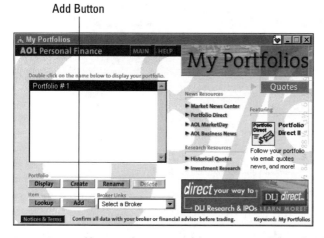

Figure 7-11. Adding a stock to your portfolio is as easy as clicking the Add button.

Your portfolio is displayed in a set format called the *default format.* You can change this format if you want to change the look of your portfolio. Double-click the portfolio name in the box or click the Display button at the bottom of the page. In the top right of the Portfolio Display box, click the down arrow of the Portfolio Column Views until you find Customize "My View." Select Customize "My View," and you will be taken to the Customize

You can display only seven columns simultaneously in your portfolio. If you already have seven columns and want to add another item, you must first remove an item by highlighting it and then clicking the Remove from Display button.

Definition

Default is a value or setting that a device or program automatically selects if you do not specify a substitute.

Portfolio Display Columns section, where you can work on changing your portfolio's appearance. By selecting a column from the Column Choices box, shown in Figure 7-12, you can add and/or remove columns. Even if you don't want to change the display right now, take a look at the list of things that you can display. One day, you might want to see the daily percentage of gain on your stocks, the 52-week high or low, or any of the other choices given.

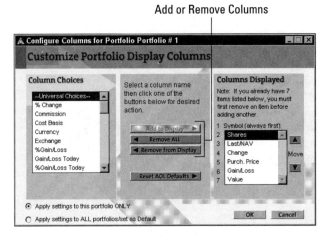

Figure 7-12. Customize your portfolio layout by adding or removing columns.

While AOL's Personal Portfolio is excellent, many on-line brokerage centers and other Web sites also enable you to create your own portfolios. AOL may be the most convenient for you; however, you can use any of them.

Financial Centers

America Online has four valuable Financial Centers (see Figure 7-13):

▸ Real Estate
▸ Insurance

▶ Mutual Funds

▶ Banking & Loans

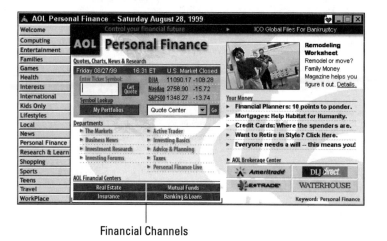

Financial Channels

Figure 7-13. AOL's Personal Finance Channel offers four valuable Financial Centers, shown at the bottom of the screen.

Real Estate

Your home is one of the largest purchases you will ever make. AOL's Real Estate Center (Keyword: **Real Estate**) can help you with house hunting. But, even more important, it provides calculators and other financial tools to help you determine home values, calculate mortgage rates, and locate other real estate resources.

All aspects of real estate are covered. Whether you are apartment hunting, buying a home, or just remodeling, you can find resources to suit your needs. Should you refinance now? How do you find a good real estate agent? How much is your home worth in comparison to your neighborhood? The Real Estate Center, shown in Figure 7-14, has the answers to many of your questions.

When you find a financial page that you like, be sure to add it to your Favorites (see Chapter 5 for instructions). The Personal Finance Channel has thousands of interesting pages, and returning to the same place is easy if you tag that page as a Favorite.

You can create more than one portfolio. One portfolio can contain stocks you own while another can contain stocks you want to monitor.

7

Investments

Figure 7-14. The Real Estate Center has the answers to many of today's real estate questions.

Insurance

The AOL Insurance Center (Keyword: **Insurance**) gives you a great way to shop for insurance, whether life, auto, home, business, health, disability, or long-term care. This area provides links to specific institutions and to general information about insurance. I don't know about you, but I find purchasing the right insurance even more confusing than purchasing stocks and bonds. So, be sure to visit the Insurance Center, which can help take the confusion out of insurance terminology (see Figure 7-15).

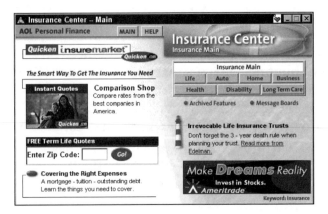

Figure 7-15. Visit the Insurance Center to learn all you need to know about insurance.

Mutual Funds

The AOL Mutual Fund Center (Keyword: **Mutual Fund Center**) explains all you need to know about mutual funds. It also provides links to various mutual funds and to information on thousands of funds, through Morningstar Mutual Funds. Extensive data is provided on the top 25 funds, and basic information is supplied on more than 8,000 other funds. Articles and commentaries on mutual funds and links to related resources are also included (see Figure 7-16).

Figure 7-16. The Mutual Fund Center explains all you need to know about mutual funds.

Banking & Loans

AOL created the Personal Finance Banking Center, shown in Figure 7-17 (Keyword: **Banking**), to provide its members with safe, secure, online banking services. It partners with over 30 financial institutions that you can access by clicking a button. If the bank you're interested in isn't there, another click will call up a complete list of banks.

7

Investments

Definition

Online banking is the process of performing common banking tasks by using a PC and modem. These functions include checking balances, transferring funds, paying bills online, communicating with the bank via e-mail, and learning about your bank's financial products.

Tip

The password you use for financial transactions should be different from any you might use to access other Web sites. Don't use the same one for both purposes.

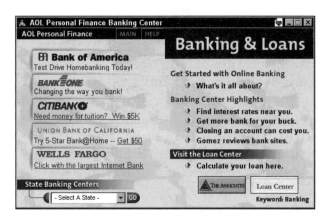

Figure 7-17. The Banking Center provides safe, secure, online banking services.

Online banking, also known as *PC banking* or *home banking,* is now available to millions of consumers. Close to 5 million people already bank online, and by the end of 2001, the number is expected to grow to about 22 million.

Online banking has become a valuable tool for millions of computer users. Financial institutions of all sizes offer the service, not just large banks. More than 1,000 financial institutions offer online financial transactions on the Internet, and the number is growing daily. Most popular is Web-based banking, which offers customers visiting a bank's Internet site the ability to log on to the bank's online banking server with an ID and a password.

Using a personal finance software package, such as Intuit's Quicken or Microsoft Money, is often the easiest way to start banking online. This type of banking offers direct updates of financial records with information from your bank account. Although you use a software program to enter and conduct transactions, the Internet access communicates between your bank and you.

The Benefits of Online Banking

- ▶ You have better access to financial information 24 hours a day.

- ▶ You can perform routine banking transactions from any location.

- ▶ Paying bills is quicker and more convenient.

- ▶ Consumer fees are often discounted.

- ▶ Online banking is one of the most secure ways to complete a financial transaction.

Tip

Check with your bank before you purchase Quicken, Microsoft Money, or any financial tracking software. Some banks prefer a certain program, or they may have their own proprietary program.

Some banks have software-based online banking that relies on a small program that they provide. This type of software may have to be downloaded from your bank's Web site or mailed to you on a CD-ROM or floppy disk. These programs offer only basic online banking functions, but in most cases, they're easy to use.

If you doubt the security of online banking, remember that for years money has been moving electronically between banks and brokerage houses around the world.

As with most real banks, the AOL online Banking Center has its own Loan Center (Keyword: **Loan**). Just click the Loan Center button (lower-right corner) for the current loan rates for different types of loans. Mortgage, home equity, new car, and used car loans are all covered here. You can calculate how much you can borrow, find information on loans, and even apply for a loan online. If you don't want to pay too much for a loan, check out the current rates here before you sign on the dotted line.

7

Investments

Online Trading Through the AOL Brokerage Center

Note

Be sure to click on SEC: Risks and Rewards of Online Trading on the Brokerage Center screen to be fully aware of the ins and outs of trading online. It is a bit different than calling your broker.

After you feel confident about your investment strategies and have done some research, you're ready to start investing and trading online. At that point, you'll probably wonder how you ever got along without a computer!

The AOL Brokerage Center (Keyword: **Broker**) is the location to buy and sell securities online (see Figure 7-18). Several brokerage houses have set up shop on AOL at the Brokerage Center — among them, DLJdirect, Waterhouse Securities, Ameritrade, and E*TRADE. AOL customers can shop and compare one brokerage to another and decide which best suits their needs. Like the banks, each of the brokerage houses has set up its own procedures for online trading, so you may want to check them all out before you make a decision.

Figure 7-18. The Brokerage Center is the location to buy and sell securities online.

Online Trading Offers Many Advantages

▶ Convenience

▶ Cost savings

▶ Fast, dependable, research updates

▶ Access to your investment information 24 hours a day

▶ Access to tax records, which are just a click away

Information is given on online broker ratings, the advantages of investing online, and the risks and rewards of online trading. Links take you to bookshelf locations and other resources.

Choosing an Online Broker Through AOL

Use the utmost care to choose an online broker — he or she can be even more important than a dry cleaner or a grocery store. Here are a few things you should consider:

▶ *How easy is it to sign up?* Many brokers require paperwork to be signed and mailed, in addition to their online signup. Just be sure that the process is as easy as possible.

▶ *How reputable is the company?* Using a reputable broker will make all of your transactions easier and more carefree. If you have used a brokerage house before and have been happy with its service, its online arm may be a good place to start. If you are going to be dealing with a brokerage house that you know nothing about, be sure to check it out. The U.S. Security and Exchange Commission (SEC) at www.sec.gov

is a good place to start (see Figure 7-19). The NASD Institute for Professional Development (www.nasdr.com) is also an excellent place to get information about online brokers.

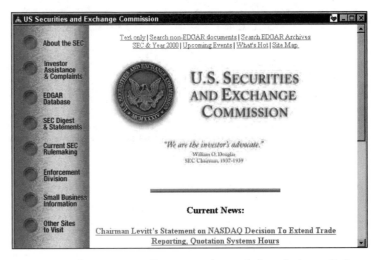

Figure 7-19. The SEC is an excellent starting place to check out background information on the many brokerage firms.

- ▶ *What are the fees?* As I write this book, the average commission on an online trade is about $15. Most online brokers are candid about their fees, but you should check their Web sites in depth to be sure there are no hidden fees.

- ▶ *Are their quotes in real time or delayed?* The Web site will give you this information, but you may have to search a little to find it.

- ▶ *How easy is the Web site to use?* Because each brokerage house has a unique interface, if all else is more or less equal, you may find that you simply like one site better than another. What you find easy may be difficult to someone else, but what matters is your own personal comfort level. Work with the information on the site and make sure you find it easy to use.

▶ *How much is the initial cash requirement?*
This varies from broker to broker. Be sure to
check this out.

Placing Your First Order

You've picked a broker, done your research, and you
are now ready to place your first online order. How
hard is it? How do you do it? What types of orders
can you place?

Without a doubt, your first online order will be a
bit scary. Mine was! But it really is easy. It all comes
down to a single mouse click. After you sign up with
a broker and put money in your account, you simply
enter the symbol and the quantity for the stock that
you want to purchase. If you want to put a limit on
the buy (usually a good idea for online trading; see
the comments in the next section), you enter that,
too. Then, you click the appropriate button to send
the order on its way.

When I made my first trade, the realization that I
had just spent a good deal of money with one click
of the mouse was somewhat overwhelming. The
first thoughts that ran through my mind were "Did I
do this right?" and "What if I made a mistake?"
However, after I saw the confirmation on the screen
acknowledging that I had purchased the correct
stock in the correct amount, I felt good. In fact, it
was an empowering experience; I felt *really* good!

So, if you feel any apprehension, don't worry, it's natural. You'll be on your way in no time at all. But, before you make that first trade, be sure to read the
simple but valuable tips in the next section.

Tip

The most expensive online
broker may not be the
best, and the cheapest
may not be the worst.
Investigate your online
broker thoroughly before
you commit your funds.

7

Investments

Hands-on Trading Tips

Online investing is different than any other kind of investing that preceded it. Even if you are an experienced trader, you may need a few tips to make the most of your new online experience.

Be Both Quick and Wise

Online trading is quick and easy, but to be a wise investor, you must spend time doing your research. Do your preparation before the trade; know the risk of each investment and be confident of your motivation to buy or sell. Invest quality time in your homework. After you do that, the split second it takes to click your mouse to buy or sell a stock will make your online trade both a quick and wise (and hopefully profitable) experience.

When You Can't Access Your Online Account

Computers are, as we all know, not the most stable devices ever created. Computers crash. Computer glitches happen. Although brokerage sites have very good track records, some do occasionally go down. Should you be concerned? Yes, but not overly concerned. If you find yourself with no access to your account online, most online trading firms offer you a choice of alternatives for placing your trade: touch-tone telephone trades, faxing your order, or doing it the old-fashioned way, by calling your broker on the phone. You may want to find out whether using this option for placing a trade will increase the cost of the trade.

Don't "Double Do"

It is a serious mistake to place a second order because you have mistakenly assumed your first order was *not* executed. You could either buy or sell twice as much stock as you intended. Get specific instructions from your online brokerage firm on how to handle the situation when you're not sure whether the original order was executed. Also, if you cancel an online trade, it is very important to confirm that your cancellation actually went through. Even if you receive an electronic receipt for the cancellation, do not assume that confirms the trade was canceled. Ask the online broker you are using how you can confirm that a cancellation order was correctly executed.

Set Price Limits

The SEC (its Web site was shown earlier, in Figure 7-18) recommends that you place *limit* orders rather than *market* orders:

> ► **Limit order:** You set a specific price that triggers the buy or sell. A *buy* limit order can only be executed at the limit price *or lower,* and a *sell* limit order can only be executed at the limit price *or higher.*

> ► **Market order:** You can't control the price at which your order will be filled. If the Web site goes down for a few hours and your order is not placed immediately, you could wind up buying or selling at a far different price than you intended. Placing limit orders can cover that possibility.

For example, if you have your eye on a hot IPO stock initially offered at $10, but you know that you don't want to pay more than $20, place a limit order to buy the stock at any price up to $20. By entering a limit order rather than a market order, if the market moves against you before your order is executed, you won't wind up paying $50 and then biting your nails while the stock drops back down to $20 in the days ahead.

Definition

IPO is an abbreviation for *initial public offering,* a stock that is being brought to the market for the first time.

The SEC Oversees the Securities World

The U.S. Securities and Exchange Commission is an independent regulatory agency charged with administering the federal securities laws. The purpose of these laws is to protect investors and make sure they have access to full disclosure of information concerning publicly traded securities. A second purpose is to make sure the securities markets operate fairly. Firms purchasing or selling securities, people providing investment advice, and investment companies themselves are also regulated by the SEC. The SEC is both nonpartisan and quasijudicial.

A limit order may never be executed if the market price surpasses your limit before your order can be filled.

Understanding Execution Speed

Online trading firms brag about the speed of their execution of stock trades. Is this for real? Although the SEC has no regulations requiring a trade to be executed within a set period of time, brokerage firms must not exaggerate the speed at which they can execute trades. Also, brokerage firms have an obligation to inform their investors of the possibility of significant delays.

Successful Complaining

The most important recommendation is to act promptly if anything adverse and out of the ordinary happens to you. You have only a limited time to take legal action. Check the SEC's Web site (www.sec.gov/consumer/onlitips.htm) for a four-step process for seeking satisfaction if you have a complaint.

Choosing Other Online Brokers

Although AOL gives you plenty of online brokers to choose from, you may want to check out others, as well. Charles Schwab (www.schwab.com) has been highly rated by several magazines and services.

Ameritrade (www.ameritrade.com) markets its brokerage house as being friendly with superior customer service positioned on the cutting edge of technology. This company offers a large choice of trading options with low commissions.

Merrill Lynch (www.ml.com) and Suretrade (www.suretrade.com) are two other online brokers who have developed Web sites that are attractive, easy to use, and filled with great information.

Coming Up Next

Now that you've seen how AOL can help with your investments, we next look at how AOL can help in another decision: retirement. The following chapter looks at how to search AOL and the Internet for retirement information and advice.

In this chapter, you learned the following:

► Before you invest in anything, you need a strategy that considers your goals, the amount of money you have to invest, your tolerance for risk, and how much time you can spend managing your portfolio.

- ▶ AOL's Personal Finance Channel supplies financial information to help you make intelligent decisions on both investing and everyday money matters.

- ▶ The Motley Fool gives investing tips and tools, but presents the information in a lighthearted, entertaining manner.

- ▶ AOL's Banking Center provides its members with safe, secure, online banking services.

- ▶ The Brokerage Center is the AOL location to buy and sell securities online.

CHAPTER

8

RETIREMENT

Quick Look

▶ **ThirdAge**   **page 236**

ThirdAge on AOL (Keyword: **ThirdAge**) has an excellent site found in their ThirdAge Money section that is focused on retirement and financial issues. It also offers daily news, chats and message boards, and a marriage center.

▶ **AOL Financial Retirement Calculators**   **page 239**

AOL offers answers to so many of our questions with their Financial Retirement Calculators, found under the Advice & Planning section of the Personal Finance channel. From there you can get answers to all of your nagging retirement questions: What will my expenses be after I retire? Am I saving enough? What can I change? What if I underestimate my expense? What happens if tax laws change? What if Social Security no longer exists? AOL's retirement calculators and the entire Retire in Style section will arm you with many planning resources to help make planning for your later years a little bit easier.

▶ **MoneyWhiz**   **page 247**

Online information can help you locate the retirement haven of your dreams. MoneyWhiz (Keyword: **MoneyWhiz**) can help you find the answers to all of these questions plus some excellent articles on retirement.

▶ **Retirement Net Online**   **page 248**

Retirement Net Online (www.retirenet.com) is a great starting point for finding the right place for retirement. You have a choice of searching by the state or by the type of lifestyle you are considering. Find the retirement communities that are known for their active lifestyles, or search for places that offer assisted living or nursing care.

Chapter 8

Retirement

IN THIS CHAPTER

Make the most of AOL's retirement resources

Understand various retirement plans

Project the impact of taxes

Choose your retirement lifestyle

As society changes and progresses, certain words and concepts take on entirely new connotations. *Retirement* is one of these evolving words. Retirement is no longer looked on as simply the cessation of work. As life spans increase and healthy living and wellness become committed goals for a larger number of our population, the connotation of rocking chairs, early-bird specials, and inactivity in retirement have been replaced with a vision of retirement as a new age of life filled with many different activities.

Today, many view retirement as an opportunity to spend more time with family, pursue interests and hobbies, volunteer to improve society, and, in some cases, even start their own business. Retirement, which used to be the long pause at the end of life, has now become the stage in life when you can fulfill your dreams.

If we define today's retiree as a person 65 and older, the retired segment of our population represents a sizeable percentage:

 Note

A recent study conducted for the AARP Research Group by Roper Starch Worldwide showed that 80 percent of adults aged 33 to 52 plan to work during their retirement.

> ▶ The retired segment of our population numbers approximately 34 million and represents 1 in every 8 Americans, approximately 13 percent of the U.S. population.

> ▶ Since 1990, the percentage of Americans 65 and older has more than tripled.

> ▶ A child born in 1996 can expect to live approximately 76 years, about 29 years longer than a child born in 1900.

> ▶ Today, 12 percent of people over 65 are in the workforce.

> ▶ Today's retirees are, on average, more financially secure than their predecessors.

Baby boomers refers to the generation born from 1946 through 1964 who are now adults aged 33 to 52, according to an AARP news release of June 1, 1998. Predictions of the baby boomer generation's impact forecast an explosion in the "retired generation of the future."

> ▶ The most rapid increase in the 65-and-older age group is expected to occur between 2010 and 2030, when the baby boomer generation reaches age 65.

8

Retirement

Retiree is one who has completed his or her active working life. A *baby boomer* is a person born from 1946 through 1964.

▸ By 2030, the U.S. will have about 70 million older persons (those aged 65 and older), more than twice the number in 1996.

▸ Only 26 percent of those in the baby boomer generation expect not to work for pay at all during their retirement years, while more than 33 percent expect to work part-time mainly for interest or enjoyment. Another 23 percent expect to work part-time mainly for the income.

▸ Most boomers do not see retirement as being the end of their productive years. Seventeen percent expect to start their own businesses. More and more workers dream of launching a second career in their late fifties as a means of easing into retirement.

▸ Baby boomers are often described as a generation that sees itself as "forever young."

Your Retirement Plan

A word to the wise: fulfilling your dreams cannot be done without some planning. Retirement planning gives you the opportunity to be the designer, shaping everything from the timing of your retirement to your retirement lifestyle. Although we never have complete control over the results, it doesn't hurt to have a good plan. Whether you are planning for your future retirement or you are already retired and need to decide what you want to do during your retirement, AOL, your computer, and the Internet are resources that can help you.

Financial Matters

Money is an inevitable consideration. Although retirement planning and living is not completely about financial matters, money does play an essential role. When should I retire? Will I have enough money? What should I do with the money I have? These are all pertinent questions.

The diversity of needs, goals, and opinions makes the financial end of retirement planning a very individual thing. Some folks want very badly to leave a nest egg for their children. One follower of the opposite philosophy, the live-it-up-and-don't-die-with-any philosophy, sports a bumper sticker that reads, "I'm spending my children's inheritance and enjoying every minute of it." So, your financial plan should be very personal, based on your own needs and goals.

I suffer from a case of nearsightedness when it comes to planning ahead. Talking about how much money I will have next week or next month is about all I can handle. When it comes to planning for years ahead, a lot of number crunching has to be done. The task demands more number crunching than I want to do, even with the help of a calculator. Because the computer is a natural at mathematical calculations, it can serve as a valuable aid for any financial projections. You just need to know where to go for help.

AOL's Retirement Resources

Type the Keyword: **Retirement**, and you will be instantly taken to some of the best online retirement resources. The retirement section is called Retire in Style (see Figure 8-1). This area will give you information on building your retirement plan, supercharging your 401(k), choosing a place to retire, and just about everything else needed to make the vision of the golden years come to fruition.

Thanks to AOL, charting your future is easier than ever. AOL is ready to help you build a plan, invest your assets, and find the best ways to finance your long-term care. AOL's Plan Well Now section will test your retirement IQ, point out tax implications, show you model retirement portfolios, and review the top ten retirement funds.

After you visit Retire in Style, you will find that this site links you to valuable resources both in AOL and on the Web. It also makes you address the difficult questions that the idea of retirement calls to mind.

Figure 8-1. Retire in Style (Keyword: *Retirement*) is one of the best online retirement resources and is found in the Life Stages area of the Personal Finance Channel.

Be sure to visit ThirdAge (Keyword: **ThirdAge**), which has an excellent site found in their ThirdAge Money section that is focused on retirement and financial issues (see Figure 8-2). AARP (Keyword: **AARP**), which serves over 32 million members, also has excellent information on retirement at its AARP Webplace (www.aarp.org), as shown in Figure 8-3. Both of these groups concentrate on the needs of older people.

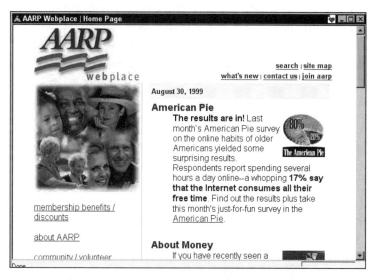

Figure 8-2. ThirdAge has an excellent site found in their ThirdAge Money section that focuses on retirement and financial issues.

Figure 8-3. The AARP site concentrates on the needs of older people.

Keyword: **Retirement** has more retirement calculators. They are located through the drop-down list.

What You Need to Know About Retirement

As with every topic, the more background you have, the better prepared you are to make important decisions. Everyone wants his or her retirement years to deserve the designation "the golden years." Quality of life is very important, so let's look at some of the things that will affect your golden years.

What Is Your Life Expectancy?

Let's start with the obvious. First, you need to determine theoretically how long you are going to live. Although this is something that no one knows for sure, the computer can come up with a calculation based on statistics and current charts. You may be surprised by the number of years your savings will need to cover during your retirement. Did you know your life expectancy goes up as you get older? Your money needs to last as long as you do.

The Life Expectancy Calculator at MoneyCentral (www.moneycentral.msn.com) will tell you what you need to know. Life expectancies are calculated using an average figure for someone your age as the starting point. Next, years are added or subtracted according to your inputs to the calculation. These adjustments are based on research about the effects of various heath habits on longevity. Generally, your life expectancy is influenced by several factors, ranging from your family history to your personal lifestyle. While you're at MoneyCentral, check out its other articles and information on creating a retirement plan, planning your estate, minimizing estate taxes, and preparing a will (see Figure 8-4).

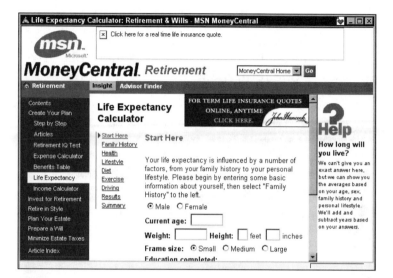

Tip

The result of the life expectancy calculation is just an average, which means you could wind up living a significantly longer or shorter span of years.

Figure 8-4. Life expectancies are generally influenced by several factors, from your family history to your personal lifestyle.

How Do I Project What My Needs Will Be?

AOL offers answers to so many of our questions with their Financial Retirement Calculators. Found under the Advice & Planning section of the Personal Finance channel, click Retire in Style. From the drop-down box, select Retirement Calculators. Just look at all the questions AOL can calculate the answers to: What will my expenses be after I retire? Am I saving enough? What can I change? What if I underestimate my expense? What happens if tax laws change? What if Social Security no longer exists? How much can I invest before taxes each year? How will each of my accounts grow? and many more.

Start by entering the information requested. Then let AOL's Financial Retirement Calculator do all the work to give you future projections (see Figure 8-5). Not only this calculator but also the entire Retire in

Style section will arm you with many planning resources. Lots of additional information is given on other topics such as creating a retirement plan, two spouses — one retirement, and retirement troubleshooting.

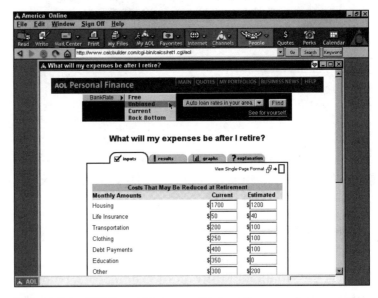

Figure 8-5. Let AOL's Financial Retirement Calculators figure out what your expenses will be after you retire.

How Much Will the Government Help Pay?

To plan your retirement, you need to know how much you have invested in Social Security. Requesting your Personal Earnings and Benefit Estimate Statement (PEBES) at the Social Security Administration's Web site (www.ssa.gov/pebes) is one of the easiest ways to obtain the information that you need. The site is clean and uncluttered (see Figure 8-6). Just complete and return the online form provided, and your PEBES will be sent to you by mail.

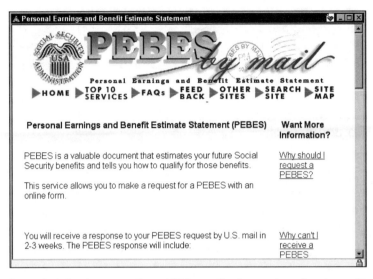

Figure 8-6. Request a copy of your PEBES to confirm how much you have invested in Social Security.

What About IRAs and 401(k)s?

Individual retirement accounts, such as Roth IRAs, traditional IRAs, rollover IRAs, and Keogh plans, are all popular retirement plans today. Many people also have a 401(k) plan through their employer. You must make decisions regarding which plans to use and which options will make the most of your retirement savings.

Research is helpful in tackling the intimidating details regarding retirement plan choices. AOL provides you with comprehensive information explaining retirement plans. Get a good lesson detailing each of these various plans at AOL's Retire in Style location. Special articles deal with 401K's, Roth, and standard IRA's. Such topics are offered in the drop-down list at Retire in Style as Making the Most of your 401K, New Rules of Money, IRA's in your 40's, 50's, 60's, and 70's and the Whiz.com 401K.

IRAs have detailed, some-
times complex, rules and
regulations on with-
drawals and contributions.
Be sure you understand
the rules before you invest.

Use Your Computer to Untangle Confusion Over IRAs, 401(k)s, and Keogh Retirement Plans

A clear understanding of the difference between an IRA, a 401(k), and a Keogh retirement plan is a good start:

- **401(k):** A retirement savings vehicle offered by employers that is named after the Internal Revenue Code section in which it is covered. This plan offers certain tax advantages, and sometimes corporate matching (when your employer matches part of your contribution) is possible.

- **IRA:** A savings account into which a stipulated amount may be deposited each year, with these deposits being deductible from your taxable income, and both deposits and interest being taxable after retirement.

- **Keogh:** A special type of IRA that doubles as a pension plan for a self-employed person. The self-employed person can put aside up to $30,000 a year, significantly more than the normal $2,000 cap on an individual IRA.

These retirement plans are all popular choices today, but you should rely on your computer and the Internet for further research to correctly match the right plan to your individual needs. Be sure to check out the Retire in Style screen (Keyword: Retirement) for informative articles on the different retirement plans.

For further research, you can get a good understanding of the basics of the varying retirement plans at the Retirement Planning Center at the

Strong Capital Management Web site, called Strong
On-line (`www.strong-funds.com`). At this site,
Strong Capital offers assistance in building your
investment knowledge, determining your risk levels,
and putting your financial goals in perspective.

How Do You Set Up and Manage a Plan?

One of the easiest retirement planners is found at
Quicken.com (`www.quicken.com/retirement/`).
The Quicken Retirement Planner walks you through
several screens of questions, as shown in Figure 8-7,
and presents you with a simple plan of action.

When Quicken computes your retirement future,
you might even be told, "your plan is not succeeding,"
like I was. If this happens, don't despair. Quicken
jumps into action and offers some suggestions and
"what-ifs." Its program even makes some suggested
changes to certain assumptions and then recalculates
the figures to show you how your plan can be improved. Another impressive and convenient feature
about Quicken's Retirement Planner is that if you use
Quicken's online portfolio tracker, you can easily link
your portfolio to your retirement plan. Now all you
have to do is be conscientious and stick to the plan.

If you want a more intricate plan, a free retirement
planner is available at the Vanguard Software
Center (`www.vanguard.com/planningcenter/`
`software/software.html`). Rather than an online
planner, this is an actual software program that you
download to your computer. Vanguard's program
offers general investing information as well as retirement, estate planning, and calculators to help you with
your retirement number-crunching. Further, Vanguard
offers you a choice of either a quick path for easy planning or a more detailed path for more advanced planning. A nice feature of the Vanguard program is
targeted to the current retiree. This segment focuses

 Find It Online

Check out IRA and 401K
Planning on the AOL
Personal Finance Channel
for information on funding
your retirement.

8

Retirement

on those who are already retired and helps them determine what is needed to maintain their present standard of living throughout retirement.

Tip

As your first step in retirement planning, many certified financial planners recommend that you determine exactly how much money will be required to live at the retirement lifestyle level you have selected.

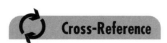

Cross-Reference

See Chapter 13 to learn how to download software.

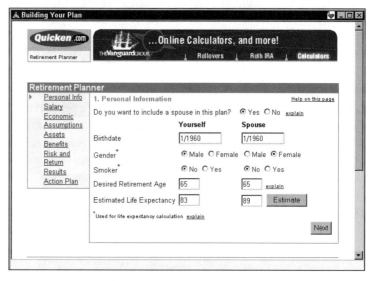

Figure 8-7. After walking you through several screens of questions, Quicken's Retirement Planner presents you with a simple plan of action.

The Motley Fool is a finance-specific area run by the Gardner brothers, who are dedicated to educating, amusing, and enriching individuals in search of the truth. The brothers add a lot of humor to their financial information. And, luckily for the older investors, AOL teams up with this pair in a special section called The Motley Fool: Finance & Folly (Keyword: **Fool**). This area has a comprehensive retirement section, as shown in Figure 8-8, which covers all aspects of retirement, from dealing with financial implications to deciding on a second career. This site also includes an excellent retirement planning primer with plenty of useful information.

Cross-Reference

See Chapter 7 for more information on how The Motley Fool can help in making investment decisions.

Figure 8-8. The Motley Fool has a comprehensive retirement section.

What About Taxes?

Taxes have a big impact on our finances. Reducing retirement taxes is within your reach if you do the proper planning. Many of the online financial resources discussed here and in Chapter 7 cover tax planning relating to investments and retirement. Because the tax laws change frequently, it is important to make sure that the information you are viewing is based on the most current laws. It is not unusual to find outdated information on the Internet, so be sure to find an up-to-date financial site.

SmartMoney (www.smartmoney.com/ac/ retirement) has an answer center where you can get responses to many of your financial retirement questions (see Figure 8-9). Tax ideas and tax planners are among the many topics covered in the answer center. This Web site also features calculators and worksheets that you can use to help with your financial decisions.

8

Retirement

Tip

Putting a child's name on the title to your home or leaving your tax-deferred retirement account to an heir may not be a good idea. Be sure to check out the tax implications before you make a decision on matters such as these.

Figure 8-9. Smart Money responds to your financial retirement questions at its answer center.

Choosing a Retirement Lifestyle

Although the financial side of retirement may seem the most daunting, other retirement-related decisions are also quite important. How far your dollar stretches can vary greatly depending on your choice of a retirement address. Often, retirement dictates downsizing or moving to a smaller home. Sometimes, the longing for a warmer climate means a move to a new community, or the lure of unseen places means time to be spent on the road.

Choosing a new lifestyle is something that can occur several different times during the course of the retirement years. Many retirees find that these lifestyle decisions are not always easy to make. Comparing notes with others often helps, which is why chat rooms about retirement-related subjects are both plentiful and popular.

Choosing Your Retirement Haven

Although the majority of retirees do not relocate, many do choose a new location to live in during their retirement years. According to theWhiz, an online publication of Intelligent Life Corp., one American in ten relocates after they retire. Others find that having a second home or apartment in a different location can offer a needed renewal or respite from the weather. Climate, recreational opportunities, and proximity to family are major considerations for most.

Finding a new location may be as easy as returning to an area that was once a vacation spot or moving to a location where children reside. On the other hand, finding a new location may be as time-consuming as using a Web site map of the U.S. to click the state or states in which you want to search for active retirement communities. Even after you have narrowed down the mind-boggling choices by location, some research remains to be done.

First, there are financial considerations. Will there be a difference in the cost of living for the new location? Will the cost of medical insurance and hospital care be different?

You have other considerations besides financial ones. What kinds of hobbies, volunteer activities, or part-time job opportunities will be available? Are retirement communities or adult real estate developments available? What about assisted living and continuing care facilities?

Online information can help you locate the retirement haven of your dreams. The MoneyWhiz (Keyword: **MoneyWhiz**) can help you find the answers to all of these questions plus some excellent articles on retirement (see Figure 8-10).

Find It Online

Some of the best chats about retirement-related subjects are found on America Online. Check out the chat schedules at Keyword: **People**. AARP holds regular chats on AOL that are both interesting and informative.

8

Retirement

Figure 8-10. MoneyWhiz, found on theWhiz on AOL's Main Screen, can help you locate the retirement haven of your dreams.

The Retirement Net Online (www.retirenet.com) is a great starting point for finding the right place for retirement. You have a choice of searching by the state or by the type of lifestyle you are considering. Find the retirement communities that are known for their active lifestyles, or search for places that offer assisted living or nursing care. Although the Retirement Net site is cluttered by advertising, it has information that can lead you to the right place whether you are looking at an international retirement community or seeking a seasonal or annual retirement community rental unit. In fact, it even lists many recreational vehicle resorts, just in case you're the traveling sort of person.

Alternative Living Options

Improved medical procedures and greater emphasis on healthy lifestyles have increased our life spans well beyond those of our parents or grandparents. Yet, we must all face the fact that a time may come when we will need help on a daily basis. Today, many retirement communities offer active lifestyles in addition to assisted living and nursing home facilities, should they become necessary.

Staying Put

Suppose you want to stay where you have always lived, near your children and around people of all ages, yet want to plan for the needs that additional years will bring. Recent developments in housing concepts have focused on retirees with the creation of the *age-friendly house*. Called a "universal design home," these ideas are on the cutting edge of an architectural concept targeted at an aging population. These ideas are easily incorporated into a renovation design of your current home, for the overwhelming majority of people who prefer to grow old in their own home in their own community. The advertising theme of "don't move, improve" plays on the concept of aging in place. The relocating retirees who are designing and constructing their retirement dream homes also can use these design concepts.

At the AARP Webplace (`www.aarp.org/universalhome/`), you will find a comprehensive list of all the components that go into making a home comfortable and useful for aging adults. These simple architectural specifications can make a home and its surrounding grounds more user-friendly to an aging population (see Figure 8-11).

An Age Friendly House calls for a single-story floor plan with no steps. The walkways are gently graded, and the doors and hallways are extra-wide to accommodate wheelchairs, and so on. Well-thought-out accessories include lever door handles, outlets and fuse boxes at a central height, and even height-adjustable closet rods. Grab-bars are found in the

Note

The Center for Universal Design at North Carolina State University and several other prominent universities have done extensive work on age-friendly house design concepts.

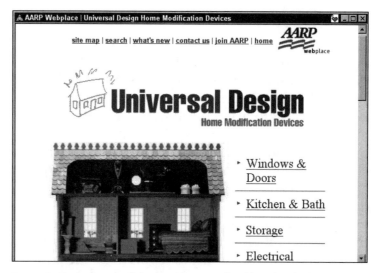

Figure 8-11. Components that make a home comfortable and useful for aging adults can be found at the AARP Webplace.

tubs in the bathrooms as well as hand-held shower-heads and lever- or pedal-controlled faucets. Skid-proof tile is perfect in the bathrooms. Don't forget the kitchen for side-by-side refrigerator and freezer, cabinets with pullout shelves, and lever or pedal faucets.

Architects have recognized the need to accommodate the requests of retirees in designing a home to serve as the ideal spot for the rest of their lives. The AARP Web site will give you all the information that you need plus links to other resources.

Assisted Living

Aging America's desire for new housing options sends retirees searching for everything from residences offering minimal services to those with attached nursing homes. Sustaining an estimated 15 to 20 percent growth rate per year over the past several years, assisted living is the fastest growing type of senior housing in the U.S. With its emphasis on personal dignity, autonomy, independence, and privacy offered by the concept of assisted living, this industry is booming.

Generally, "assisted living" is used to describe a residential facility that provides personal care, 24-hour supervision, both scheduled and unscheduled assistance, social activities, and many times some health-related services. Assisted living facilities strive to provide a homelike atmosphere and accommodate a resident's changing care needs and preferences. "Assisted living" is commonly used to describe several tiers of senior living:

> ▶ **Independent living**: A community of seniors living on their own in their personal residences or apartments with no supervision, meals, or personal services.

> ▶ **Congregate care**: A community of seniors living in rental apartments with a communal dining room and enjoying limited personal services.

> ▶ **Freestanding assisted living**: Seniors living in rental apartments, usually for a monthly fee that covers dining room service for three meals per day, onsite nurses, and assistance with personal needs such as bathing and medications.

> ▶ **Continuing care retirement community**: Seniors living in a community that enables residents to age in place by including the full range of living choices, from independent living to skilled nursing and a nursing home on one campus. Accommodation can be by monthly fee or by purchase.

8

Retirement

The rapid growth of the assisted living industry is thought to be a result of the increase in the population of persons age 85 and older, the desire of older persons to "age in place," and changes in America's family structure, which have increased the number of older persons living by themselves with more limited family support.

Also, because today's retirees are more financially secure than their parents, many have the means to demand and pay for assisted living. State governments have a keen interest in the assisted living options. As state governments continue to search for alternatives to expensive nursing home care and increased Medicaid expenditures, the possibilities of lower costs in assisted living facilities may become an attractive option.

Coming Up Next

AOL and the Internet offer a wealth of health-related information, which is the focus of the following chapter. In this chapter, we focused on retirement and how AOL can help you locate the information and advice you may be looking for. You learned the following:

- ▶ Planning for and enjoying retirement can be enhanced through the resources of AOL and the Internet.
- ▶ Online tools can help you calculate how long you can expect to live, as well as how much you can expect to receive through Social Security.

▶ Financial-planning sites will assist you in understanding various retirement plans and managing your taxes.

▶ Whether you retire near home or move across the country, Internet resources can help you explore options from your living room.

▶ A range of retirement lifestyles is available, from independent living through various levels of care.

Quick Look

▸ **A-Z Health Index**   **page 259**

For easy access to medical and health information, use AOL's A-Z Health Index, found at Keyword: **Health Index**. This expansive index will enable you to find almost any health-related topic quickly and easily. This index has an alphabetically tabbed format to help you look up everything from acne to ulcers.

▸ **AOL's Seniors Health**   **page 261**

Everyone wants to live longer and have a better quality of life. So, one of the focuses of the Seniors Health area is healthy living and healthy aging. It includes anti-aging techniques, fitness tips, and related topics. You can visit the Fitness for Seniors area by clicking this topic in the Information, Support, News, and More box found in the Seniors Health area (Keyword: **Seniors Health**). This area gives more in-depth information on the importance of staying active and the benefits of exercise.

▸ **drkoop.com**   **page 268**

For years, Dr. Koop, former Surgeon General of the United States, has devoted considerable resources and efforts toward consumer education. Dr. Koop's Web site (www.drkoop.com) offers a wide range of information, including a drug-interaction database that enables visitors to find out dangerous side effects of various medications. drkoop.com is a fast-growing site that hosts a "coffee shop" where you can chat with others, an online library, and a medical encyclopedia. This site also rates other medical Web sites and can be an excellent guide to medical Internet resources.

▸ **WebMD**   **page 269**

WebMD (www.webmd.com), which identifies itself as the homepage of health, is an Internet company devoted to improving healthcare. WebMD is a network connecting physicians, hospitals, and patients to a virtual world of medical information, tools, and services. It offers easy access to its free online Health and Wellness Center, which gives medical information from trusted sources, current health news, online communities, a physician directory, and a wealth of information on virtually anything that has to do with health.

Chapter 9

Health

IN THIS CHAPTER

Educate yourself about health issues via the Internet

Find information about using alternative medicine

Search great medical sites

Research specific diseases

Use AOL Chat for medical information

S eventy or eighty years ago, the average person didn't think much about health. People just went about their daily lives until some disease or disaster forced them to see a doctor. The doctor's pronouncements were official and incontestable.

Times change quickly. Today, health is a popular topic. Healthy people are reevaluating their lifestyles and researching ways to stay healthy. Sick people are searching out additional opinions and learning everything they can about their illnesses. Overall, the general public is becoming better informed about health issues, and this is changing the balance of power between doctors and patients.

AOL and the Internet are having great impact on people's lives as they use online resources to learn about health issues in the rapidly expanding medical field. America Online has been developing health-related resources since its inception and now provides people with the latest information available.

Using AOL's Health Channel

The AOL Health Channel is a vast resource for family health information and an excellent place to start any exploration into health-related topics. It offers many resources that will help you take an active role in your own healthcare, whether you enjoy robust health or have a specific health concern.

The main screen (Keyword: **Health**) is well-organized and easy to use. Near the upper-right corner, for example, you will find an excellent feature called Today in Health, shown in Figure 9-1, which brings you up to date on several of the hot health-related topics. This area also features a daily health tip, a poll in which your opinion actually counts, and a question-and-answer segment that draws out inter information from experts around the world.

Staying Healthy

For those who just want to stay healthy, the Health Channel has an almost endless array of information and advice on diet, exercise, and ways to minimize stress. The Healthy Living section is devoted to disease prevention, good eating habits, fitness, and wellness.

Figure 9-1. The main screen of the AOL Health Channel features Today in Health, focusing on current health-related topics.

Are you forever scheduling your diet to start tomorrow? Get some motivation, direction, and support from the Dieting and Nutrition area of the Health Channel (Keyword: **Diet**). In this section, you can review dieting basics and learn how to take weight off and keep it off. If you need encouragement, read the success stories of other AOL members. The Advice and Tips portion has a section on recipe makeovers that shows you how to take your favorite calorie-laden cholesterol-rich recipe and transform it to make it both nutritious and tasty. If you are adventurous and want some new recipes, the Kitchen of 1000 Pleasures gives you nutritious and delicious recipes. The Never-Say-Diet Center wants to change the way you think about food, exercise, and yourself. Learn to overcome the obstacles to good health with reformed eating habits, lifestyle changes, and a community to support you along the way.

What is that other word you always associate with diet? Exercise! The Fitness and Sports Medicine area (Keyword: **Fitness**) can help you get moving. From getting in shape to staying in shape, it has what you need to keep moving and motivated. The Exercise Match section can find just the right exercise for you. Walking is always a good, dependable exercise.

Find out how to "Walk It Off" with advice, gear, and a seven-week plan. Fitness Online (Keyword: **Fitness Online**) explores three important aspects of exercise with you: training, nutrition, and attitude.

So, now you are firm and fit and just the right size; time for some health and beauty tips. On the Health main screen (refer to Figure 9-1), click the Health & Beauty button under Taking Care of Your Health on the left side of the screen. The Health & Beauty section has plenty for the ladies, as expected, but the guys are not neglected. They will be interested in skin care and good sun habits, and there is even a section on baldness. Need to know about cosmetic dentistry? This is the spot. AOL's Health Channel is interested in taking care of you when you are healthy — and keeping you that way.

Knowledge Is the Best Medicine

If you or a loved one has lost the rosy glow of good health and has developed a challenging health-related problem, the Health Channel is there for you. This is the resource for information on almost every kind of medical condition, with facts on medications and treatments, advice from medical experts, and support groups in which you can compare notes with others.

For easy access to medical and health information, use the A-Z Health Index, shown in Figure 9-2, which will enable you to find almost any topic quickly and easily. This index has an alphabetically tabbed format to help you look up everything from acne to ulcers.

For more medical information, you can use the Specialized Medical Searches (also shown in Figure 9-1) to find drug, doctor, and medicine databases. This section (Keyword: **Medical Search**) includes an excellent medical dictionary, a vitamin, mineral, and herb index, and complete medical research going back to 1966.

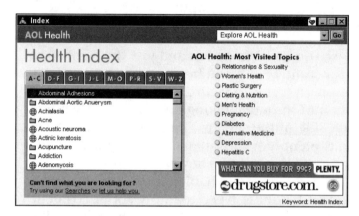

Figure 9-2. Both the A-Z Health Index and the Specialized Medical Searches will enable you to find almost any medical topic quickly and easily.

Another popular area is Conditions & Treatments (Keyword: **Conditions**), where you can use a tabbed index to find useful information on many different medical problems (and possible treatments), including cancer, osteoporosis, and arthritis (see Figure 9-3). It is a great, well-organized stepping-off point for researching any medical condition.

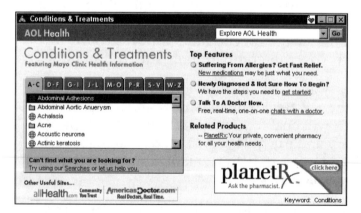

Figure 9-3. The Conditions & Treatments area has catalogued useful information on many different medical problems, including cancer, osteoporosis, and arthritis.

Aging and Health Issues

Different groups of people have different health concerns, so AOL features health issues for men, women, children, and seniors. While information is plentiful for the first three groups, the Seniors Health section (Keyword: **Seniors Health**) is especially comprehensive. With the baby boomer generation becoming the over-fifty group, large numbers of people are interested in this area and it is a rapidly expanding section. The Seniors Health area also features message boards. Chats and discussions with health experts will give you a well-rounded selection of the current opinions of trained medical professionals. Chats with others will give you valuable input from the "man on the street."

Everyone wants to live longer and have a better quality of life. So, one of the focuses of the Seniors Health area is healthy living and healthy aging. It includes anti-aging techniques, fitness tips, and related topics. You can visit the Fitness for Seniors area by clicking this topic in the Information, Support, News, and More box found in the Seniors Health area (Keyword: **Seniors Health**). This area gives more in-depth information on the importance of staying active and the benefits of exercise. If you are over 50, you'll find fitness information specifically targeted to your needs and — I hope — will also find the encouragement that you need to stay on an active and healthful path (see Figure 9-4).

Tip

It's great to talk to others and hear about their experiences in dealing with health issues. Just remember to evaluate anecdotal information of this type carefully and judge its worth cautiously and always consult your physician before acting on any advice.

Note

Fifty-Plus, an international organization, also has a great fitness site, called Our Bodies are Made to Move (www.50plus. org). This site, which is devoted to motivation toward and participation in exercise and fitness while aging, is sure to get you on the move.

Disclaimers Abound

Our disclaimer: The information in this chapter and on AOL's Health Channel serves as a resource for finding health information and as a guide to taking a more active role in your healthcare. This information is not a substitute for medical care. If you have any concerns about your own health or that of your family, contact a healthcare professional.

You will see similar disclaimers throughout the online world as you search for information. Most of these disclaimers recommend contacting a doctor or healthcare professional for evaluation of medical problems. This is good advice and should be followed.

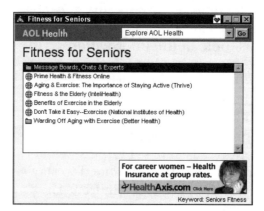

Figure 9-4. Fitness for Seniors encourages you to stay active and appreciate the benefits of exercise.

Better Health for All

The AOL Health Channel gives you many ways to take care of your health. It also gives you links to other helpful sites, such as AmericasDoctor.com (www.americasdoctor.com), which is presented through a sponsorship by Duke University Health System. If you have trouble communicating with your doctor, the Ask the Doc section may be very useful to you. The site also has real answers to many medical questions, as well as information on different hospitals, communities, and doctors.

Because many things affect our health and wellness, when you explore the AOL Health Channel, you will find numerous useful sites that expand into other areas as well. ThriveOnline (Keyword: **Thrive Medical**) not only gives you medical and fitness information, but it also contains information on nutrition, weight, sexuality, and serenity.

The InteliHealth area (Keyword: **InteliHealth**) is a joint venture between Aetna U.S. Healthcare and Johns Hopkins University and Health System. This is an award-winning site that includes very effective reference tools, databases, and search tools that are easy for the average person to use. Health insurance information can be found at HealthAxis (Keyword: **HealthAxis**).

PlanetRx (www.planetrx.com) is one of several places on the Web where you can order health products and supplies and have them delivered to your door. PlanetRX provides many useful features, such as detailed information about your prescription drugs. It also provides up-to-date advice and chats.

Another related site that is just plain fun is Test Yourself (Keyword: **Test Yourself**). Many of the tests are health-related, such as "Fitness IQ: What Does it Take to be Fit?" and "Chocolate: What Do You Know?" You can also have some fun by taking the IQ and personality tests (see Figure 9-5). Find out where you score among the 16 personality

Tip

Who is behind the stethoscope? Check out the validity of any healthcare-related site by finding out who sponsors it. This information is often found on the main page of the site, but sometimes you have to sift through several pages to find it. If a reputable healthcare organization, hospital system, or medical association sponsors the site, you may find more trustworthy information at that location.

Definition

Alternative medicine is differentiated from traditional medicine by its reliance on medical practices that are not always accepted by mainstream medical experts. These practices can include acupuncture, herbs, nutrition, and embracing wholeness of mind, body, and spirit.

types. On the more serious fitness side, you can find the best exercise for your needs, calculate how many calories you burn, or find out how many nutrients are in the foods you eat.

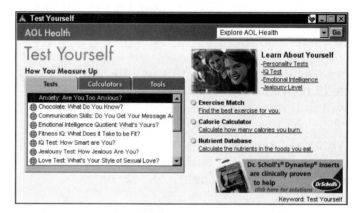

Figure 9-5. Have some fun at the Test Yourself site by discovering your personality type.

Alternative Medicine

Other popular areas in the AOL site include the Alternative Medicine section (Keyword: **Alternative Medicine**), where you can learn about natural remedies, such as acupuncture, yoga, aromatherapy, and magnetic therapy. This area will also give you information about healing practices and mixing modern medicine with natural techniques. Herbal remedies grow more popular every day. Brush up on the uses of ginkgo, St. John's wort, garlic, ginger, and aloe vera as natural remedies. Consider keeping your picnic bug-free with an herbal bug repellent containing citronella (see Figure 9-6).

More on alternative medicine can be found at `http://cgi.pathfinder.com/drweil/`. This site includes an area called Ask Dr. Weil, which features common questions with answers by Dr. Weil, a pioneer in alternative medicine. Guests include other notables, such as Bernie Siegel, who writes

columns filled with sage advice, with titles such as
"These Years Don't Seem So Golden." The site also
helps you find holistic practitioners who are located
in your neighborhood.

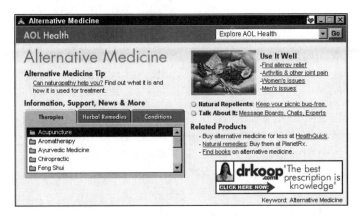

Figure 9-6. Learn about natural remedies, such as acupuncture and aromatherapy, at AOL's Alternative Medicine site.

Using Other Great Medical Sites

When you first start searching for online medical
information, the sheer volume of available data
will, without a doubt, overwhelm you. The data
can seem unorganized and confusing. Hot links
are great, but if you follow enough of them, you
can become lost and unproductive.

One of the best ways to handle all of this data is to
find a few good medical sites, add them to your list
of Favorites, and use them as anchors from which
you can fan out and find other information. You
likely have already done that with several of the
excellent AOL sites. Now, let's add a few more
Web sites to your list.

Cross-Reference

See Chapter 5 for more information about your Favorites list.

How to Diagnose a Good Medical Site

▶ Find out who sponsors the site. Do they have any health or medical expertise or training?

▶ Is the information factual or is it opinion? Determining the authenticity of the facts presented often is difficult. So, whether fact or opinion, make sure the material comes from a reputable source.

▶ Is the site trying to sell you something? Even if the site represents an excellent product, you should be aware that the producers of the site may have a vested interest and may be providing a slanted view.

▶ Is the information current?

Informative Medical Sites on the Internet

Following is a guide to some of the medical Web sites on the Internet.

Government

The National Institutes of Health (www.nih.gov/health) holds a wealth of medical information from the Government's health research institutes. The information found here is generally consumer-related. This is the place to find consumer publications, toll-free numbers for medical information, and an area containing information from the National Library of Medicine. This site gives you links to many quality resources as well as links to thousands of research articles published in biomedical journals. What a mind reader! This site also has an area offering help in spelling medical terms (see Figure 9-7).

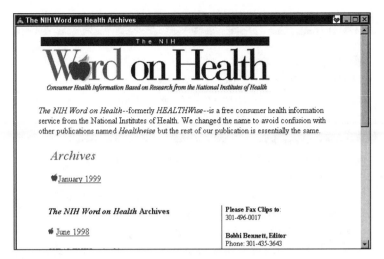

Just as the Mayo Clinic (`www.mayohealth.org`) and Johns Hopkins (`http://infonet.welch.jhu.edu/`) have their own Web sites, many other teaching hospitals and clinics have electronic information available. These medical Web sites can be found with any search engine and can be valuable resources.

Figure 9-7. The National Institutes of Health Web site holds a wealth of medical information from the Government's health research institutes.

Clinical

The Mayo Clinic is one of the most widely known and respected medical clinics in the world. The Mayo Clinic Health Oasis (`www.mayohealth.org`) carries that reputation to the online world. The online Mayo Clinic is proud of its many research centers, where you can search for a variety of topics. Several of these centers deal with common diseases, such as cancer, asthma, and Alzheimer's disease, while others focus on more general topics, such as medicine and nutrition. The Mayo Oasis has its own glossary and library. This popular medical site features an online help area called Housecall and an excellent search feature that will help you locate the topic of your choice.

Professional

The American Medical Association (AMA) has its own online health information center, called AMA Health Insight (`www.ama-assn.org/consumer.htm`). This site is an excellent place to get the most current medical news. It has a comprehensive listing of current news items. It also covers general health topics and specific conditions, and has an interactive health area that can be personalized to your needs.

Tip

For patients in small towns and for those who have rare disorders, the Internet can be a lifeline to necessary resources.

C. Everett Koop

Medical Web sites undoubtedly will have a significant impact on the healthcare system in the United States. The first highly visible person to realize this is C. Everett Koop, former U.S. Surgeon General.

For years, Dr. Koop has devoted considerable resources and efforts toward consumer education. Today, the 83-year-old doctor's opinions are shaping the way medical information reaches millions of people on the Internet. Dr. Koop's Web site (`www.drkoop.com`) offers a wide range of information, including a drug-interaction database that enables visitors to find out dangerous side effects of various medications. About 100,000 people die each year from drug reactions. Dr. Koop has made this valuable database freely available to everyone.

drkoop.com is a fast-growing site that hosts a "coffee shop" where you can chat with others, an online library, and a medical encyclopedia. This site also rates other medical Web sites and can be an excellent guide to medical Internet resources. Dr. Koop's primary message is that knowledge is the best medicine (see the following figure).

Dr. Koop's primary message is that knowledge is the best medicine.

Research

Mediconsult.com (www.mediconsult.com) has earned a reputation as an up-to-date site offering the very latest medical research. This site is packed with resources for people with chronic conditions. Information is available about clinical trials and drug therapies. Until the Web became a tool for the everyday person, doctors, hospitals, and insurers maintained an almost exclusive grasp on medical information and treatment options. Now, the "virtual medical center" at Mediconsult.com, with its medical topics search index, live events, and constantly updated articles, will continue to produce better-informed patients.

Healthcare

WebMD (www.webmd.com), which identifies itself as the homepage of health, is an Internet company devoted to improving healthcare. This site offers personalized, authoritative health and medical information. WebMD is a network connecting physicians, hospitals, third-party payors, and patients to a virtual world of medical information, tools, and services. Using the Internet's electronic data interchange, WebMD aspires to become a premier "healthcare portal," a single point of access for insurance verifications, improved communications, and healthcare resource content, as well as other Web-based offerings.

This site hopes to entice healthcare professionals to use WebMD for multiple administrative, communications, and research functions. For the consumer/patient, WebMD offers easy access to its free online Health and Wellness Center, which gives medical information from trusted sources, current health news, online communities, a physician directory, and a wealth of information on virtually anything that has to do with health.

Tip

Most Web sites post a privacy policy. Be sure to check out the privacy policy of the Web site before you give out any information about yourself or the state of your health.

Definition

A *portal* is a Web page that offers a broad array of resources and services, including search engines, online shopping, discussion groups, and e-mail, to name just a few. Many traditional search engines and informational Web sites have transformed themselves into Web portals, to attract a larger audience.

Graphic Surgery

They say that a picture is worth a thousand words, but when dealing with medical information, a picture may or may not be what you want to see. However, if you are graphically inclined, a Web site called Adam (www.adam.com) has an excellent section called Health Illustrated that features medical artwork in full color. The Adam site is based on a series of CD-ROMs created for the medical education community, so the information and drawings should be accurate (see Figure 9-8). YourSurgery (www.yoursurgery.com) is another Web site that uses photos and diagrams to represent the details of common surgeries. This site also offers animations and discusses the risks of many surgical procedures.

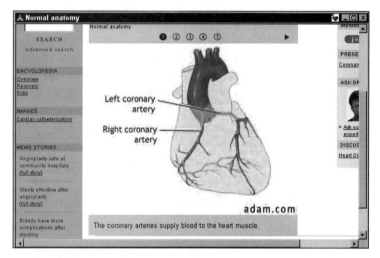

Figure 9-8. The Adam site has an excellent section called Health Illustrated, which features medical artwork in full color. (Copyright " 1999, A.D.A.M. Software, Inc. d/b/a adam.com)

If you are not the queasy type, you can even see surgery performed live on the Internet. The Health Network (www.thehealthnetwork.com), which was the first to show a live Webcast of the birth of a baby, also shows live surgeries (see Figure 9-9). A partnership between Fox TV and the America Health Network has created more reality-based programming. This Internet site is one of a new breed of Web sites trying to morph the best of television with the immediacy of the Internet.

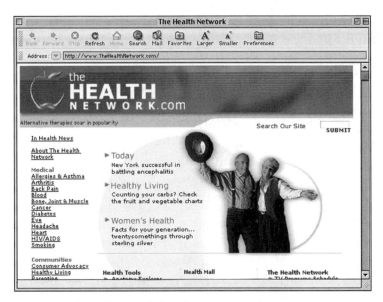

Figure 9-9. The Health Network shows live surgeries on the Internet.

Building a Network of Support

In times of confusion and need, people naturally reach out to others for support. The same disease that is confronting you or your loved one may not plague anyone else in your immediate community, but the online community spans the globe. So, from the comfort of your own home, you can find someone who faces the same difficulties, someone who can offer comfort, support, and empowerment. It is estimated that more people search online sources for information on diseases than for any other health-related topic. AOL and the Internet have become a network of support and information for thousands who are encountering health-related problems.

Knowing Where to Start

If you want help with a certain medical condition, where do you go? Start at AOL's Health Channel and then move on to any of the sites listed in this chapter.

Another possible starting point is the Health on the Net Foundation, an international initiative found at www.hon.ch. Health on the Net is a not-for-profit organization headquartered in Geneva, Switzerland. Health On the Net sponsors MedHunt, which is an excellent medical search engine. Just type the key-word you want to search, and you are presented with a list of pertinent sites and a detailed description of each one.

Other possible starting points for your search are the National Mednav.com (www.mednav.com), the Mental Health Net (www.mentalhelp.net), the National Organizations for Rare Disorders (www.rarediseases.org), and Support-Group.com (www.support-group.com).

Researching Specific Diseases

The Web is also filled with sites devoted to specific diseases. If your search is cancer-related, for example, try OncoLink (www.oncolink.upenn.edu), which is an online part of the University of Pennsylvania Cancer Center. The site is searchable and also offers screening methods, cancer prevention, and links to a wealth of cancer-related information (see Figure 9-10).

The Association of Cancer Online Resources (www.acor.org) is another site for cancer resources. Web sites are often created after a person is plunged into researching a disease that touches a loved one.

This site was created by Gilles Frydman, a French entrepreneur, while he was trying to gather information about his wife's battle with cancer. His wife recovered, and now he helps others through his network of cancer-related mailing lists (see Figure 9-11).

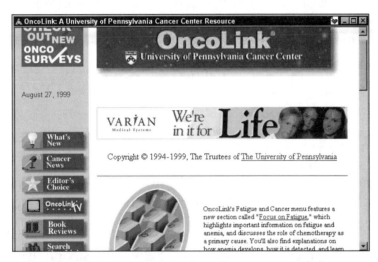

Figure 9-10. OncoLink is a cancer-related site offering screening methods, cancer prevention information, and links to a wealth of cancer-related information.

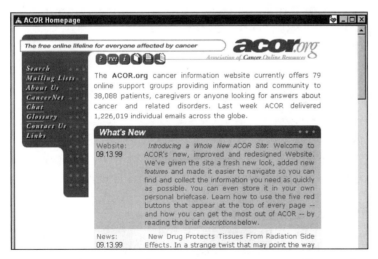

Figure 9-11. The Association of Cancer Online Resources was created by a French entrepreneur as he gathered information to aid in his wife's battle with cancer.

Chatting for Medical Information

Caution

Remember that anyone can dispense medical advice online, with or without credentials.

Even those who have tried and rejected the type of relationships that chat rooms offer have found the support of a cyber community to be a comfort when health-related problems occur. Finding a chat room or message board that you can relate to is a bit like finding a neighborhood in which you feel comfortable. Each chat room and message board community develops its own unique personality, yet each welcomes newcomers. So, feel free to stop by any chat room you find. You are welcome to just hang out in the background and see what's going on. Chats that center on diseases and cures seem to use a lot of abbreviations and unusual terminology. It may take a while for you to figure out what actually is going on, so don't be too quick to judge the usefulness of such a chat room. Also, don't be afraid to jump right in and ask questions. Most of the folks in these online groups are more than willing to help a newcomer. Also, don't forget about using an Instant Message to ask just one person a question without having to post a message to the entire group.

Coming Up Next

Many people are using the Internet these days to research their family trees. The next chapter focuses on just this: using AOL and Internet resources to help trace your genealogy. In this chapter, we focused on health issues and how AOL can help in answering many health-related questions. You learned the following:

▶ AOL's Health Channel, a vast resource for family health information, is an excellent starting place for research into health-related topics.

▶ Knowledge is the best medicine, and AOL's Health Channel supplies information on almost every known medical condition, along with facts on medications and treatments.

▶ Understanding that everyone wants to live a better-quality, longer life, AOL focuses on healthy living and healthy aging in the Seniors Health area.

▶ AOL links you to other Web sites, such as AmericasDoctor.com, to answer medical questions and supply information on different hospitals, communities, and doctors.

▶ It is estimated that more people search online sources for information on diseases than for any other health-related topic.

Online chat rooms, support groups, and discussion boards are a way for people to exchange experiences and opinions with others who share a special health concern.

See Chapter 3 for more information about Instant Messages.

Quick Look

▶ **AOL's Genealogy Forum** **page 280**

Type in the Keyword: **Roots**, and you will be at the Genealogy Forum, America
Online's vast and diverse collection of genealogical resources for family history
buffs of every experience level. The Genealogy Forum offers "how-to" guides
for the novice as well as reference articles for the professional genealogist. This
is the place to find chats and message boards as well as file libraries, extensive
surname databases, and interesting lectures.

▶ **Library of Congress** **page 286**

The Library of Congress (www.loc.gov) has one of the world's premier collections of U.S. and foreign genealogical and local historical publications. The
Library is ready for your research task with its collection of books, CD-ROMs,
and even a vertical file collection. Research training classes are offered to help
new genealogists get started. The Local History and Genealogy Reading Room
has a selected list of references compiled for the beginning genealogist that
includes introductory books for U.S. genealogical research.

▶ **Ancestry.com** **page 288**

Ancestry.com (www.ancestry.com) claims to be the first and most inclusive
genealogical online service. It provides credible and comprehensive genealogical databases for tracing family history for either the professional genealogist
or those just wondering about their family name.

Chapter 10
Genealogy

G*enealogy* is the finding of vital statistics on your ancestors and their relatives. It may at first sound boring, but few hobbies are as exciting or as fulfilling as genealogy. The search for one's history may fulfill the inborn urge for self-discovery, while, at the same time, genealogy can bring generations together.

Each and every family shares in its own part of history, and the search for ancestors can bring out the detective in all of us. If you enjoy a good mystery, you will enjoy doing genealogical research.

Why Genealogy Is So Popular

Definition

Everyone loves to hear Grandma and Grandpa's stories of long ago. Now, computers and the Internet can help to keep those stories alive. Technology has made the search for one's roots easier and, in many ways, more gratifying. For example:

Genealogy is the search for vital statistics of your ancestors and their relatives.

▶ Interest in genealogy is building nationally at a grass-roots level and is fast becoming a national obsession. (*Time* magazine, April 19, 1999.)

▶ Seventy-five percent of consumers, regardless of gender, age, region, race, or socioeconomic level, feel that staying in touch with family members is "very important." (Survey conducted by Ancestry.com, Inc., as reported by "Eastman's Online Newsletter," June 22, 1999.)

▶ "Root seeking" ranks with sex, finance, and sports as a leading subject on the Internet. (*Time* magazine, April 19, 1999.)

▶ Genealogy is the third biggest hobby in the U.S. and the second most popular topic on the Internet. (Maritz Marketing Research study conducted for *American Demographics* magazine.)

▶ At least seven "treemaking" computer programs are currently selling well, such as Family Tree Maker, Generations Family Tree, Ancestral Quest, Legacy Family Tree, Presidential Family Forest, Ultimate Family Tree, and Reunion.

▶ Nielsen/Net Ratings report that the three top genealogy Web sites had an audience of 1.3 million individuals during one month (www.nielsen-netratings.com). Tens of thousands of genealogy Web sites now exist.

Cross-Reference

More information on the Genealogy Forum is given later in this chapter, in the section, "AOL's Genealogy Forum."

Genealogy requires much patience and a lot of digging, but now you can get your computer to do a good deal of the spadework.

Starting Your Genealogy Project

As with many tasks, starting a genealogy project may at first seem to be a daunting chore, but AOL helps to make it easy. Just type the Keyword: **Roots**, and you will be at the Genealogy Forum, America Online's vast and diverse collection of genealogical resources for family history buffs of every experience level. The Genealogy Forum offers "how-to" guides for the novice as well as reference articles for the professional genealogist (see Figure 10-1). This is the place to find chats and message boards as well as file libraries, extensive surname databases, and interesting lectures.

To offer even more resources in your search, the Genealogy Forum has international research guides, broad ethnic resources, and high-level forum search features. It also has help to assist you in learning how to proceed on your own, whether you are a veteran genealogical researcher or just beginning your genealogy adventure.

Start by focusing on yourself. You are tracing *your* family tree, so this is one time that you can get away with being very self-centered. You are the beginning of the research. Record all the information you know about yourself: birth, baptism, marriage dates, and so on, as well as for your brothers, sisters, parents, grandparents, aunts, and uncles.

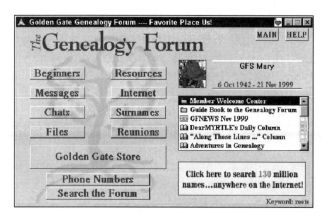

Figure 10-1. AOL's Genealogy Forum offers plenty of help to both the veteran genealogical researcher and the family history novice.

Gather all of your family records, including birth and death certificates, marriage licenses, scrapbooks, letters, newspaper clippings, military certificates, diaries, and other family histories. Bring out those old family picture albums, which may also have names and dates.

Expand your search for information to include others. Talk to relatives and gather information. Interview your family members. Tape-record or videotape your interviews.

Remember that just collecting names and dates can be a very sterile pastime. Use this information to gain an understanding of your ancestors and the lives they led, and you will be rewarded with an awareness of your rich family history that can be shared with other members of your family.

Keeping Records

Record-keeping is an important part of documenting a family history. Many different methods are used. Find the method that you are most comfortable with or develop your own. It is important to be accurate and to preserve your records in a clear, efficient, and consistent manner.

Keywords: **Gen** and **Roots** will both lead you to AOL's Genealogy Forum.

A great source of names and dates could be the old family Bible that your great-great-grandmother used to record family births, weddings, and deaths.

10

Genealogy

Definition

A *family tree* is a graphic layout of family lineage showing individual ancestors by generation, usually giving a family member's name, date of birth, marriage, and death.

Find It Online

Check out Keyword: **AOL Shop Direct** to find the special AOL edition of the Ultimate Family Tree Deluxe.

Remember to record the important events that took place in each person's life, including the place where they happened and their dates. A research log is very helpful. This is where the computer really comes in handy. The computer can put all of your information together and keep it accurate and organized. It enables you to track where you are at every stage of research and maintain a concise roadmap of your research. The computer also enables you to analyze all the parts, as well as the whole project, and keep a detailed record of your progress.

Using Genealogy Programs

If tracing your genealogy is going to be a serious endeavor for you, consider purchasing a genealogy program. AOL has teamed with The Learning Company to produce a special AOL edition of the Ultimate Family Tree Deluxe especially for use with the AOL Genealogy Forum. Other well-known genealogy software programs are Brøderbund's Family Tree Maker and Sierra Home's "Generations."

Genealogy programs give an immediate structure to your research and make it easy to organize all of your family information. They provide places to input your information, such as names, addresses, and important dates.

Genealogy programs create family tree charts where you can easily insert photographs and graphic elements. The result is that, with your personal computer and a small printer, you can produce a family tree chart that looks like it was created by a professional researcher and printed by a commercial printer. These heirloom-quality printouts make great gifts for family members. Plus, a variety of reports are available that can help you keep track of everything from family birthdays to complete family histories.

AOL's Ultimate Family Tree Deluxe is easy to use and has online tutorial and support information right on AOL at Keyword: **UFTD**. It also contains additional research tools on the CD-ROM. The included Social Security databases, world name indexes, Civil War muster rolls, and other databases can be an excellent place to begin your exploration or find missing links in your family tree.

Tip

For a quick start, check out the surname searches that most genealogy sites offer.

Understanding File Formats

Data is stored in a computer in a file. Many different types of files exist: data files, text files, program files, directory files, and so forth. Different types of files store different types of information.

Definition

A *file* is a collection of data that is stored in the computer.

Each file has a specific format that is used to encode the information in that file. Just as a person who speaks English may not understand a person who speaks Italian, a program that uses one file format may not be able to understand or to transfer data to a program that is written in another file format.

Definition

File format refers to the structure of a file that defines the way it is stored and laid out on the screen or in print.

The most common file format for genealogical information is called GEDCOM, which stands for Genealogical Data Communications. GEDCOM allows genealogy files to be opened in any genealogy software program that supports it. Computers give everyone the ability to organize their own genealogy records, but sharing that data can be very important among members of your own family as well as with the outside world. Using the GEDCOM format enables you to freely exchange your data. You don't have to know anything about this file format to use it. Just be certain that the software program that you choose supports the GEDCOM standard. (AOL's Ultimate Family Tree Deluxe supports GEDCOM.)

Definition

GEDCOM, an abbreviation for *Genealogical Data Communications*, is a file format that allows genealogy files to be opened in any genealogy software program that supports it.

10

Genealogy

Using Your Computer's Built-in Programs

Although I strongly suggest purchasing a genealogy program, the computer alone is an excellent place to input all the information that you gather, even if you don't start off with a special software program. You can use a simple word processing program, a database program, or a spreadsheet as a place to store all the information that you accumulate. However, while these programs are sufficient for accumulating information, it is difficult to show the relational links between individuals in such programs. That is why genealogy programs are so useful.

Expanding Your Search

After you get a start researching your family history, the Internet is an excellent place to expand your search. When you start your Internet search, just go with the flow. Let yourself click from one link to the next. Whether you find your ancestors on the Mayflower passenger list or on an inmate list from a British prison, I promise you an interesting Internet experience. Here are a few hints to help you expand your search.

AOL's Genealogy Forum

The AOL Genealogy Forum is a great place to start your Internet search. It spotlights a constantly updated list of top-quality Web sites as features of the week. Check out current interesting sites on Topic Site of the Week (such as LDS FamilySearch), Regional Site of the Week (such as U.S. Surname Distribution), and Mailing Lists of the Week (such as MailingLists-Surnames). AOL also offers you a choice of more Internet Web sites at New Genealogy Sites, shown in Figure 10-2.

To find New Genealogy Sites in AOL's Genealogy Forum, follow these steps:

1. Go to the Keyword: **Roots**.

2. Click the button titled Internet.

3. Double-click the title New Genealogy Sites.

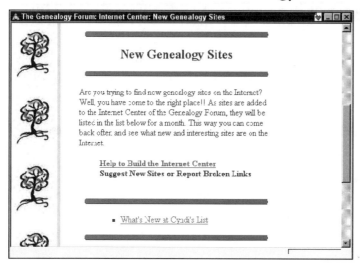

Figure 10-2. AOL updates New Genealogy Sites on a regular basis.

You will be presented with a list of great Web sites. This New Genealogy Sites list is updated on a regular basis, so be sure to visit often.

Additional Online Resources

Several other Web sites should be on your list for genealogical research.

FamilySearch

The Church of Jesus Christ of Latter-day Saints, also known as the Mormon Church, believes that by learning about our ancestors, we can better understand who we are. They also compile extensive genealogical records, because they believe non-Mormon ancestors can be converted through baptism for the dead.

Because the Mormons consider genealogy a religious mission, they maintain one of the largest collections of genealogy data in the world. It is, in fact, considered the mother lode of ancestral data. The Mormons have microfilm records of more than two billion people in their facilities in Salt Lake City. Much of this data, which was previously available only in Utah, is now available on the Internet. The FamilySearch site (`www.familysearch.com`), shown in Figure 10-3, contains more than 600 million names. These records range from marriage certificates to property deeds, ship manifests, and other important documents.

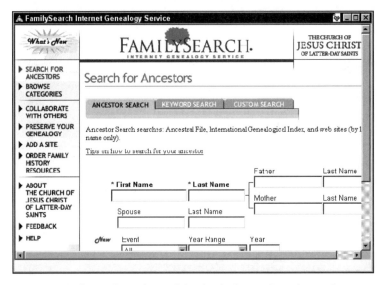

Figure 10-3. The FamilySearch site of The Church of Jesus Christ of Latter-day Saints contains more than 600 million names. (Reprinted by permission. Copyright© 1999 by Intellectual Reserve, Inc.)

Library of Congress

The Library of Congress (`www.loc.gov`) has one of the world's premier collections of U.S. and foreign genealogical and local historical publications (see Figure 10-4). The Library's genealogy collection began as early as 1815, when Thomas Jefferson's library was purchased.

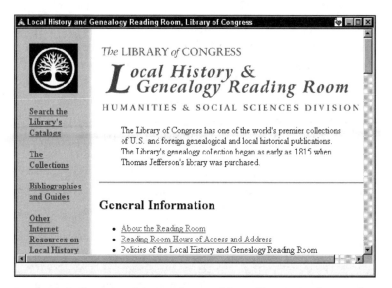

Figure 10-4. The Library of Congress has one of the world's premier collections of U.S. and foreign genealogical publications.

The Library is ready for your research task with its collection of books, CD-ROMs, and even a vertical file collection. Research training classes are offered to help new genealogists get started. The Local History and Genealogy Reading Room has a selected list of references compiled for the beginning genealogist that includes introductory books for U.S. genealogical research. As expected, research sources are also available for advanced, specialized, and foreign genealogical study. For the ambitious genealogists, the Library of Congress suggests looking through its extensive list of searchable genealogy databases.

If you would like your own family history to be a part of the Library of Congress, check out the instructions in "How to Donate Published Genealogies to the Library of Congress" on the Library of Congress Web site.

10

Genealogy

Cyndi's List

Cyndi's List (`www.cyndislist.com`) is a vast index to genealogical Web sites. It has over 40,000 links that are categorized and cross-referenced in over 100 categories. Cyndi Howell started working on the list just to show others how much information the Internet had to offer. She says that she still adds to the list daily to continue in her effort to catalogue the many online genealogical resources. This Web site is a great starting point that will lead you to many of the best Internet sites for researching your ancestors.

Ancestry.com and MyFamily.com

Ancestry.com (`www.ancestry.com`) is a Web site that was launched in 1996 when the Internet as we know it was in its infancy. Ancestry.com claims to be the first and most inclusive genealogical online service (see Figure 10-5). It provides credible and comprehensive genealogical databases for tracing family history for either the professional genealogist or those just wondering about their family name.

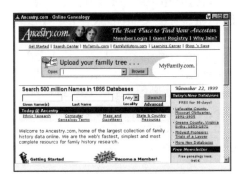

Figure 10-5. Ancestry.com claims to be the first and most inclusive genealogical online service.

As part of a family network, which includes MyFamily.com (`www.myfamily.com`), Ancestry.com enables consumers to go beyond genealogy and use their family history research to enrich their relationships. MyFamily.com, shown in Figure 10-6, offers families an excellent communication experience for keeping in touch and strengthening the family bond. This Web site bridges gaps in time and space through free, private Web sites where families can hold family discussions, create online family photo albums, and maintain a calendar of family events. Ancestry.com offers a wealth of free information. It also has various levels of yearly membership on a fee basis. Membership in Ancestry.com may be worthwhile if you are heavily into your search, because it offers access to over 240 million names and a subscription to the informative *Ancestry* magazine.

Figure 10-6. MyFamily.com offers free private Web sites where families can enjoy a rich communication experience for keeping in touch and strengthening the family bond.

Message Boards, Chats, and Forums

After you start your research, you are sure to be overwhelmed by the amount of information and seemingly endless resources available in the genealogical area of the Web. Why not call out for help from others who have struggled before you? AOL and

Definition

Message boards are valuable research tools where genealogists can post questions about their search and benefit from pertinent information shared by others.

Cross-Reference

See Chapter 2 for an in-depth discussion of message boards and how they work.

the Internet offer numerous opportunities to enlist direction and aid from others in your ancestral research. The fun part is that after someone has helped you, you can return the favor by sharing your findings with others. Help of this type is just waiting for you on the many Web sites offering message boards, chats, and forums.

Message Boards

Message boards allow you to post questions about your search and read others' postings that might contain pertinent information (see Figure 10-7). They are a way to glean precious gems of information that you might otherwise miss. I recently posted a question on a message board about Germans who lived in Russia, in an effort to find a missing segment of my husband's family tree. Although no one could directly answer my question, some wonderful people led me to several great Web sites about Germans in Russia that I did not even know existed. One simple posting led me to a gold mine of information. So, although message boards may seem overwhelming, don't underestimate their power.

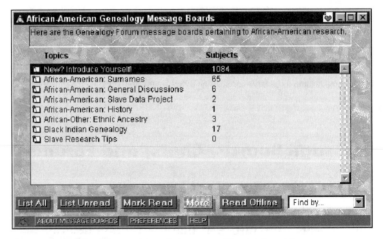

Figure 10-7. AOL offers a variety of topics on its Message Board Center.

Message boards often have the ability to handle different topics, or *threads,* as they are called. In the genealogical area, this means that a message board can be threaded to have what actually becomes thousands of family history message boards. There are boards that are devoted to surnames and other genealogy-related topics. The surname boards can often be very helpful, especially if you are just starting out in your quest (see Figure 10-8).

Tip

If your research gets bogged down, post a question on a message board or in a chat room.

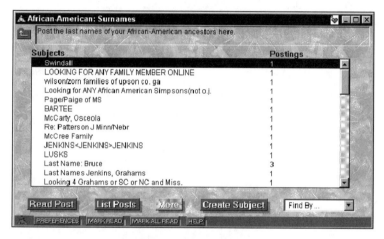

Figure 10-8. A sample message from a message board.

The AOL genealogy message boards are a part of the Genealogy Forum, which can be accessed by typing the Keyword: **Roots**. These boards are especially effective because you can post messages about your research in specific states or in other countries. The Genealogy Forum also has special surname boards, and boards that cover different ethnic or religious groups. The Message Board of the Week is also very interesting, because it offers specific topics such as French Huguenots, the Alamo, and African-American surnames.

10

Genealogy

The Genealogy's Most Wanted Web site (`www.citynet.net/mostwanted/`), shown in Figure 10-9, was designed to put researchers in touch with each other through e-mail or postal addresses. Researchers can post their surnames and the information they know on their subject in the hopes that another user can make a connection with them. In the site's first year, it received over 12,200 listings comprised of over 7,000 surnames, and 96 people were successful in locating a "most wanted" person.

Figure 10-9. The Genealogy's Most Wanted Web site located 96 "most wanted" people in the site's first year.

Chat Rooms

Chat rooms are another powerful tool for genealogical research. Chat rooms offer the chance to talk directly with others, not just through message board postings. Sometimes known as *conference rooms* or *meeting rooms,* chat rooms are a way for AOL members to meet each other one-on-one to discuss topics of common interest. You will often find both chat rooms and message boards available.

AOL's genealogy chats are lively and informative. Chat rooms, such as Ancestral Digs, Root Cellar, and the Family Treehouse, are often filled to capacity. To visit any of these three, type the Keyword: **Roots** and select CHATS from the menu. You will find links to all three chat rooms ready for your input.

Chats are often informative, hosted chats with a wide variety of experts in attendance. Each of these AOL-based chat rooms posts schedules of when chats will be held and the featured topic of each chat. After you enter a chat room, you can participate in the conversation with other genealogists.

Forums

A *forum* is an online area that is devoted to a common interest. It is a place where participants with common interests can exchange open messages. In the Internet world, forums are sometimes called *newsgroups*. Often, a forum is a conglomeration of message boards and can also include chat rooms.

Trained staff members who have expertise in different areas of genealogy host many of the chats sponsored by Genealogy Forum Special Interest Groups. Forum topics might cover such things as ethnic groups, countries or U.S. regions, computer-related topics, or topics of historical interest.

Anyone can post to these forums and immediately have their data shared with other researchers. GenForum (`www.genforum.com`) features chat rooms and welcome messages claiming to be the Internet's largest genealogy message board site with over 1.8 million messages. This site will check out your surname and then run a national or international search. If you are interested in forums, GenForum even divides them into topics for you: general topics, specific topics, and computers and software. Here, over 8,200 forums are

Tip

You can post the same question on several message boards.

Definition

Chat rooms, sometimes known as *conference rooms* or *meeting rooms*, are another powerful tool for research where genealogists meet each other to discuss topics of common interest.

Cross-Reference

See Chapter 2 for more information about chat rooms.

Definition

A *forum* is an online area that is devoted to a common interest.

10

Genealogy

devoted to specific surnames, states, countries, and general topics.

This is typical of sites where genealogists can gather and talk live about their research, experiences, and hints. It is also a place for beginners to ask questions and have fun. Many sites even offer a list of regulars on the genealogy page, with their nicknames, e-mail addresses, and homepages.

Message boards, chats, and forums are the places to enjoy the success stories of others as well as your own. Titles such as "10 Generations in One Day (287 years)" and "I Found My Bio-Dad" speak of happy endings.

Genealogy Classes Online

The Internet offers the opportunity to participate in online genealogy classes. Courses range from 4 to 12 weeks and are provided by top teachers and professionals across the country. Most classes feature online assignments, online lectures, daily message boards, and e-mail support. Many of the classes are free, although some require a registration fee.

American Online has the most extensive offering of classes. A particularly popular course, Genealogy and Family History Center, is for those who have a beginning knowledge of the Family History Center and want to learn more (see Figure 10-10). This class is targeted at advanced genealogists and beginners alike. Online interaction with instructors can help solve specific research problems and exposes students to a wide variety of resources.

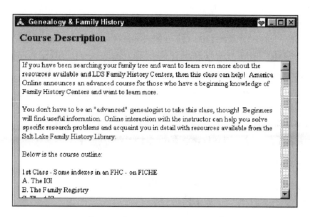

Figure 10-10. The Family History Center at Salt Lake City, Utah, has the largest genealogy library of its kind in the world.

Family History Center

The first Family History Library of the Church of Jesus Christ of Latter-day Saints was established in 1894 at Salt Lake City, Utah. Today, it has grown into the largest library of its kind in the world, with collections of millions of microfilm, thousands of microfiche and books, and innumerable other records. The microfilm program began in 1938. Because of the great importance of family history research to members of the Mormon Church, it has established many Family History Centers throughout the world. These extended Family History Centers provide access to a majority of the Family History Library's extensive genealogical holdings.

10

Genealogy

The scope and variety of genealogy courses vary. The following list is an example of the content of one minicourse, held in four 2-hour sessions every other week. The course outline of Genealogy and Family History Center, offered by American Online, covers:

▶ Indexes in the Family History Center of the Salt Lake Family History Library

▶ Indexes on computers

▶ How to submit or donate information you have gathered to the FHL

▶ The importance of documentation

▶ Using vital records

▶ A section on obscure indexes

▶ Questions and answers

Besides AOL, other online courses are available on the Web. Genealogy.com (`www.genealogy.com`) sponsors an Online University that offers genealogy classes and new lessons every few weeks. The available courses include Beginning Genealogy, Tracing Immigrant Origins, Beginning Internet Genealogy, and Advanced Internet Genealogy.

Ancestry.com's Learning Center (`www.ancestry.com`) contains useful information to make your family history work easier. Under its Help for Beginner's section, which can be accessed by selecting Learning in Library Link, and then choosing Learning Center, you will discover an online class called The History Lesson. This course gets you started on the right foot with a helpful introduction to family history research.

Free online classes are even offered where parents and children or grandchildren can learn genealogy together. What a great idea for quality family time! WorldGenWeb For Kids (`www.rootsweb.com/~wgwkids/`) has printable forms designed so

that your children can print them and start on
the family tree (see Figure 10-11). At this same site,
teenagers and young adults who are interested in
genealogical research can join a mailing list. Teenagers
included on the list will receive information about
general genealogical concerns, keeping records, and
finding information as well as clues.

Caution

When typing a URL or
Web address, you must
type the address exactly
as given.

Figure 10-11. Whether you are a parent or grandparent, genealogy is an excellent
way to make history come alive for children.

From this WorldGenWeb For Kids site, a hot link
takes you to Genealogy Instruction: Beginners,
Teenagers, and Kids, a Web site sponsoring an
online class, The Present Meets the Past, (`http:
//home.earthlink.net/~howardorjeff/
instruct.htm`). Here, teenagers and kids are
given research questions to ask their parents,
grandparents, aunts, and uncles to start the family
tree. Projects are designed to involve children
and grandchildren in the world of family history.
Games, quizzes, scavenger hunts, races, contests,
and riddles will stimulate your child's interest in
family. Whether you are a parent or grandparent,
 genealogy is an excellent way to make history
come alive for children. Kids gain new insight
into the development of this country, as well
as the part their ancestors played in its growth.

Expanding Your Genealogy Network

Definition

Networking is a series of people, computers, or organizations connected together to perform a specific function, such as sharing genealogy information. This interest in exchanging information results in a vast network of societies, projects, and genealogical communities.

Networking is an important part of genealogy. It can take place in the form of online classes, chat rooms, message boards, or real live attendance at conferences or society memberships. Most people who dabble in genealogy realize the difficulty of the search and are eager to share their findings and research with anyone who needs the help. This interest in exchanging information results in a vast network of societies, projects, and genealogical communities. When you start your research, you will invariably be drawn to some of these special groups. They can be beneficial in increasing your productivity as well as encouraging you to adhere to time-tested research methods. They can even help you learn the etiquette involved in researching your family history.

Finding online genealogy groups will be easy, and you can also use the Internet to find leads to groups that meet in your own neighborhood, for real live networking. FamilyTreeMaker.com (`www.familytreemaker.com`) posts a schedule of upcoming events that lists annual genealogical society conferences, genealogy and family history conferences, and gravestone studies conferences (see Figure 10-12). Joining one of these groups can help you enjoy the camaraderie that a hobby such as genealogy produces.

When you think of genealogy and your own family's history, you can't help but think of the events that shaped the lives of all our ancestors: war, religion, and, above all, technological change. Technology fueled the endless migrations of the last centuries, atomizing communities and even families. Now, technology is bringing them, living and dead, back together again.

Figure 10-12. FamilyTreeMaker.com keeps a current schedule of upcoming genealogical events posted on its Web site.

Searching for your ancestors is, without a doubt, a worthwhile endeavor. Be sure to have patience with your research. Sometimes, the search seems endless, and getting results can take a long time. That's why genealogy is often referred to as a hobby that lasts a lifetime.

Whether you start your quest because you want to create a legacy for your children and grandchildren or just want to disprove tales about your ancestors being notorious criminals, researching your family tree is worth the time you will invest. Your computer, AOL, and the Internet are tools that will shorten your journey and make the trip more rewarding.

Coming Up Next

In the next chapter, we look into the world of hobbies on the Internet and discover all that AOL and the Web has to offer.

In this chapter, we learned that AOL and the Internet provide many options for research and help when putting together a family tree or otherwise researching your family history. We saw that:

- ▶ Staying in touch with family members is very important to many people.
- ▶ The resources for online genealogical searches are almost endless.
- ▶ Networking along with your computer, America Online, and the Internet will make your genealogical efforts more rewarding.

Quick Look

▶ **MusicStaff.com** **page 308**

Sites devoted to learning musical instruments abound on the Internet. At
MusicStaff.com (www.musicstaff.com), you can search for a music teacher
by specifying the instrument, location, and level of instruction. This site also
provides links to hundreds of university music programs throughout the world
and has a selection of online music lessons, complete with animated graphics
and sound samples.

▶ **WebMuseum** **page 311**

The WebMuseum (http://sunsite.unc.edu/wm/) is one of the oldest and
largest online museums, which, as explained by its creator, Nicholas Pioch,
makes the artistic fruits of human civilization freely available 24 hours a
day throughout the year. Collections include more than 100 works of
Impressionist painter Paul Cézanne, an illuminated medieval manuscript,
and the Famous Paintings sections, which can be browsed by artist, country,
or period.

▶ **HobbyWorld** **page 323**

If you are on the lookout for a hobby, check out HobbyWorld (www.
hobbyworld.com). This Internet site bills itself as having "the most extensive
variety of online Hobbies & Web sites." The site features an excellent beginner's corner in which you can learn how to make either a corkboard from
used wine bottle corks or a Native American dreamcatcher. It also features
links to more than 80 other sites, including aerobics, aquariums, barbershop
harmony, bonsai, hang gliding, magic, origami, skydiving, and woodworking.

Chapter 11
Hobbies

Chess, arts and crafts, cooking, flying, bridge, music — these are a few of the activities that adults pursue in their spare time. You may already be active in a favorite hobby, or you may have a hidden love, a personal project that you have always longed to pursue. Whether you are retired and have finally found the time to follow your dream or you are just dabbling, the computer, America Online, and the Internet can offer you a convenient starting point.

A hobby can provide a creative outlet, a break from routine, intellectual stimulation, emotional satisfaction, and just plain fun. Besides, as recent research has shown, leisure and recreation are crucial to our physical, mental, and emotional well-being. Although no hobby can guarantee a longer or healthier life, those who keep mentally and physically active do seem to find more pleasure.

Even if you don't have a hobby as such, you probably have an area of interest that online resources can help you develop into a full-fledged hobby.

Find It Online

Type the Keyword: **Hobbies** and you'll have instant access to a broad range of hobby links.

Enjoying AOL's Treasure Chest of Hobbies

The resources of America Online and the Internet can open a wide world of hobbies, both for those who want to add a fresh dimension to a favorite pastime and for those hoping to spark new interests. And, as many cyber-enthusiasts have already discovered, computers and the Internet can even develop into fascinating and stimulating hobbies all by themselves.

Whatever your interest, the AOL Hobbies page has a site for you. Start with the Keyword: **Hobbies**, from which you will find links to everything from Antiques and Astronomy to Railroading and Rock Collecting (see Figure 11-1).

At AOL Hometown, you can even take up a new hobby of designing Web pages. Build your own Web page or enjoy looking at the Top Picks of Web pages created by other subscribers.

11

Hobbies

Find It Online

To get to AOL Hometown from the Hobbies screen, click the link in the upper-right corner labeled "personal hobby web pages."

Figure 11-1. AOL offers hobby sites for a wide variety of interests, ranging from antiques to woodworking.

How to Be a Tightwad

Saving a buck is always a great goal. Type the Keyword: **Tightwads** and join in the fun of economizing: plan a yard sale, draw up a weekly budget-meal plan, and even print coupons redeemable at your local grocery store (see Figure 11-2).

Figure 11-2. At the Tightwads screen, share saving strategies and join in the fun of economizing.

Developing Your Love of Music

Music, the elixir of the ages, is an enjoyable and soothing hobby for millions. Not only is music therapeutic and relaxing, but research has shown that the mental exercise and muscle movement of playing an instrument tones both your mind and your body.

The multimedia capabilities of your computer can turn it, too, into an effective *instrument* in your pursuit of music pleasures. You can use it to find concerts, locate a teacher, meet with others who share your love of music, or order CDs without going to the music store.

The computer can also play music and can even hook up with digital instruments to create a unique audio environment.

Definition

An *instrument* is a tool used to make music, but it can also be anything used to further a particular end. In that sense, your computer becomes a musical "instrument" when you use it to learn about music through AOL.

The AOL Music Page

Attack the mountain of music resources at AOL (Keyword: **Music**) and check out sound samples and reviews of featured artists in a range of musical categories: classical, jazz, country, rock, R&B, pop, and more. You will find links to countless sites devoted to every imaginable musical style. You will even find photos and concert schedules for your favorite artists. Click the drop-down Music Index menu, as shown in Figure 11-3, and choose from Today's Web Events, AOL Hear and Now, Concert Tours, or another category.

11

Hobbies

Figure 11-3. The Music Index drop-down menu links you to Today's Web Events, Concert Tours, AOL Hear and Now, plus other interesting choices.

You Are Never Too Old for Music

Have you always wanted to play an instrument, but have never taken the time to learn? Whether you want to find a teacher and take face-to-face lessons or use the computer to bring the music lessons to you, learning can be fun.

Sites devoted to learning musical instruments abound on the Internet. At MusicStaff.com (www.musicstaff.com), you can search for a music teacher by specifying the instrument, location, and level of instruction (see Figure 11-4). This site also provides links to hundreds of university music programs throughout the world and has a selection of online music lessons, complete with animated graphics and sound samples:

The Art Department's Piano on the Net site (www.artdsm.com/music.html) is another spot for brushing up on your musical skills, with a series of 35-minute lessons. Divided into Starter, Intermediate, and Advanced sections, many of the lessons are enhanced with QuickTime video and RealAudio sound clips.

Note

Research has shown that the mental exercise and muscle movement of playing a musical instrument tones both the mind and the body.

Figure 11-4. At MusicStaff.com, fine-tune your search for a music teacher by specifying the instrument, location, and instruction level.

When searching for an instructional site, you can search by instrument, such as piano, organ, or flute. However, don't forget to also search by type of music, such as classical, jazz, or reggae. This type of search often leads to a gem such as Jazclass (`www.ozemail.com.au/~jazclass/#02`), an instructional site by Michael Furstner from the Sunshine Coast (Australia). Jazclass will help you learn the basics of modern music principles, blues and jazz improvisation, and saxophone techniques.

Following Your Artistic Inclinations

The Internet has a vast assortment of resources for those interested in art as a hobby. This is one case where the Internet not only offers stay-at-home information, but also gives you everything that you need to plan the cultural evening of your dreams.

11

Hobbies

One of the not-to-be-missed Web sites for planning this type of adventure is Digital City at www.digitalcity.com/arts. The Digital City site gives you information on the best exhibits and performances in cities and towns all over the country. Just select a city, and you will be given all the information needed to create a cultural excursion. Digital City highlights dance perfomances, theater schedules, classical music concerts, and museum exhibits.

If you love art, the Internet is filled with exciting resources that can turn your computer into a virtual art museum. The National Gallery of Art in Washington, D.C. (www.nga.gov) offers an overview of its collection, descriptions of current exhibits, and a variety of virtual tours, which can be tailored to your interests and available time (see Figure 11-5). A series of In-Depth Study Tours lets you focus on a single artist's work, or even on one particular painting.

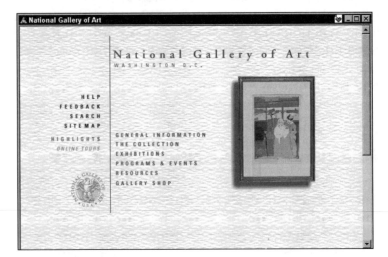

Figure 11-5. The National Gallery of Art in Washington, D.C., sponsors In-Depth Study Tours that can focus on a single artist's work or even on a particular painting.

A Web Museum

One of the oldest (debuting in 1994) and largest online museums is the WebMuseum (`http://sunsite.unc.edu/wm/`), which, as explained by its creator, Nicholas Pioch, makes the artistic fruits of human civilization freely available 24 hours a day throughout the year. Collections include more than 100 works of Impressionist painter Paul Cézanne, an illuminated medieval manuscript, and the Famous Paintings sections, which can be browsed by artist, country, or period. The WebMuseum network is constantly expanding to accommodate hundreds of thousands of visitors every week. It has over 10 million documents! Be sure not to miss the Famous Paintings and Medieval Art sections.

Lovers of other types of art will find no lack of online resources. Whether you like Spanish, Romanesque, or contemporary art, you'll find plenty of online museums and resources. Many traditional museums present portions of their collections via the Internet, but you'll also find many virtual galleries designed to exist only on the Internet.

I've always had a love for anything French, so I found the virtual visit to France very exciting. The Centre Georges Pompidou in Paris (`www.centrepompidou.fr/english/`) offers an excellent collection of modern and contemporary painting, sculpture, and other art, as well as exhibits on design and architecture. At its Web site, you can click the Museum link to explore past and current exhibitions, or follow the Works Online link to learn about the museum's current showings. And, while we're talking about French art, you won't want to miss the virtual tour of the Louvre (`http://mistral.culture.fr/louvre/`), as shown in Figure 11-6.

Figure 11-6. The Web site of the Louvre has a wonderful virtual tour of its famous museum.

Becoming an Internet Gourmet

Whether you are interested in cooking or eating food (or maybe even both), you will find the online food-related resources very appetizing. Ready to try your hand at a new recipe? AOL's online kitchen (Keyword: **Food**) is the place to start. In addition to a heaping portion of illustrated recipes, the opening screen, as shown in Figure 11-7, will guide you to sections on Healthy Eating, Vegetarian Living, Drinks, Desserts, Grilling, and more. Then, after you've experimented enough to satisfy your hunger for the chef's role, click the Local Dining link and go out and enjoy someone else's cooking (see Figure 11-8).

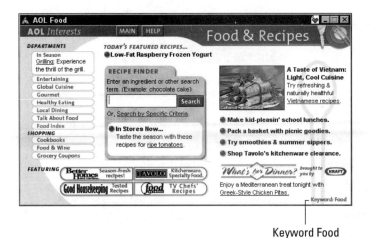

Keyword Food

Figure 11-7. The starting point for online food-related resources is AOL's kitchen, found under the Keyword: *Food*.

For an Internet site with just about everything a novice or experienced chef could want or need, try Cooking.com at `www.cooking.com`. This highly rated site features sections on Shopping, Recipes, and Cook's Tips. Its comprehensive approach is likely to make your mouth water — and your credit card may get some use as well. For instance, a recent feature on Tex-Mex cooking started with an overview of this tasty cuisine, illustrated with a photograph of the grill and other accessories necessary for success. Each item in the photo was then listed, with links to detailed descriptions and the opportunity to purchase each item online through Cooking.com's shopping cart utility. A sidebar on the screen added links to several Tex-Mex recipes, as well as Cook's Tips on buying a grill and roasting peppers.

11

Hobbies

Tired of being your own chef? Find your city in AOL's extensive list under Digital City Dining Guide, and be ready to surf through a list of tempting restaurants to find that one great place to eat out.

Figure 11-8. Let AOL's Digital City Dining Guide help you find the perfect restaurant if you are hungry for someone else's cooking.

For the Epicurious . . .

The Epicurious Food site (www.epicurious.com) is a database of culinary delights. It is also home to *Gourmet* and *Bon Appétit* magazines. This site has cookbook reviews, cooking tips, restaurant reviews, and interviews with famous chefs. You'll find that cooks love to share their tips and tricks as well as their recipes. The Epicurious forum is a great place to meet other chefs (see Figure 11-9).

Whether you want to create a gourmet meal or just a quick snack, see the massive recipe indexes at the SOAR Searchable Online Archive of Recipes (http://soar.berkeley.edu/recipes/). SOAR contains over 55,000 recipes. But don't worry; it's easy to find the one you want. You can search for any recipe by name or ingredient. You can also browse by topics, such as main dishes or baked goods, or by regions and ethnic groups, such as African, Jewish, or Greek. Another favorite place to shop for recipes is Culinary.com (www.culinary.com), with more than 73,000 recipes in its collection (see Figure 11-10). Once you start scouring the Internet, you are sure to find enough recipes to last a lifetime.

Find It Online

Try www.cooking.com for a whole series of features and links dealing with every aspect of cooking. Updated periodically.

Figure 11-9. The Epicurious Food site is home to *Gourmet* and *Bon Appétit* magazines.

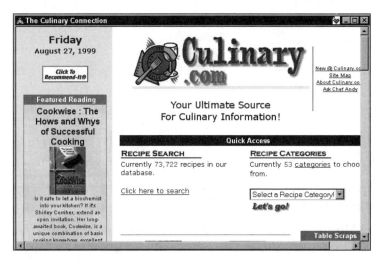

Figure 11-10. Culinary.com can keep you busy with more than 73,000 recipes from its collection.

Blooming as an Internet Gardener

If gardening is your hobby, you know how satisfying it can be to get your fingers off the keyboard and into the dirt. But first, check out the resources available to you through America Online and the Internet.

Just type the Keyword: **Garden** and you'll be off and running. America Online gives you a plant encyclopedia, a weather zone map, and numerous gardening tips, plus message boards, chats, and a member area. The latter features home pages of members who are avid gardeners, which gives you a great chance to find out what others are doing in this extremely fertile area (see Figure 11-11).

Figure 11-11. America Online supplies you with all the resources you need to become an expert gardener.

In *Modern Maturity* magazine, Mark Wexler says, "for computer-literate gardeners, *www* might stand for water, weeds, and a wealth of information." He is so right! Literally thousands of Internet sites devoted to gardening can help you learn to grow just about anything. Type the word **gardening**

into any search engine and you will find an overwhelming list of links. For a more targeted list of
Internet gardening resources, look at Microsoft's
SeniorsSearch topics (`www.seniorssearch.com/`
`sgardening.htm`). This great site will give you
links to garden products, garden centers, gardening
guides, organic gardening, vegetable gardening, and
more. Whether you are looking for hydroponic
garden supplies or information on growing garlic,
you'll find plenty to like at the SeniorsSearch site.

Another very interesting online resource is Bloom
(`http://homearts.com/bloom`), shown in
Figure 11-12, which is dedicated to cultivating the
gardener in all of us. Here, you can swap seeds, tour
gardens, and find links to the popular Rebecca's
Garden (`www.rebeccasgarden.com`) and the
Country Living Gardener (`http://homearts.`
`com/clg/toc/00cghpcl.htm`).

Tip

AOL and the Internet
are great resources for
weather forecasts, as
well as weather zone
information that is always
helpful when performing
gardening tasks.

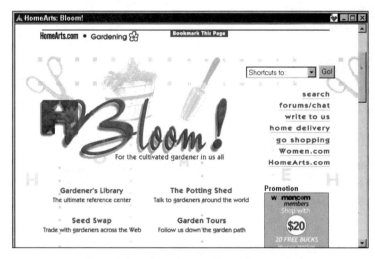

Figure 11-12. Bloom, dedicated to cultivating the gardener in all of us, is an
excellent site to swap seeds and tour gardens.

11

Hobbies

Don't hang up your hoe yet. Another great site, called GardenWeb (`www.gardenweb.com`), describes itself as "The Internet's Garden Community." Boasting an impressive catalog of discussions on every aspect of gardening (it includes eight subcategories of forums on roses alone), GardenWeb also gives you a dictionary of plants and a gardening glossary. Other main links within the site take you to a directory of gardening organizations, a calendar of events, national and regional weather forecasts, a shopping bazaar for purchasing all of your gardening needs, and a Mystery Plant Contest (see Figure 11-13).

Figure 11-13. Need to dig up some plant names? GardenWeb provides a dictionary of plants as well as a gardening glossary.

Finding the Right Craft

If you're ready for a real hands-on hobby, explore America Online's craft resources (Keyword: **Crafts**). The main screen will take you to Message Board Discussions on anything from crochet to stained glass and from pottery to woodworking (see Figure 11-14).

If you're feeling adventurous and ready to take up
a new craft, follow the Learn How to Quilt link to
AOL's step-by-step instructions and advice.

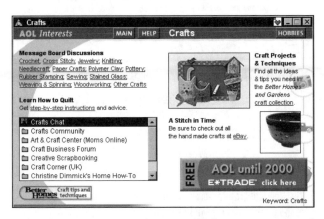

Figure 11-14. AOL's main Crafts screen will link you to Message Board Discussions
on anything from crochet to stained glass and from pottery to woodworking.

The Crafts Collection at the Better Homes and
Gardens Web site (`www.bhg.com/crafts`) hosts
a virtual community of crafters through six discussion groups: quilting, cross stitch and needlework,
general crafts, decorative painting and woodcrafts,
upcoming craft events, and downloadable projects.
You can also browse a glossary of crafting terms, get
tips on craft techniques, and subscribe to any of the
BHG publications devoted to arts and crafts.

The National Crafts Association is the "Information and Resource Center for the Professional
Arts & Crafts Industry," and its Web site (`www.
craftassoc.com`) offers you resources on
wholesale supplies, marketing information, tips
and tricks, an arts and crafts message board, and
listings of craft and trade shows. Its Internet Tools
section provides business-minded crafters advice
on how to take advantage of online resources for
displaying and marketing their creations (see
Figure 11-15; the "Internet Tools" section appears
in a lower portion not shown in this screen capture).

11

Hobbies

Figure 11-15. The National Crafts Association has served as the information and resource center for the professional arts and crafts industry since 1995.

Gaming Is Not Just for Kids

How did families pass the time before the computer moved into the living room? They played board games, for one thing. Even here, though, the technology revolution has had an impact. America Online provides plenty of opportunities for playing games on the computer, which can be exciting entertainment. The AOL Games area, shown in Figure 11-16 (Keyword: **Games**), offers nonstop fun for all ages. The opening screen shows you exciting information from the game world, including all the latest insider news. From the main Games screen, click Game Shows Online (Keyword: **Game Shows Online**), where you will find all types of free games to play. A broad range of games is available, including some unusual but interesting variations. For instance, Strike a Match asks you to find a common thread in two or three words displayed on a game board to move to the next level. Out of Order is an unscrambling game featuring progressive levels of difficulty — a word, a phrase, an entire quotation, and the originator of the quotation. Puzzles, casino games, and word games of all types are available. An area called Games Paradise includes trivia games that you can play online with others. The one characteristic that these games all seem to have in common is that they are quite addictive. Once you start playing them, you just can't stop.

Figure 11-16. America Online provides nonstop fun with plenty of gaming opportunities for computer users of all ages.

Game Parlor (Keyword: **Game Parlor**) is another area that tempts you with card games, board games, and more. You can play online games for $.99 an hour, including Backgammon, Bridge, Casino Blackjack, CatchWord, Classic Cards, Cribbage, Gin, Hearts, Online Casino, Poker, Spades, Splatterball, and Tetris, to name just a few.

USCF Chess (see Figure 11-17), which is one of the top-rated computer chess games and is endorsed by the U.S. Chess Foundation, is also available in the Game Parlor. You can get it on CD-ROM for $49.95, but you can also play it online at AOL for $.99 an hour (Keyword: **USCF**).

11

Hobbies

Figure 11-17. USCF Chess is one of the top-rated computer chess games and is endorsed by the United States Chess Foundation.

When you enter the Lobby for the chess game, you can chat, observe a game, get assistance from an AOL Game Operator, or play a game. It's like being part of an entire chess community. When you are ready, you can play chess against the computer or offer (or accept) a challenge from another player who's logged on at the time. Be careful, though, because some of these online opponents are accomplished players.

Other games of this type include Jack Nicklaus Online Golf, and Virtual Pool. Although you pay a fee to play these games, you may save money in the long run, because you get to try them out before you plunge in and buy them. In some cases, before playing a game, you might need to download some game files to your computer. Don't worry, though, because a Help screen explains how to do this.

When you search for games online, you'll find a lot of old board games with revamped images. For example, it's not your parents' Monopoly game anymore. Monopoly has become a colorful, animated experience. Learn more at www.monopoly.com. Scrabble (www.scrabble.com) and many other board games have online editions. Some require you to buy the game, but several offer demos to play before you pay. It's a great way to mesh the old with the new and to show the grandchildren how much fun games from the past can be.

On the other hand, if "cards" means bridge to you, a game is always waiting for you on the Web. Sharpen your bridge skills at the Play Bridge Hand Generator (`www.playbridge.com`).

Developing Unique Online Hobbies

Even if you think you don't have an "officially approved" hobby, you certainly have some areas of interest that could evolve into a more focused pastime. You'd be surprised at the number and variety of hobbies found on the Internet. Many dedicated hobbyists have made their experience and expertise available at thousands of Web sites.

If you are looking for a new hobby, surf to Hobby-World (`www.hobbyworld.com`), which bills itself as having "the most extensive variety of online Hobbies & Web sites." The opening screen links you to sites on topics such as hunting fossils in West Virginia and making homemade apple cider. It also features an excellent beginner's corner in which you can learn how to make either a corkboard from used wine bottle corks or a Native American dreamcatcher. However, this site's most impressive feature may well be its extensive collection of links to other hobby sites on the Web. It features links to more than 80 other sites, including aerobics, aquariums, barbershop harmony, bonsai, hang gliding, magic, origami, skydiving, and woodworking.

11

Hobbies

Appreciating the Computer as a Hobby

Once you plunge into the online world, you will find that the computer itself can be a great hobby. The average desktop computer today is many times more powerful than the computers that were used to send the first man to the moon. Learning to take full advantage of such a powerful machine can be an interesting and exciting endeavor.

However, as you may have already found out, much of the computer information available today is written in complex technical terminology that is difficult for the average computer user to digest. America Online comes to your aid with the Computing Channel (Keyword: **Computing**), which is dedicated to helping you make the most of your computing experience. It provides a guide for new computer users and a special area in which you can get answers to your computer questions. The online classroom and online computing communities will also be helpful to all levels of computer users.

Much computer information can be found at the ThirdAge tech area (`www.thirdage.com/tech/`) of AOL, which features the ThirdAge School of Online Learning. Free online courses are offered on topics such as homepage basics, Web skills, and even how to meet people online. These types of classes enable you to expand your computer knowledge without leaving the comfort of home.

You can also find great help for computer users at the AARP Computers & Technology Webplace (`www.aarp.org/comptech`). This is the place to go for in-depth tutorials on everything computer-related. Learn how to install software, deal with computer viruses, or buy a scanner. It also includes current computer news with a perspective on how it will affect you, product reviews, and feature stories on everything from keeping in touch through hometown news to using your computer to search for ET or old Army buddies (see Figure 11-18).

Cross-Reference

Search engines can provide useful links to all sorts of unusual hobbies. See Chapter 5 for more information on how to conduct a search.

Tip

If you are thinking of taking on a new hobby, the computer itself can be an educational and very useful hobby. Learning to take advantage of this powerful tool can be an interesting and exciting endeavor.

Figure 11-18. The AARP Computers & Technology Webplace offers help for computer users with its in-depth tutorials on everything computer-related.

Want to find a class to help you learn about computers? Or maybe you would like to volunteer to help teach such a class? Be sure to check out SeniorNet (`www.seniornet.org`), a nonprofit organization that teaches the over-50 group to use computers and the Internet at over 160 Learning Centers nationwide. The SeniorNet Web site is titled, "Bring-ing Wisdom to the Information Age." Don't you just love it?

11

Hobbies

Looking for easy-to-understand computer information? Don't miss my own Compu-KISS Web site (`www.compukiss.com`). Using the Keeping It Short and Simple approach, my computer tips and tricks, columns, and RealAudio clips are filled with good basic information that will make your computer experience more enjoyable and more fulfilling (see Figure 11-19). Recognizing the growing popularity of the personal computer with the *BCs* (those schooled *Before Computers*), a special section of my Web site focuses on people from this generation who are adventurous enough to learn computerese on their own! Check out Compu-KISS to see how easily computer benefits can be applied to your daily life.

Figure 11-19. Get a KISS (Keeping It Short and Simple) from Sandy Berger, and you will agree that using the computer is quick and easy — and fun!

Many people think that the computer is a machine that does all the thinking for you. However, anyone with hands-on computer experience quickly realizes that the person interacting with the computer must actually do most of the thinking on his or her own. The computer user must plan strategy, figure out how to do things, and then implement the plan. Using a computer can help keep an older person's brain active, just as walking or golf will keep his or her body active.

Coming Up Next

Now that we've explored how to further your hobbies with AOL and the Internet, we next look at how to search for information and conduct research online — with speed and ease. In this chapter we discovered the following:

- ▶ The resources of AOL and the Internet can add a fresh dimension to a favorite hobby, or spark interest in a completely new one.
- ▶ The Internet is filled with exciting resources that can actually turn your computer into a virtual art museum.
- ▶ Whether your interest is in cooking or eating food (or maybe both), you will find the online food-related resources very appetizing.
- ▶ For gardeners, *www* brings to mind water, weeds, and a wealth of information. If you are eager for a real hands-on experience with your hobby, explore AOL's craft resources for step-by-step instructions and advice.

11

Hobbies

CHAPTER

12

RESEARCH AND LEARNING

Quick Look

▶ *Keyword:* **Research & Learn**　　　　　　　　　　**page 331**

America Online has collected and organized a vast array of resources for those who want to stretch their minds through exploring familiar or new topics of interest. The place to start is the Research & Learn Channel (Keyword: **Research & Learn**). With its Research & Learn Channel, AOL finesses us into being smarter, one step at a time, one day at a time. This channel opens by offering you a fact-a-day, such as a new word to expand your vocabulary, or an overview of what happened on this date in history.

▶ **Merriam-Webster Dictionary**　　　　　　　　　**page 332**

Keyword: **Merriam-Webster** or Keyword: **Dictionary** is a quick way to access AOL's online version of the Merriam-Webster Collegiate Dictionary. Just enter a word to define, and read a typical dictionary entry for that word. Or, choose the Full Text option to see a list of all the dictionary's entries containing the word you're investigating. Wow! I checked out the word "investigate" and found that it was mentioned 120 times in the Full Text listing of the entry.

▶ **AOL's Electronic Library**　　　　　　　　　　**page 342**

You won't want to miss the Electronic Library @ AOL (Keyword: **ELP**), a gateway to millions of online documents: magazines, books, newspapers and newswires, television and radio transcripts, as well as drawings, photographs, and maps. Conducting a search on a term will lead you to a page of annotated links connected to a variety of resources in the Electronic Library database.

▶ **Ask-A-Teacher**　　　　　　　　　　　　　　**page 344**

America Online puts you a little closer to some human sources of knowledge in its Ask-A-Teacher section (Keyword: **Ask-A-Teacher**). Separate areas exist for elementary, middle, and high school, as well as college and beyond. Here, you gain access to AOL's huge Knowledge Database of brief essays prepared by experts in a range of fields in response to questions submitted by AOL subscribers. You can browse the questions and answers already posted (and arranged by subject), or you can pose a new question of your own.

Chapter 12

Research and Learning

IN THIS CHAPTER

Get started with research on AOL

Learn how to search for information on the Internet

Visit virtual libraries and museums

Learn how to go back to school while staying at home

Find sources of practical help

Just because you don't get up every morning and head off to school anymore, that's no reason to stop learning. According to Aristotle, "All men by nature desire knowledge." F. Scott Fitzgerald summed up this continuing process when he described his novel *This Side of Paradise*: "To write it, it took three months; to conceive it — three minutes; to collect the data in it — all my life."

You may already appreciate the truth of these quotations. We are all born with the need for knowledge seated deeply in the core of our being. Satisfying that need takes us on a lifelong quest. Many components of learning have remained constant throughout the centuries. But, as with all other areas of our lives, the computer and the Internet are changing the way we learn — both in and out of school.

Whether you want to check the definition of a word, read a brief introduction to a topic, pursue an interest in greater depth, or take a full course in an academic subject, the tools to do so are as close as your keyboard.

Getting Started with Research on AOL

Most homes are equipped with at least one dictionary and perhaps even a set of encyclopedias. Such standard reference books may continue to have a place in research, but they have their limitations. How often does an encyclopedia article on a scientific topic need to be updated? How many new terms from technology and foreign languages should be added to the dictionary? (For that matter, where *is* the dictionary?)

With electronic technology, reference works can be updated on a regular basis, and online texts are available night and day. America Online has collected and organized a vast array of resources for those who want to stretch their minds through exploring familiar or new topics of interest. The place to start is the Research & Learn Channel (Keyword: **Research & Learn**), which is shown in Figure 12-1.

With its Research & Learn Channel, AOL finesses us into being smarter, one step at a time, one day at a time. This Research & Learn Channel opens by offering you a fact-a-day, such as a new word for expanding your vocabulary, or an overview of what happened on this date in history. I have always

Find It Online

Go to Keyword:
Encyclopedias to ac-
cess several popular en-
cyclopedias: Compton's
Encyclopedia and
Columbia Concise
Encyclopedia, among
others.

enjoyed these little tidbits of information. They are a great way to expand one's knowledge and can also come in handy if you like to play Scrabble or Trivial Pursuit, two of my favorite board games.

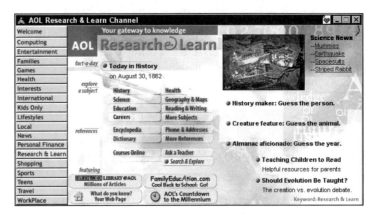

Figure 12-1. America Online has collected and organized a vast array of resources that are available to you night and day at its Research & Learn Channel.

Encyclopedia and Dictionary

If you want to get down to more serious research, the Research & Learn Channel also has choices for exploring a particular subject (history, science, careers, and so on) or consulting a general reference work, such as an encyclopedia or dictionary.

Go to Keyword: **Encyclopedias** to access Compton's Encyclopedia, the Columbia Concise Encyclopedia, and others. AOL's dictionary (Keyword: **Merriam-Webster** or Keyword: **Dictionary**) is an online version of the Merriam-Webster Collegiate Dictionary. (The Merriam-Webster dictionary is also available directly on the Web at www.m-w.com/netdict.htm.) Just enter a word to define, and read a typical dictionary entry for that word. Or, to take full advantage of electronic technology, choose the Full Text option to see a list of all the dictionary's entries containing the word you're investigating. Wow! I checked out the word "investigate" and found that it was mentioned 120 times in the Full Text listing of the entry.

Phone & Addresses

In addition to these standard reference works, you can also open the doors to other kinds of information with AOL's Phone & Addresses area (Keyword: **PhoneBook**). Or, try the More References section (Keyword: **More References**), where you can check out calendars and holidays, foreign language dictionaries, a medical dictionary, quotations, statistics, and more. Need to brush up on procedures for running a meeting? Get help from the leading resource on parliamentary procedure, Robert's Rules of Order. Your guide for the correct way to preside over a meeting can be found by going to the Keyword: **More References** and selecting Robert's Rules of Order from the scrollable box.

Geography & Maps

I have always loved geography. Just the thought of all the different places that exist in the world is appealing to me. If, like me, you haven't been able to travel to all the exotic destinations that you've heard about, you can use the Geography & Maps area (Keyword: **Geography**) of AOL to explore the world from your armchair.

Or, maybe you just need to find directions to a friend's home. You can get step-by-step directions from one location to another, complete with a map, simply by typing the two addresses on the form at Keyword: **Mapping**. You are also given options to create a map of the immediate vicinity of a given address, as well as city, regional, state, and international maps. You can also use this section for information about weather and time zones, and can click a link to take you to map games. You no longer have an excuse for waking up your uncle in Australia in the middle of the night because you didn't account for the time variation before dialing his phone number.

Click Geography — US & World in the Geography Maps section, as shown in Figure 12-2, to find a wealth of information, including a list of all the states and their capitals. You'd better refresh your knowledge before you try to help the children or grandchildren learn the state capitals.

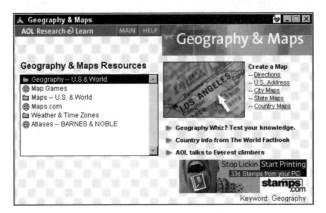

Figure 12-2. In addition to a wealth of other information, the Geography & Maps section offers a list of all the states and their capitals.

More Subjects

Among the topics covered in More Subjects (Keyword: **More Subjects**) are The Arts, Business Research, Consumer & Money Matters, Law & Government, and Sports & Leisure. There is something for everyone in this section.

Searching for Information on the Internet

The resources for research and learning available on the Internet are truly mind-boggling — and getting more so every day. The Internet includes perhaps two billion Web pages. You can think of the Internet as one huge digital reference source, exceptionally vast and varied, and ever-expanding.

Part of the attraction of the Web, and a key to its richness as a repository of information, is the fact that no one individual or institution controls its content. At the same time, this openness often manifests itself as chaos. The Internet can be frustrating when you're trying to find a particular piece of information and all you can stumble upon are irrelevant sites and dead-ends.

Note

As many as two billion Web pages are on the Internet, and more are appearing every day.

Using Online Resources Requires Discernment

Anyone can create a Web page. That's one of the things that make the Internet so extensive and exciting. However, this situation creates a dilemma for millions of wired knowledge seekers. How do we know that the information we find on the Internet is factual? How do we know that it is not slanted to advance some hidden agenda? How do we differentiate between fantasy and reality?

We do this by developing our sense of discernment. We must always determine the source of information and decide whether that source is reputable. We must develop our critical faculty of judicious reasoning so that we will always question and judge the veracity of the information we are presented with.

If we are dealing with important information, we need to double-check our data. We shouldn't accept as true everything that we read on the Internet. The Internet is filled with accurate information, but it also includes a lot of garbage. Only our own keen insight, good judgment, and common sense will be able to discern the difference.

Tip

The Internet was designed to survive nuclear war. Earlier communications systems were vulnerable to attack, because a break at one point in the communications chain disconnected the two ends and many related areas of the entire chain. The Internet was designed so that every point was connected to every other point, like a spider web — a web of information. For this reason, the Internet has survived attempts at regulation, control, and, as we see, even organization.

Fortunately, the flexible structure of the Web makes it possible for resourceful souls to index Internet resources, update their findings on a regular basis, and share these reference tools with the rest of us.

If you end up doing much research on the Internet, you're likely to find yourself drawn to one or another of the many sites — catalogs, portals, or search engines — attempting to impose order on chaos. AOL is one of the best at organizing and making things easy to find and to use. In this section, I'll give you an overview of a few of some other popular and extensive sites.

Ask Jeeves

Ask Jeeves (www.ask.com) is one of the newer search engines that combine various search tools to answer questions that can be typed in everyday English. At Ask Jeeves, you can type any question, such as "What is the population of Japan?" and Jeeves will come up with a quick link to the correct answer. If you have children or grandchildren who ask a lot of questions, Ask Jeeves also has a special area just for children.

Excite

The Education directory at Excite (www.excite.com/education) is subdivided into such classifications as Alumni, Career Planning, Continuing Education, Libraries, Reference, Teacher Resources, and Universities & Colleges.

HotBot

The Reference section at HotBot (http://directory.hotbot.com/Reference) features search forms linked to Encyclopedia.com and the Merriam-Webster Online Dictionary, as well as its own categories of resources for learning. Just a few of the possibilities are archives, geography, management, science, and style guides.

Netcenter

The home page of Netscape (`http://home.netscape.com`), creator of one of the most popular Web browsers, is also a directory for a whole range of Internet resources. Its Research & Learn section (`http://webcenters.netscape.com/webcenters/research/home.adp`), shown in Figure 12-3, links you to easy forms for an encyclopedia, a dictionary, and a reference collection. It also has departments for such topics as science, history, and education, plus a collection of Essentials: maps, quotations, phone directories, online newspapers, and more.

Definition

A *portal* is an organized gateway or starting point to information on the Internet. Most portal sites enable you to customize your own home page or start page, including the news, topics, and categories that you want to begin with every time you enter that site. A home page or start page is a site's main page, the one you see when you first access the site.

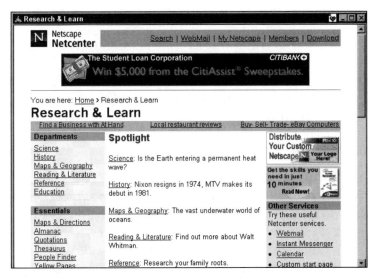

Figure 12-3. The Research & Learn section of Netscape's Netcenter links you to an encyclopedia, a dictionary, and a reference collection, in addition to departments on specific topics.

12

Research and Learning

Definition

An *annotated link,* more than simply a title that is hyperlinked to a Web page, includes a brief description of the Web site in question.

Tip

Although using search engines is a great way to find information, you may also want to try some Web sites that are designed to help you find specific resources, such as My Virtual Reference Desk (`www.refdesk.com/facts.html`).

Yahoo!

Yahoo! was one of the earliest search engines on the Web. (Its name is an acronym for Yet Another Hierarchically Organized Oracle.) The Reference area at Yahoo! (`http://dir.yahoo.com/Reference/`) is subdivided into some 40 categories, each of which leads to another page (or several pages) of annotated links to applicable Web sites. Some useful topics here include Almanacs, Environment and Nature, Flags, Quotations, and Web Directories.

Yahoo! also has an education section (`http://dir.yahoo.com/Education/`), which leads to academic links, conferences, higher-education resources, a K-12 page, instructional technology links, and a teaching section.

Reference Sites

In addition to the reference and education sections of these general search sites, many Web sites have been designed specifically with the online learner in mind, where you may find a more selective arrangement of resources.

My Virtual Reference Desk

At My Virtual Reference Desk (`www.refdesk.com/facts.html`), you will find an organized way to link to many different types of information sources. If you can't find your dictionary, thesaurus, or almanac, don't fret. You'll find it here. You can also find links to newspapers, quotations, encyclopedias, world facts, statistics, stock quotes, yellow pages, Internet resources, comics, maps, and much more. This site even has a money converter for travelers, and an atomic clock, which enables you to set your computer clock precisely to the correct time.

Dictionary.com

As its name suggests, Dictionary.com (`www
.dictionary.com`) specializes in resources
about words in the English language. Each page of
the site contains an easy-to-use form to look up the
meaning, pronunciation, etymology, and usage of a
word — but that's not all. Although the study of language is not normally thought of as a mind-expand-
ing endeavor, it has certainly proven to be just that.
If you love language and words, you can use this
area to find online discussions about words, learn
the word of the day, play word games, and consult
Dictionary.com's own Web Directory for other reference sites on the Internet. Links are also included to
foreign language dictionaries, *Roget's Thesaurus,*
and *Bartlett's Familiar Quotations.*

StudyWeb

StudyWeb (`www.studyweb.com`) is an interesting
site that styles itself "The Learning Portal." It has
more than 30 major categories, plus hundreds of
topical subcategories to support this description.
The collection of over 100,000 "research-quality"
URLs, each accompanied by a brief description, is
exhaustively thorough. If you want to explore anything from agriculture and architecture to meta-
physics and transportation, this could be the
place to start.

One of the most appealing features of StudyWeb
is its flexibility of organization. The opening screen,
shown in Figure 12-4, offers an overview of major
categories, but you can also browse the entire
alphabetical table of contents. At any point in your
research at this site, you can open up the Study
Buddy, a small window with icons for such reference
aids as an encyclopedia and dictionary, as well as the
CIA World Fact Book, currency and measurement
converters, calendars, and maps.

Figure 12-4. StudyWeb is an interesting site that styles itself "The Learning Portal" and has a collection of over 100,000 research-quality URLs.

WWW Virtual Library

The WWW Virtual Library (www.vlib.org) has a certain claim to fame, describing itself as "The oldest catalog of the Web." Started by Tim Berners-Lee, one of the original Web pioneers, this site is orderly and well-structured. Its opening screen and various category pages may not overwhelm you with flashy graphics or hundreds of links, but the quality of the chosen sites is consistently high. Each category is maintained by a volunteer who is an expert in that field.

LibrarySpot

LibrarySpot (www.libraryspot.com) is a site that professional librarians may want to consult, but it's also valuable for the ordinary learner (see Figure 12-5). A sidebar on the opening screen features links to specialized libraries (law, music, and so on), as well as a list of popular categories: acronyms, business information, phone books, statistics, and more. LibrarySpot also has links to Special Stacks for parents, students, teachers, and business. LibrarySpot is a division of StartSpot (`www.startspot.com`), which also sponsors BookSpot, EmploymentSpot, GourmetSpot, GovSpot, ShoppingSpot, and TripSpot.

Special Stacks

Figure 12-5. Special Stacks for parents, students, teachers, and businesses is a feature of Library Spot, a site for both professional librarians and the ordinary learner.

Visiting Virtual Libraries and Museums

No exact substitute exists for the experience of actually walking through a museum exhibit or browsing the stacks of a library. But, when you're willing to use the onscreen equivalents of these locations, a whole new world of learning opens to you.

America Online's Search & Explore feature for the Research & Learn Channel (Keyword: **Research**) is a good way to get started researching a topic, or even

12

Research and Learning

discovering a new subject to learn about. This A-Z guide collects resources in a wide variety of interest areas. The Arts link (Keyword: **RL Arts**) categorizes resources about music and theater as well as fashion and film. In the Business section (Keyword: **RL Business**), you can search copyrights and patents, consult a glossary of financial terms, or browse the trade show database. The Reading & Writing link (Keyword: **Reading**) enables you to learn about writing as a hobby, read book reviews and literary criticism, or check grammar and style guides.

Electronic Library @ AOL

You won't want to miss the Electronic Library @ AOL (Keyword: **ELP**), a gateway to millions of online documents: magazines, books, newspapers and newswires, television and radio transcripts, as well as drawings, photographs, and maps. Conducting a search on a term will lead you to a page of annotated links connected to a variety of resources in the Electronic Library database. To gain full access to these documents (and the entire collection of Electronic Library resources), you may sign up for a free 30-day trial period. If you decide to continue to use the Electronic Library as an online resource, the charge is $9.95 per month or $59.95 for a full year, as of this writing. (The Electronic Library is also available directly on the Web at `www.elibrary.com`.)

Library of Congress

The Library of Congress, generally understood to be the nation's most extensive collection of books, maps, photographs, documents, and other resources, also boasts one of the Web's richest sources of online information. At its opening page (`www.loc.gov`), shown in Figure 12-6, you can jump to a section

explaining how to take advantage of numerous collections, browse one of the library's exhibitions,
or enjoy the American Memory project. A link
also is provided to the THOMAS site (`http://`
`thomas.loc.gov`), the definitive starting point
for U.S. legislative information on the Internet.
This is also the address to use to e-mail your
senator or representative.

Figure 12-6. The Library of Congress boasts one of the Web's richest sources of
online information.

Smithsonian Institution

Another national treasure with an extensive online
presence is the Smithsonian Institution Web site
(`www.si.edu`). Its Museums and Organizations
page (`www.si.edu/organiza/start.htm`) features links to 18 separate museums and 13 research
centers. Whether you're interested in space exploration at the National Air and Space Museum, Orien-
tal art at the Freer Gallery, or dinosaurs at the
Natural History Museum, the Smithsonian can be
the beginning of a great learning adventure.

Going Back to School While Staying at Home

Do you remember that alarm clock going off at 5:30 a.m. and getting up early to get to school? I am from the Windy City of Chicago, and I can remember many days of standing on a snowy street corner in subzero temperatures at 6:30 a.m. waiting for the bus to take me to school. Well, with AOL and the Internet, you can go to school without ever leaving the comfort of your home. Whether you want to continue your formal education or just want to explore some subject that you love, the computer will be a valuable aide.

Ask-A-Teacher

America Online puts you a little closer to some human sources of knowledge in its Ask-A-Teacher section (Keyword: **Ask-A-Teacher**). Separate areas exist for elementary, middle, and high school, as well as college and beyond (see Figure 12-7). Here, you gain access to AOL's huge Knowledge Database of brief essays prepared by experts in a range of fields in response to questions submitted by AOL subscribers. You can browse the questions and answers already posted (and arranged by subject), or you can pose a new question of your own. (Before submitting a question, you'll be asked to review the postings already available on the message board for that particular topic.)

Courses Online

Distance learning. Have you seen it advertised by your local college or community college? Just what is it? With AOL's Courses Online (Keyword: **Courses**), you can take advantage of one of the

latest developments in contemporary education:
distance learning. Forget about driving across
country and moving into a dorm room; use your
computer and a connection to America Online
to take courses on virtually any subject, many
for college credit.

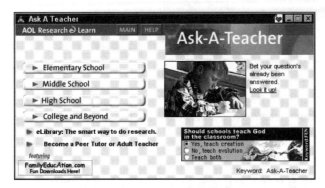

Figure 12-7. AOL offers Ask-A-Teacher, which is divided into separate areas for elementary, middle, and high school, as well as college and beyond. Students can browse questions and answers already posted by teachers, or pose a new question of their own.

Online Campus

AOL's own Online Campus (Keyword: **Online
Campus**), shown in Figure 12-8, provides enrichment courses on a range of topics, including academic, professional, and special interests. Courses run
from 4 to 12 weeks and are presented by top teachers and professionals. Classes offer online lectures,
daily message board and e-mail support, and supplementary materials available only to AOL students.

The Online Campus Course Catalog presents learning opportunities in 13 categories, including arts,
education, mathematics, and even spiritual growth
and the supernatural. If you're interested in learning
more about the history of classical Greece, an AOL
course on that topic "meets" for two hours each
Monday for eight weeks, for a registration fee of
$40. A section of free courses also is offered.

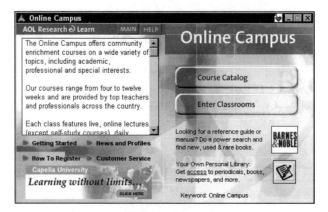

Figure 12-8. AOL's own Online Campus provides enrichment courses on a range of topics, including academic, professional, and special interest.

Finding Sources of Practical Help

We have talked about a lot of book sense. How about practical or common sense? My mother taught me to cook a turkey, and my dad taught me to tie a knot. But, if I hadn't picked up these everyday skills in my childhood, I could get instructions at a great Web site called Learn2.com (`www.learn2.com`). Need to fix a leaky faucet? Want to keep wasps out of the hummingbird feeder? Wish you could keep a cat from walking on your car? This is the Web site to visit.

At Learn2.com, shown in Figure 12-9, you can learn to do just about anything. Featuring hundreds of free online "2torials" in addition to low-cost online courses, this site is a rich source of practical information. In the Automotive Channel, for example, you can take a 2torial on jump-starting your car or changing a tire, read "learnlets" (brief bits of handy advice) on removing bird droppings or dealing with a chipped windshield, and join an online discussion about automotive topics. Other channels at

Learn2.com include Arts & Crafts, Family & Pets, Style & Grace, and Writing & Speech.

Figure 12-9. At Learn2.com, you will find hundreds of free online "2torials" that are rich in practical information.

Learning About Computers and Technology

While you're in the process of educating yourself via computer about one or another of your previous interests, you may find yourself wanting to learn more about this vast and rapidly changing technology. Not surprisingly, one of the best places to learn about the Internet is the Internet itself. It's also no surprise that the abundance of sites devoted to learning about the Internet can be overwhelming. Here are a few places to start your "Webucation."

AOL's Computing Channel

At America Online, type the Keyword: **Computing**. You will find an abundance of computer-related resources. Whether you want to get help with your computer questions, chat with others, or build your own Web page (it's not as hard as it sounds!), the

Tip

A great way to learn about computers and the Internet is to use AOL and the Internet as a learning guide. Many of the Web sites listed here will help you do just that.

AOL Computing Channel will be a valuable tool. If you want to learn more about computers, you will want to visit the Online Classrooms (see Figure 12-10). If you have never tried online learning before, this is a good place to start, with an excellent explanation of how the classes work as well as a list of basic classes that you can take.

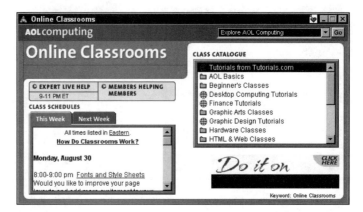

Figure 12-10. Whether you want to get help with your computer questions, chat with others, or build your own Web page, the AOL Computing Channel will be a valuable tool.

Microsoft's Seniors & Technology

Another place to look for resources on computers, the Internet, and related technologies is Microsoft's Seniors & Technology site (`www.microsoft.com/seniors`). Giving technology a human face, a collection of Profiles offers the thoughts of individuals with particular experience and expertise. They explain how contemporary developments are affecting seniors, from gaining access to local resources to establishing nationwide networks. You can even share your own story, "If you or a senior you know has gained new skills, broadened their horizons, or found inspiration through computing and technology . . ."

Part of the Microsoft Senior site is the Microsoft Senior Training Resource Guide (`www.microsoft.com/seniors/content/resources/trg_main.asp`), which features a database of over 1,500 community programs offering introductory computer classes, including community centers, senior centers, and community colleges.

AARP's Webplace

You won't want to miss AARP's extensive Webplace (`www.aarp.org`), which includes a wealth of resources specifically aimed at the over-50 age group. With vast numbers from this age group entering the online world, AARP has also developed a special area called Computers & Technology (`www.aarp.org/comptech`), with yours truly, Sandy Berger, as your online host.

SeniorNet

The mission of SeniorNet (`www.seniornet.org`) is to provide older adults education for and access to computer technology to enhance their lives and enable them to share their knowledge and wisdom. SeniorNet is a nonprofit organization that has established over 160 Learning Centers nationwide. If you would like to learn the computer in a classroom setting where you can meet others, SeniorNet is for you. And, if you are already computer-literate, why not volunteer to help teach computers?

The computer is a powerful tool that can help you find the answers to many of your questions and aid you in the unending quest for knowledge. The knowledge that you amass every day has concrete value. Your accumulated knowledge and wisdom is, without a doubt, useful in your daily life. Perhaps some day, like F. Scott Fitzgerald, you'll even write a book about it all.

12

Research and Learning

Coming Up Next

In the next section of the book, we look into the various shortcuts and helpful hints to make your computing adventure easy and enjoyable. The chapter that follows begins with instructions on how to deal with e-mail attachments and how to download files from the Internet.

In this chapter, we looked at how AOL and the Internet can be used as tools for learning and research, including the following:

- ▶ AOL has convenient tools for all levels of research — from looking up a new word to taking an online course.
- ▶ Many helpful starting points on the Web give you a handle on the vast store of information on the Internet.
- ▶ You can visit the world's great libraries and museums without ever leaving your living room.
- ▶ Distance learning is the latest revolution in education, and your computer makes it possible for you to join in.

Quick Look

▶ **AOL's Download Center**   **page 358**

America Online makes downloading files easy. Many of the potentially time-consuming and complicated steps of locating and downloading files have been eliminated or simplified for you by AOL. The place to start is the Download Center (Keyword: **Download**), which offers all you need to gain proficiency with downloads.

▶ **Keyword: *VBRUN***   **page 367**

Often, when you first try to download a file, you may get a message that says that the program you are trying to download needs a file called VBRUN300.DLL (or something similar) for the program to work. Your first thoughts will probably be: Does my computer have this file? How would I know? How do I get it if I don't already have it? Luckily, AOL has a detailed discussion of such files (Keyword: **VBRUN**), which officially are called Visual Basic Runtime Modules and are necessary to run many software applications. Some may already be installed on your computer if you've loaded certain other programs. Otherwise, you can download everything you need from AOL.

▶ **ZDNet**   **page 376**

For a site with an emphasis on shareware, try ZDNet's shareware site (www.zdnet.com/swlib). In addition to Hot File of the Day and Weekly Top Ten categories, you can search for a title or a type of file, and improve the usefulness of your results by choosing the platform (or operating system) you use: various versions of Windows are available, as well as Macintosh, DOS, OS2, and several others.

▶ **TUCOWS**   **page 376**

Check out the Web site TUCOWS at www.tucows.com if you want to specialize in software related to the Internet itself. The acronym stands for *The Ultimate Collection Of Winsock Software,* but the site also takes advantage of the bovine implications of its name: a typical review rates a program by awarding it not stars but *cows* — up to five of them. Each review also gives you a brief description of the program and links for downloading the file from TUCOWS or visiting the Web site of the file's creator.

Chapter 13

Downloading with Ease

IN THIS CHAPTER

Learn how to download files from AOL

Learn where to store files after they are downloaded

Learn how to download files from the Internet

See where to find good sites for shareware

What exactly does your friend Mary mean when she says, "I just downloaded a great new program from the Internet"? How did she do it? Where did it come from? How did she know where to look? What happened once she got it onto her computer? Most important, how can you download a great program yourself?

These questions and related topics are the focus of this chapter. Although the process of downloading a file may be a little strange at first, you'll soon have the knowledge and the confidence to join this world of online file sharing.

What Is Downloading?

Whether you know it or not, every time you log on to America Online or visit a Web site, you're downloading files to your computer. Every screen in AOL and every Web page you view is a compilation of several files — text files, image files, and perhaps sound files — arranged for your viewing and listening pleasure by your AOL software or your Internet browser. But, because this fairly complex process happens in the background, all you notice is the multimedia experience of the online world.

Usually, when we speak of "downloading a file," we mean something more specific: copying a file from another computer to our computer so that we can use it. (The opposite of download is *upload,* which means to copy a file from your own computer to another computer.)

At this point, we should pause for some definitions and distinctions. A *file* is a single entity existing on a computer's hard drive (or on some other storage medium). You're already familiar with some kinds of files. If you use a word processor to type a letter to print and mail to your brother in Kansas, that letter is a document file. When you save it on your computer, it gets stored in the particular *file format* associated with your word processor.

Different word processors save their files in different formats (as you may have discovered if you've had trouble reading someone else's floppy disk with your computer), and many other formats exist for all the different kinds of programs in your computer: spread sheets, photographs, musical tracks, video clips, and so on.

Definition

Download is the process of moving a copy of a file from a remote computer to your computer. A link is created between the two computers, usually by telephone lines, and one or more files are transferred from one computer to the other. Many different kinds of files can be downloaded, including programs, pictures, and data.

Definition

A *browser* is a software program that enables you to view Web pages on your computer.

Definition

A *file* is a collection of computer data or information — a program or a document — stored on a computer and identified by a filename.

Definition

A *program* is a file or collection of files working together to accomplish a particular computing task (or several related tasks).

Definition

A *folder* is a collection of programs or documents created on a computer for the purpose of organizing related files. A folder may include subfolders as well as individual files. Folders are sometimes called *directories*.

A computer program (such as the word processor you used for your letter, or an arcade game for blasting alien ships) is actually a collection of files — hundreds of files, in the case of a complex program — all working together to accomplish the program's purpose. Fortunately, we don't need to know about all of these files to run the program!

All the files that make your computer function — both program files and document files — are arranged on its hard drive in *folders,* analogous to the paper folders in a file cabinet. Having some familiarity with the organization of folders on your computer will make it easier to keep track of the files you download.

Downloading Files from AOL

Successfully downloading a file from America Online basically requires three steps:

1. Locate the file you want to download.
2. Copy the file to your computer.
3. Install the program and/or use the file appropriately — balance your checkbook, play a game, add colorful images to your reports, and so on.

America Online makes downloading files easy. Many of the potentially time-consuming and complicated steps of locating and downloading files have been eliminated or simplified for you by AOL. Start at the Download Center (Keyword: **Download**), which offers all you need to gain proficiency with downloads (see Figure 13-1).

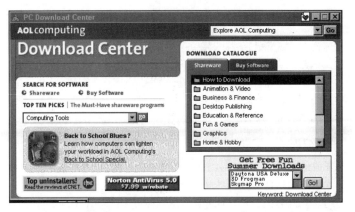

Figure 13-1. AOL's Download Center offers all you need to gain proficiency with downloads.

The opening screen of the Download Center presents you with a quick list of its Top Ten Picks in several software categories: Computing Tools, Fonts, Fun & Games, Music & Sound, and so on. The Download Center also has a Download Catalogue section, where you can browse and download a wide variety of shareware, as well as purchase and download commercial software.

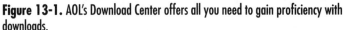

Definition

To *install* a program is to make it available for use on a computer by choosing a location for it to reside and copying the files that enable it to function.

Downloadable Software Comes in Different Flavors

You can download both commercial software and shareware from the Internet. *Commercial software* is just like the software programs that are available from a software company or a retailer. Rather than purchase the package at the store, you pay for it online (usually by credit card at a secure site) and then transfer the necessary file (or files) to your computer. Some companies distribute programs this way without supplying the paper manuals usually accompanying the software; others will mail you the manuals after you place your order. (If you can wait for what may be a very large file to download through

Continued

Downloadable Software Comes in Different Flavors *(continued)*

your modem, this can be a convenient alternative to store shopping.)

Shareware is a generic term often used to describe three general types of programs:

▶ **Freeware:** Programs that are free to download and free to use indefinitely, made available by programmers who simply want to share their creations with the online community.

▶ **Shareware:** Programs available to use freely for a trial period. After that period, if you don't want to continue to use the program, you must delete it from your computer. If you want to keep it, you are asked to pay the programmer a fee — often significantly lower than prices for similar commercial products. (While some shareware may still work after the trial period, continuing to use it without paying for it deters programmers from developing and making such shareware available.)

▶ **Demoware:** Programs produced by commercial software vendors to let you try out, or "demo," their products before you buy them. A demo is similar to the full package you can purchase in your local computer store, but it's limited in one way or another — it may have only a few features of the full version, or it may have a built-in time limit that makes the program unusable after a certain number of days.

The first choice on the Shareware tab is How to Download (refer to Figure 13-1). Double-click this option to view and listen to a series of animated

13

slide shows that will give you a very clear introduction to the process. You'll learn how to find files on America Online and how to use AOL's handy Download Manager (which enables you to choose either to download files immediately or to add them to a list of files for downloading at a later time).

To save space on AOL's computers and to reduce the transfer time of files coming in to your computer, programs are stored (or *archived*) in a compressed or "zipped" format. Mastering the process of decompressing or "unzipping" the files to use them used to be one of the trickiest parts of online file transfers, often requiring special software and an intimate knowledge of your computer's file structure.

But no longer! America Online has designed its software so that after you choose a program to download, it is automatically stored in a Download folder (part of the AOL folders on your hard drive). In fact, after you sign off from AOL, a subfolder with an appropriate name is created within the Download folder, and the file will automatically be decompressed in that subfolder, ready to install and run.

AOL's download tutorial also gives you essential information about computer viruses and how to protect your computer against them. The staff at America Online will carefully check for known viruses in any files that it offers, but new viruses are being created all the time. The tutorial explains how to get antivirus software, if you don't already have such a program, and how to update its virus-protection capabilities on a regular basis.

Definition

Zip is a popular data compression format for Windows. Files that have been compressed with the Zip format are called Zip files and their filenames usually end with the .zip extension.

Definition

A *stuffed* file is the Macintosh equivalent of a Window's zipped file. The filenames of these files usually end with a .sea or .sit extension.

Definition

An *archive* file is one that is in a compressed, zipped, or stuffed format.

Beware of Viruses

Computer viruses are nothing more than malicious lines of computer code written by some unscrupulous person and spread to your computer through shared files. A virus is a parasitic program written intentionally to attack a computer without the computer user's knowledge. Because of the popularity of the Internet, new and more-damaging virus strains are constantly appearing. These viruses can spread quickly through today's intricate cyber world.

An once of prevention . . . The best way to deal with viruses is to prevent them from entering your computer by using a good anti-virus program. McAfee'sVirusScan from Network Associates is one of the best virus protection programs. Symantec's Norton Anti-Virus is another good program.

After you purchase and install an anti-virus program, simply set it to scan for viruses in the background. The program will then look at each file that you download or copy to your computer including each e-mail attachment that you open. After "scanning" that file for viruses, should an infected file be found, the anti-virus program will pop up and advise it has found a virus before that file has a chance to infect your computer. A good anti-virus program will also detect and eliminate any viruses that were already residing in your computer.

One important thing to note is that destructive people are literally working day and night to spread their loathsome viruses. Because new viruses are constantly unleashed, you should regularly updates your anti-virus program to make sure it can find and eradicate all the current viruses.

Instructions for updating your anti-virus program will be included with the original program. Updates can be downloaded from the Internet. I recommend updating your antivirus program at least once a month, more often if possible.

Note

The download process for Macintosh users is similar to the one described here for Windows users. However, the choices for games and other files will differ.

Step by Step

Now, let's go through the download process step by step.

Suppose I know that I want to try a new computer game, but I don't have a specific title in mind. From the Shareware categories in the Download Catalogue (Keyword: **Download**), I can double-click Fun & Games, and the next screen offers me an option for a variety of game styles — everything from adventure and arcade games to flight simulators and sports (see Figure 13-2).

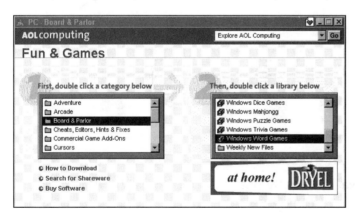

Figure 13-2. Fun & Games offers options for a variety of game styles — everything from adventure and arcade games to flight simulators and sports.

This screen is typical of all the software offerings at AOL. In the left window, you scroll down a list of categories. Double-clicking a category brings up a more specialized list of libraries in the right window.

Note

Because of the fluid nature of the online world, a title may not always be available at the same location from one month to the next. Nevertheless, you should be able to find similar games (or other files) to your liking. Explore the scrolling menus and try the Search feature.

Libraries, in turn, come in two flavors: if the icon for a library is a series of diskettes, double-clicking it will take you directly to files for that topic; if the icon is a file folder, double-clicking it will lead to a further set of choices — eventually you get to the files!

For now, I've decided that I want to try Board & Parlor Games. Double-clicking that category opens up a list of file libraries, including one of my favorites, Windows Word Games. When I double-click that topic, AOL's Download Manager opens, as shown in Figure 13-3, offering me a choice of about 20 games. Because I can't tell much from the filenames themselves, I click one called Hangman and then click the Read Description button. This opens a new window in which I learn that this program is a "kinder, gentler" version of the popular guess-which-word-I'm-spelling game: no capital punishment, just spell the word correctly before all the apples fall from the tree.

▲ Windows Word Games			
Upld	Subject	Count	Download
5/13/98	TRYWORD2: v1.0 Word Game	548	8/16/99
4/30/98	TRACKER: v1.0 Fill In Crossword	1300	8/17/99
4/30/98	TRACKER: v1.0 Coded Crosswords	190	8/7/99
4/16/98	WORDZAP: v3.65 16-bit Word Game	873	8/18/99
3/25/98	MORAFF: v1.00 Phrase Detective	1097	8/17/99
10/27/97	XWORD: V1.30 Crossword Challeng	5935	8/18/99
10/19/97	WORDPLAY: v1.0 Word Games	1907	8/17/99
6/11/97	FUNLIBS: v1.1 Word Game	3918	8/18/99
5/13/97	CRYPTOGR: v3.0 Cryptogram game	2312	8/17/99
4/14/97	HANGMAN: v1.0 The Apple Tree	4974	8/18/99
3/24/97	MIXWORD: v2.0 Unique Letter Gam	2220	8/18/99

Read Description   Download Now   Download Later   Upload   List More Files

Sort Order: Upload Date

Figure 13-3. About 20 games are available for download under Windows Word Games. Hangman is our choice.

I think I'll try the game. Because I'm impatient to play (and I've also learned from the description that it should take less than two minutes to transfer the file), I click the Download Now button. A window appears prompting me to save the file "Apple" in my Download directory, so I click the Save button. As the file is being transferred from AOL to my computer, a small status window shows me the progress of the download. When the file has arrived in its entirety, a message onscreen (and on my computer speakers) announces "File done," and I'm ready to install the game.

I sign off from AOL (you are recommended to close all programs before installing new software) and look for my new file. It's not hard to find! Back at my Windows desktop, I click the Start button and choose Find and then Files or Folders (Mac users: pull down the File menu and choose Find).

Because I remember that the filename of the downloaded file is Apple, that's what I type in the Named box (capitalization doesn't matter). Checking to make sure that the Look in box has the icon and letter of my hard drive (C), I click the Find Now button (see Figure 13-4). (Mac users: be sure that the location to search and other options are correct. Type the name to locate, and then click the Find button.)

Tip

It's important to close all open programs before installing a new program. Also, signing off from AOL helps to automate the installation process.

Find Now

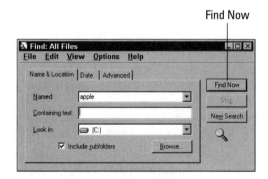

Figure 13-4. After typing the name of your downloaded file in the Named box and making sure the Look in box displays the icon and letter of your hard drive, click the Find Now button.

The results of my search are displayed in the bottom section of the window. Several items have "apple" in their names, but I want the one with the file-folder

Tip

When you choose a file to download, be sure to write down its filename. It may seem obvious at the time, but if you download several programs before installing them, or if you install a program at a later time, it's easy to forget.

icon, because that's the new folder created by my AOL software to simplify the installation process (see Figure 13-5).

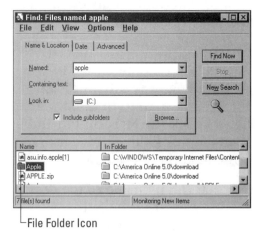

└─ File Folder Icon

Figure 13-5. When searching for an installation or setup file, first choose the item marked with a file folder icon.

Double-clicking the file-folder icon opens a new window, which displays the entire contents of the folder, as shown in Figure 13-6, including one called Setup (indicated by an icon of a computer monitor with installation disks). Double-clicking that icon brings up the opening Apple Tree Setup screen, with a prompt for me to install the program in a new folder on my hard drive, C:\Apple (see Figure 13-7).

I click the Next button, and a succession of windows guides me through the process, and informs me of the status, of the installation. In a minute or so, the game has been installed, and I'm ready to play.

After guessing a few words before all the apples fall off the tree (and missing a few more), I click the Place an Order button on Hangman's opening screen and discover that the game's creator is asking about $20 for the program. Options are provided for credit card orders by phone or fax, as well as a mailing address for cash orders. I'll think about it . . .

Figure 13-6. The entire contents of a folder are displayed by double-clicking the folder icon.

Figure 13-7. The Apple Tree Setup screen suggests installation of the program in a new folder on the hard drive, C:\Apple.

What if you're not interested in word games? AOL's Download Center has more than enough to keep you busy and stimulated. If you're interested in drawing and painting, the section on Graphics will introduce you to a range of programs for editing existing images and photographs, or for creating your own from scratch. The Internet Tools area offers utilities for transferring files and even for designing your own Web pages. For the musicians out there, you can download guitar music for your favorite songs, or a sound clip from a big-band recording.

Tip

When you first try to download a file, you may get a message that says that the program you are trying to download needs a file called VBRUN300.DLL (or something similar) for the program to work. Your first thoughts will probably be: Does my computer have this file? How would I know? How do I get it if I don't already have it?

Luckily, AOL has a detailed discussion of such files (type Keyword: **VBRUN**), which officially are called *Visual Basic Runtime Modules* and are necessary to run many software applications. Some may already be installed on your computer if you've loaded certain other programs. Otherwise, you can download everything you need from America Online. Read all about it!

E-Mail Attachments

Caution

One of the fastest and most dangerous ways computer viruses are spread is through e-mail attachments. Be sure you are familiar with the sender of the message before you download an attachment. (It is also wise to scan every attachment with an updated antivirus program before opening. Follow your program's instructions to set it to automatically scan and disinfect e-mail message attachments.)

A handy way of acquiring downloads is by saving a file that someone has sent to you as an attachment to an e-mail message. When you open an incoming e-mail that has an attachment, you will see a button at the bottom of the e-mail screen that says Download Now (see Figure 13-8). Don't download an attachment unless you personally know the sender of the message! As you may know, one of the fastest and most dangerous ways in which computer viruses are spread is through e-mail attachments. Scan your inbox before opening a message, delete anything suspicious, and be wary of what you allow into your computer.

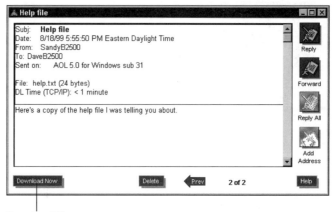

Download Now

Figure 13-8. Incoming e-mail with an attachment can be downloaded by using the Download Now button found at the bottom of the e-mail screen.

Help from AOL

Don't forget that you can always get help from America Online in numerous ways. Two ways to keep in mind if you get stuck downloading are Get Help Now (Keyword: **Get Help Now**) and PC Help Chat, which is held every night from 9 to 11 p.m., EST.

Downloading Files from the Internet

As explained in the tutorial on downloading (see the previous section), some of the options you'll see when browsing for downloads will take you away from America Online's computers and onto the World Wide Web. (You'll know this is happening because AOL's Web browser opens with the label World Wide Web temporarily displayed in the title bar.) If you decide to download files from the Web, several other considerations come into play.

First, the chances of encountering a virus are higher on the Internet, so be sure to keep your antivirus software running (and updated) and limit your downloading to the more reputable and reliable sites. (I'll recommend a few antivirus programs later in this chapter.)

Second, the automated features of AOL downloads (finding the right folder on your hard drive, unzipping the files, and so on) will not be functioning when you acquire files from the Web. Therefore, you need to know something about the organization of files on your computer's hard drive and how to find your way from one point to another.

Recalling the process we went through to install the Hangman game, picture your hard drive as either a tree with branches, an outline with subcategories, or a file drawer with folders and subfolders. Experiment with the windows and scroll bars until you feel comfortable moving around the structure of folders. (Remember, if you double-click a folder icon, you'll simply open that folder to view its contents. You can't hurt anything on your computer or accidentally run any programs if you confine your clicks to folders.)

Definition

A *virus* is a software program designed to "infect" computers by disrupting other programs, erasing files, or otherwise damaging a system. A virus can spread to other computers through infected e-mail attachments or diskettes.

Cross-Reference

See Chapter 2 for more about chatting on AOL.

Decide Where to Save the File

Before you download a file from the Web, decide where you want to save it prior to installation. Feel free to keep it in your AOL Download folder. Some people prefer to create a folder on their hard drive just for these downloaded files.

If you want to create such a folder, minimize or close all windows so that you can see the desktop. In Windows, double-click the My Computer icon and then double-click the icon for your hard drive. (For Mac users: double-click the Macintosh HD icon.) You'll see a display of the existing folders on your hard drive. To create a new folder in Windows, select Folder from the File, New menu, as demonstrated in Figure 13-9. (Mac users select New Folder from the File menu.)

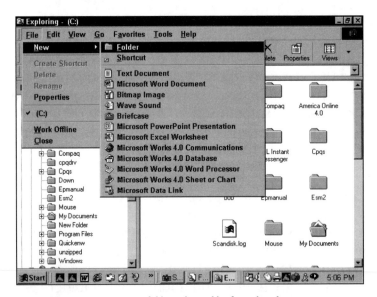

Figure 13-9. To create a new folder, select Folder from the File, New menu.

A new folder will be added at the bottom of the window (temporarily named "New Folder" in Windows and "untitled folder" on the Mac). You may have to resize the window or scroll down to see the new folder. You can give it a new name (for this example, use **Download**) by typing over the high-lighted label. (If the label is no longer highlighted in Windows, right-click the New Folder icon, choose Rename from the shortcut menu that appears, and type the new name.)

Find the File You Want to Download

Now, you're ready to hunt for files to download! The first program that you need is essential for almost all the other programs you download: an unzip program, which is a utility program that is used to compress and — more essential for your immediate purposes — uncompress files. (In the Mac world, *zipping* is referred to as *stuffing*.) One of the most popular programs of this type for Windows users

is called WinZip. For Mac users, the counterpart is StuffIt Expander.

WinZip is an excellent shareware program from Nico Mak Computing, Inc. You can download WinZip without any fee, but you are asked to pay for it later. You can visit the WinZip Web site at www.winzip.com, or download it easily at AOL's Download Center by clicking MIME Help and Software from the Computing Tools, PC Computing Tools menu. There you will find the latest version of WinZip along with earlier versions and an explana-tion of Mime and Zip files.

StuffIt Expander is a freeware program available from Aladdin Systems at www.aladdinsys.com, as well as from many other download sites.

Let's go to CNET's extensive software site called Download.com (www.download.com) to try to find WinZip (see Figure 13-10). Because you know what you're looking for, you can use the Search

Note

Remember: To go to a site on the Web, type the URL or Web address in the lo-cation bar, the long white rectangle near the top of your AOL screen, and click the Go button.

feature: type **winzip** and click the Go button.
The next screen gives you a list of hyperlinked
file titles. Click a title, and the next page provides
a full description of the program, along with links
to Related Resources and a link for you to
Download Now (see Figure 13-11).

Figure 13-10. Download.com has a Search feature to help locate specific files
to download.

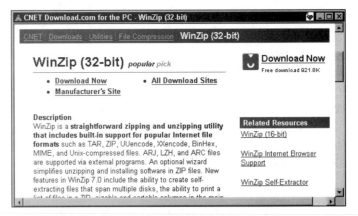

Figure 13-11. Download.com provides a full description of the program, along with
links to Related Resources.

When you click Download Now, a window labeled
File Download appears, with options to run the program or save it (see Figure 13-12). Selecting Save this
program to disk and then clicking OK opens a Save

As window, which may indicate the most recent folder opened by an application. To change to your download directory, click the down arrow to the right of the Save in box and choose the hard-disk icon labeled (C:), as shown in Figure 13-13.

Figure 13-12. At the File Download screen, you are given two options: run t he program from its current location or save the program to disk.

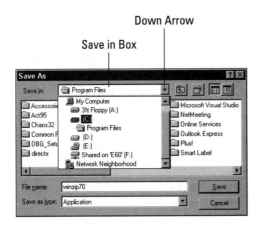

Figure 13-13. Clicking the down arrow to the right of the Save in box brings up an overview of your computer's disk drives.

The Save As window now displays all the folders on the hard drive; find the one you renamed Download and double-click it. Now, clicking Save will start the download of the WinZip file to your computer. A status window lets you know the progress of the download (Figure 13-14), and, after the transfer is complete, you can install WinZip. (The process for locating and downloading a copy of StuffIt Expander for Macintosh users is essentially the same. Download.com does have an extensive collection of Mac files, as well as an area for the UNIX-like operating system Linux.)

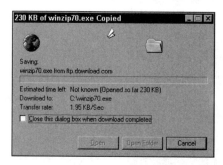

Figure 13-14. A status window indicates the progress of the download.

You may be wondering, "How am I going to unzip the WinZip file if I need the WinZip program itself to unzip files?" Good question. The folks at WinZip have a good answer: The file you just downloaded is a *self-extracting archive.* In other words, you don't need to run another program to unzip the files compressed in the archive — simply running this file automatically unzips its component files into the folder where it's located.

To unzip WinZip, you first need to find it. Select Find on the Start menu and then click Files or Folders. Type **winzip** in the Named box and click the Find Now button. The search results will include the icon and name of the file that you downloaded, noting that it's located in the Download folder of the C drive.

Now that you have found WinZip, you are ready to unzip and install it. Double-clicking the icon will unzip the file and begin the installation process, which is generally a process of clicking a series of buttons. At one stage, you'll need to confirm where the program should be installed. The default is to install it in a new folder within the Program Files folder, and this option is fine (see Figure 13-15). Some computer users like to create a different folder so that all their applications won't be buried in Program Files, but that's up to you.

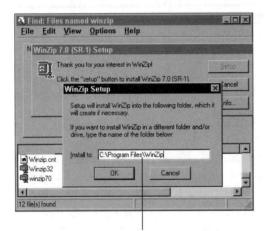

Type in folder name and location here.

Figure 13-15. New programs are installed in the Program Files folder by default, but you may select a different folder location simply by typing its name in the Install to box.

You'll be asked to look at the WinZip license agreement, with a reminder that this is a shareware program that you should register and pay for if you decide to keep and use it. You probably will! (Some freeware programs also are available to uncompress files, and you can locate them at download sites.)

After WinZip is installed, an entry for the program appears on the Start menu. Another great feature of the installation process is that any zip files on your computer now will be "associated" with WinZip. This means that when you look at a folder's contents with Explorer, any zipped files will be displayed with the WinZip icon (a yellow file cabinet being compressed in a vise), and when you double-click the icon, WinZip will run automatically and

start the uncompression-and-installation process,
which makes the process easier for you.

More Download Options

Okay, now for some other files to download. Back at
Download.com, you can jump to any one of several
categories for software — from business and education to home and multimedia. You can also browse
a list of the most popular titles at Download.com,
check out new releases, or review the editors' picks.
Both shareware and commercial products are listed.

For a site with an emphasis on shareware, try
ZDNet's shareware site (www.zdnet.com/swlib).
In addition to Hot File of the Day and Weekly Top
Ten categories, you can search for a title or a type
of file, and improve the usefulness of your results
by choosing the platform (or operating system)
you use: various versions of Windows are available,
as well as Macintosh, DOS, OS2, and several others.

If you want to specialize in software related to
the Internet itself, one of my favorites is TUCOWS
(www.tucows.com). The acronym stands for
The Ultimate Collection Of Winsock Software,
but the site also takes advantage of the bovine implications of its name: a typical review rates a program
by awarding it not stars but cows — up to five of
them. Each review also gives you a brief description
and links for downloading the file from TUCOWS
or visiting the Web site of the file's creator (see
Figure 13-16).

As with most of the large download sites, TUCOWS
offers software for several different operating systems: Windows (in all its varieties), Macintosh,
and others.

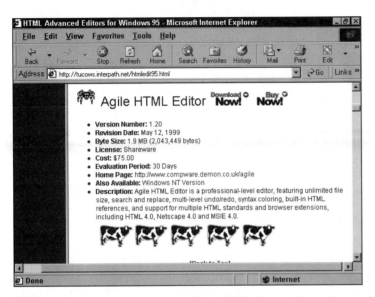

Figure 13-16. TUCOWS recognizes quality in a software program by awarding cows rather than stars. Only the best programs get five cows.

Many excellent download sites are available on the Web. Try a few and then pick your favorite. I like the sites that review the programs and give you some information about them. You will also want to look for a site that gives you consistently fast downloads. Although a program such as WinZip or StuffIt can be downloaded from any number of different sites, you will often find that some sites provide speedier downloads.

Many large collections of software for download also maintain *mirror sites* at different locations around the country and sometimes around the globe. The computers at these sites reproduce the file collections of the company in question; choosing a mirror site geographically close to you usually means faster downloads.

Most of the main search sites have categories for shareware and freeware, as do Web sites such as FILEZ (www.filez.com) and CNET's Shareware. com. Many commercial software companies, such as Microsoft (`www.microsoft.com/downloads`) and Apple (`http://asu.info.apple.com/`), offer free utilities to enhance their primary products or otherwise spruce up your computing experience. You can also find a plethora of sound files, screen-savers, and even specialized icons that you can use on your computer.

Look around and have some fun!

Coming Up Next

In the next chapter, we take a look at how to work with graphics and photos online. In this chapter, you saw how to download files from e-mail, AOL, and the Internet, which included the following information:

- ▶ AOL makes downloading easy by eliminating or simplifying many of the potentially time-consuming and complicated steps of locating and downloading files.

- ▶ The software found on America Online auto-matically stores programs you download in a folder called Download, within your AOL folder.

- ▶ Don't download an attachment unless you personally know the sender of the message, because computer viruses are often spread through e-mail attachments.

- ▶ An unzip or unstuff program is a utility pro-gram used for compressing and uncompress-ing files, and is essential for almost all the programs you download.

- ▶ Great sites for shareware are Shareware.com, TUCOWS, and ZDNet. Many commercial soft-ware companies, such as Microsoft and Apple, offer free utilities at their Web sites to enhance their products.

Quick Look

▶ **You've Got Pictures** **page 386**

AOL 5.0 includes a new feature called You've Got Pictures, which enables AOL
members to access their photographs on their own computers as the film is
developed. You simply take your film to be processed as usual, check the AOL
box on the film envelope, and fill in your AOL screen name. Then, pick up
your prints and negatives as you normally do. When you get home, sign on to
AOL and click the You've Got Pictures button. Your roll of pictures will arrive
under the New Rolls tab on the You've Got Pictures screen. You can instantly
share your pictures by e-mail by clicking the E-mail Picture button, and you
can store them in picture albums by clicking the Create New Album button.

▶ **Paint Shop Pro** **page 389**

Check out the information on AOL at Keyword: **PSP** in the Graphic Art area to
learn more about Paint Shop Pro, a popular image-editing program that delivers professional-quality graphics and photo-editing tools. It is an excellent program for business users and home hobbyists.

▶ **Keyword: *Graphics*** **page 394**

After you start working with photos and graphics, you'll quickly realize that
this is an art form that you can use to express yourself. AOL's Graphic Arts
Community has resources to help you create your own original works of art.
Start at the Keyword: **Graphics** and check out the Explore Graphic Arts section, which includes tutorials, resources, and information on special
interest groups.

Chapter 14

Working with Graphics and Photos

IN THIS CHAPTER

Learn what it means to digitize photos and images

Learn how to work with digital cameras

Learn how to edit photos with software

See how to enhance your work with clip art

Learn how to e-mail images

Ezra Pound, a famous American poet and critic, said, "The image is more than an idea. It is a vortex or cluster of fused ideas and is endowed with energy." With that in mind, it's no wonder that, as our society progresses, images become more and more important. We live in the colorful graphic world of video and multimedia. We are accustomed to movies and television with constantly moving, colorful pictorial images.

The computer and the Internet extend that visual world even further by making it easy for us to create our own powerful images. Working with electronic images is easier and neater than working with paint-brushes or pencils. No messy brushes to clean up. No need to wash the ink or glue off your hands. Even more exciting is the fact that creating and working with images on the computer is often chea-per and faster, as well. A photograph can be taken with a digi-tal camera and reproduced on the compu-ter within minutes, without any film or processing fees. If a shot doesn't turn out, just delete it and try again!

First-time grandparents, living far away, see their new grandson moments after he is born. A picture of a forgotten object from the attic is posted at an online auction site, and the unknown treasure fetches an unbelievable price. A cherished family photograph is pulled out of an old shoebox, recon-ditioned, and shared with the entire family through e-mail. The computer and online resources make all of this possible.

Working with images and photographs is easy, but before you can have fun with pictures and graphics, you have to know a little about how they work and how you can work with them.

Having Fun with Digital Photos

A computer understands only bits and bytes, mean-ing that the computer can work only with items that are digital in nature. To access a photograph with a computer, the photograph must be input by a digital piece of equipment or translated into a *digital* format.

Definition

Digital information is data measured at discrete intervals. Today's clocks are digital devices when they use numerals rather than the hour and minute hands to display time.

Definition

A *scanner* is a device that attaches to your computer and reads text, illustrations, or photographs printed on paper and translates the information into the digital form that the computer can use.

Photos and Image Files Are Quite Large

Simple text items, such as letters and address books, don't take up a lot of room in your computer. However, photograph and graphic image files are quite large and take up a lot of hard disk space. If you plan to work with images, be sure to purchase a computer with a large hard disk. If you are running out of room on your hard disk, the easiest solution might be to buy another hard disk. You can leave your original hard disk with all of your information intact and simply add a second hard disk for extra storage. The installation of a second hard disk might be within your scope if you are mechanically inclined, but in most cases, having a professional install the hard disk is best.

Scanners

A *scanner* is a device that attaches to your computer and reads text, illustrations, or photographs printed on paper and translates the information into the digital form that the computer can use. A scanner works by digitizing an image. Although this may sound complex, it is seamless in its operation.

A scanner works like a photocopier. You simply insert your newspaper or magazine clipping, document, or photo into the scanner, and a digital picture of the item appears on the computer screen.

Scanners come with their own software. The software enables the scanned image to be reproduced on the computer screen and saved in digital format on your hard drive. However, the scope and the quality of the software vary greatly and should be investigated when purchasing a scanner.

Digital Cameras

A *digital camera* is a tool that has recently come of age. Although a digital camera looks like a regular camera, it has one big difference — no film. You point and shoot digital cameras just like ordinary cameras, but the image is stored in the camera itself or on a removable data storage unit that, unlike film, can be used over and over again. Some digital cameras use floppy disks to hold the image data, while others use smart cards (which in computer-speak is a circuit board with built-in memory and decision-making capabilities) or another rewritable medium.

Recent enhancements and events have brought the quality of digital cameras up and the prices down. Digital cameras now not only take excellent photos, but also have other dynamic features, such as a small built-in screen, where you can view the picture right after you take it. If you don't like the photo, you simply press the Delete button and retake the photo. If the digital camera uses a floppy disk, or other storage medium compatible with your computer, you can simply remove the disk from the camera and insert it into the computer. However, most digital cameras come with a cable that enables you to transfer the pictures to your computer.

Note

If you want to scan slides into the computer, purchase a scanner with an attachment specifically made for scanning in slides, or have your slides developed as prints.

Tip

A wonderful way to store copies of your important papers (deeds, birth certificates, insurance policies, and so on) is to scan them and organize them on a disk. This takes up very little room and, in case the originals are destroyed or misplaced, you know where your copies are.

Connecting Your Scanner and/or Digital Camera to Your Computer

A variety of different connections are available for attaching a scanner or digital camera to your computer. One of the fastest and easiest to set up and to use is a universal serial bus (USB) connection. If you have a fairly new computer or an iMac, it has a USB connector. To take advantage of the USB port, you will also need to be running Mac OS 8 or newer or Windows 98 or higher.

Continued

14

Working with Graphics and Photos

Note

Digital cameras don't use film. The quality of a digital picture is based on resolution, just like traditional photography. But, in the digital world, resolution is based on tiny electronic squares, called *pixels*. The more pixels a picture has, the higher its resolution and the sharper its image.

Connecting Your Scanner and/or Digital Camera to Your Computer (continued)

Many digital cameras have built-in microphones that you can use to produce an instant audio caption. Most cameras can also be plugged into a television. Recently, I took my digital camera along to a party. I was able to take photos of the partygoers and then use the cable that came with the camera to hook it up to the television and create an instant slide show of the pictures that I had just taken. Some digital cameras can also be hooked up directly to a printer, so you can even print your photos without a computer. If you happen to be purchasing a camera and a printer at the same time, you will want to verify that they are compatible for performing this function.

Digital cameras, like scanners, come with software that runs on your computer and enables the photographs to be transferred from the camera to the computer and then displayed and manipulated on the computer. If you plan to purchase a digital camera, ask for a demonstration not only of the camera, but also of the included software.

You've Got Pictures

Perhaps you don't want to incur the cost of a digital camera or scanner right now, or you would like to see what digital images are all about before you purchase another piece of equipment. AOL 5.0 includes a new feature called You've Got Pictures, prominently displayed right on the Welcome screen (see Figure 14-1). You simply take your photographs with your regular camera, as usual. Then, drop off your film as you usually do, but make sure that you check

the AOL box on the film envelope and fill in your
AOL screen name. Then, pick up your prints and negatives like you always do. When you get home, sign
on to AOL and click the You've Got Pictures button.

Tip

You can have your pictures
developed as slides or
prints, as you normally
do, and also have them
sent to your America
Online account in a digital
form, via You've Got
Pictures.

14

Working with Graphics and Photos

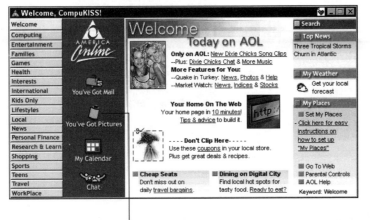

You've Got Pictures

Figure 14-1. You've Got Pictures is a new feature that allows AOL members to access
their photographs on their own computers as the film is developed.

Your roll of pictures will arrive under the New
Rolls tab on the You've Got Pictures screen. You
can instantly share your pictures by e-mail by clicking the E-mail Picture button. You can store them
in picture albums by clicking the Create New
Album button. You can also click the Download
Pictures button to store the pictures on your own
computer, so that they are available when you are
not online. Click the Order Prints & Gifts button to
have your favorite picture reproduced on a mug or
other novelty item (see Figure 14-2). Have someone
take your picture in front of the computer, label it
cybergranny or *cybergrandpa,* and put it on a
mug for the grandchildren. It's fun, it's easy, and
it can really help with that hectic holiday and
birthday shopping.

Note

You probably won't have any trouble finding a participating film developer, because over 38,000 film processors are participating in the AOL program. However, if you want to check on the location of a participating developer, simply click the You've Got Pictures button on the main AOL screen (refer to Figure 14-1). Or, type the Keyword: **Pictures** and use the easy online search to find a participating You've Got Pictures photo developer near you.

Order Prints & Gifts

Figure 14-2. Ordering reprints and personalized photo gifts is as easy as clicking Order Prints & Gifts.

Photo-Editing Software

After you get your photos into your computer, the fun begins. With your pictures onscreen, the possibilities are endless. Enhance, organize, customize, share . . . get more out of your pictures in every way.

You can use simple photo-editing software to improve your photos and/or to manipulate them to your heart's content. Get rid of that unwanted red eye. Zoom in on your favorite person in the crowd. Put Aunt Edna's head on Uncle Phil's body. Make the sky bluer, create a collage, or put a border around a great photograph. You can make a screen saver out of your favorite photo, print it on photo paper, create a family newsletter, make personalized greeting cards, or even purchase special transfer paper so that you can put your favorite photo on a T-shirt.

PhotoDeluxe and Picture It

Many different levels of photo-editing software
are available. You will want to start by experiment-
ing with the software that comes with your AOL
pictures. If you find that you enjoy working with
photos, you may want to graduate to a full-fledged
photo-editing piece of software. Two of the best are
Adobe's PhotoDeluxe and Microsoft's Picture It.
These two dynamic programs are easy to use and
full of fun projects. They give you the ability to add
special effects and to correct the imperfections in
your photos. They also have plenty of creative activities, from designing postcards to producing slide
shows. These two programs enable you to do fun
things with photographs. They are full of quality
features, and they are fairly easy to learn and use.

Paint Shop Pro

If you have more serious graphic ambitions, try
Paint Shop Pro, a popular image-editing program
that delivers professional-quality graphics and
photo-editing tools. Although Paint Shop Pro is
more powerful than most other image-editing
programs, it is still relatively easy to use. It is an
excellent program for business users and home
hobbyists. The Graphic Art area of AOL provides
a lot of information on Paint Shop Pro, including a
list of online classes, found at Keyword: **PSP**.

Print Shop

To create greeting cards, signs, newsletters, postcards,
and other graphic projects, you may also want to
try a program such as The Print Shop Deluxe from
Brøderbund. Print Shop and other similar graphics
programs enable you to work with photos, but they
do not have as many photographic editing tools as
the previously mentioned programs. However, Print
Shop excels at graphic layouts for simple home and

14

Working with Graphics and Photos

Note

For a list of additional graphics programs, check out keyword: **AOL Shop Direct.**

small-business projects and also has an abundant amount of clip art, Web graphics, and images.

Photoshop

Professional artists and those of you who aspire to be professionals and have the time to invest will want to acquire Adobe's Photoshop, which is hailed by many as the granddaddy of all graphics programs. Photoshop is expensive and has a steep learning curve, but it is extremely powerful and enables you to manipulate photos in many different ways. Photoshop keeps getting better and more powerful with each new version.

Clip Art

Working with photographs is fun, but that's not the only way to enjoy computer graphics. One of the most common types of graphics is called *clip art.* These are electronic illustrations that can be inserted into a document. Many clip art packages are available, some general and others specialized for a particular type of clip art or a particular subject. For instance, you can get clip art of people, food, flowers, birds, animals, and about a zillion other topics (see Figure 14-3).

Be Careful of Copyrighted Material

Some clip art and graphics found on the Web and in shareware collections are copyrighted and may not legally be used in any way (including placing them on a Web page or sending them in e-mail) without the author's permission. To get the author's permission, you must contact him or her. Using others' copyrighted art without prior permission, whether for commercial or personal purposes, can expose the user to legal action with stiff fines.

Note: America Online strictly prohibits the transfer or posting of sexually explicit images online. Doing so may lead to immediate and permanent termination of your account. See Keyword: **TOS** for more information and for directions on how to report violations.

Definition

Clip art is a form of electronic illustration that can be inserted into a document.

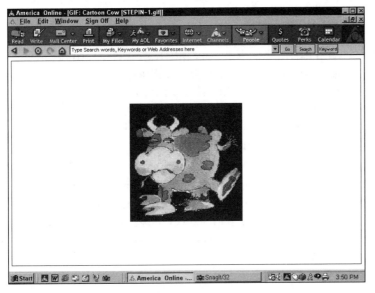

Figure 14-3. Clip art packages contain illustrations on general areas or on specialized areas, such as people, food, flowers, birds, animals, and so on.

Finding clip art is easy. Your word processor may contain some clip art. If you purchase a photo-manipulation program, it will almost certainly have clip art in it. Look at any of the shareware sites that were mentioned in Chapter 13 to find good clip art. You should also check out AOL's resources at Keyword: **Web Art**. Although much of what you find there was created for use in Web pages, it is also useful for adding to letters, creating greeting cards, and developing your other artistic creations. Find clip art software at keyword: **AOL Shop Direct.**

14

Working with Graphics and Photos

File Formats

Definition

Wallpaper refers to the background of the computer screen. In both Windows and Mac systems, the wallpaper can be changed to suit your fancy. Both Windows and Mac systems allow you to choose from a variety of wallpaper styles through the Control Panel. In Windows, click Start, click Settings, and then click Control Panel. Next, click the Display icon. In Mac, click the Apple symbol, click Control Panel, and then click Appearance. Select the Desktop tab.

Not all graphics are created equal and, unfortunately for the end-user, many are not compatible with each other. Here is a quick rundown on the common types of graphic file formats:

- ▶ **GIF** (pronounced "JIF," as in the word *jiffy*) is an image that was created to be displayed on a computer screen. These types of files are often used in Web pages for line art and drawings.

- ▶ **JPEG** (pronounced "J-peg") is actually more of a compression format than a true image format. JPEG stands for *Joint Photographer's Expert Group.* The JPEG format compresses image files to a smaller size, which may cause some image quality to be lost. JPEG is also a common format used on Web pages, particularly for photographs.

- ▶ **BMP** is a bitmap image used primarily in Windows programs and often as Windows wallpaper. Due to its excessive size, this format generally isn't used for photographs or Web pages.

- ▶ **TIF** or **TIFF** files can also be quite large. This format is commonly used for photographs, but numerous variations of the TIF format exist, and not all software will view all variations.

- ▶ **PICT** is a format that is common among Macintosh users, but can be a problem for Windows users to display.

E-Mailing Images

E-mailing images can be fun if all goes well, but occasionally, because of incompatibilities and other details, problems do occur. You can avoid most problems by understanding a few simple facts:

- Limiting the size of your images will help them travel more quickly and will cause fewer headaches in the long run. An image that takes up the entire screen will undoubtedly be too large to e-mail.

- The format of the image greatly affects its size. GIF and JPEG images are the recommended formats for e-mail. You can often change the format of the image by starting the program that it was created in and choosing Save As to save the image to another format. When the Save As screen appears, click the drop-down arrow to choose a JPEG or GIF format (see Figure 14-4).

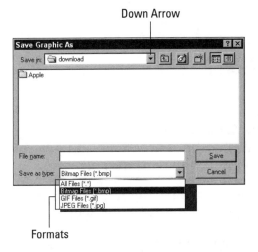

Figure 14-4. Click the Down Arrow of the Save As screen and choose a JPEG or GIF format to change the format of an image you want to save.

- Some digital cameras save images in a *proprietary format,* which means that the recipient needs the software used to create the image to view it. If that is the case, simply convert images to GIF or JPEG format, as just noted, to share with others.

Cross-Reference

See Chapter 13 for more information about where to find and download compression software from the Internet.

▶ If you receive an e-mail attachment that you cannot easily see, you may need a *viewer.* You can find viewers for the various file formats in the Graphics Arts Resource Center. From the main menu of the Graphic Arts Community at Keyword: **Graphics**, select Graphic Arts Resources from the box labeled Explore Graphic Arts. You will find Viewer Recommendations in the list offered on the Graphic Arts Resource Center page.

▶ If you do need to send a large image as an e-mail attachment, be sure to use a compression program, such as WinZip for PCs or StuffIt for the Mac, to bring it down to a workable size.

Coming Up Next

In the chapter that follows, we take a look at what to do if your computer doesn't behave as it should. We learn how to troubleshoot problems, and where to find help both on AOL and the Internet.

In this chapter, we looked at having fun with graphics and images online, including the following:

▶ To access a photograph with a computer, the picture must be translated into a digital format.

▶ Digital cameras have no film, but instead store the image in the camera itself (later downloaded to a computer with a cable) or on a removable data storage unit.

▶ AOL 5.0 has a new feature called You've Got Pictures that gives members computerized access to their photographs.

▶ Photo-editing and graphic-design software is available for those of you with serious graphic ambitions.

▶ E-mail can be enhanced by attaching photographs.

CHAPTER

15

TROUBLESHOOTING
AND FINDING HELP

Quick Look

▶ **AOL Help**   **page 408**

America Online has developed an amazingly comprehensive and accessible
system of online help to guide you through problems you may encounter with
your computer and AOL. Much of the information available assists you with
beginner, intermediate, and advanced features of the vast AOL community, but
there are also extensive sections on more general computing activities. Go to
Keyword: **Help** to access Member Services Online Help, which is the most
complete starting point for getting assistance. Offline Help is also handy to
read when you are not connected to AOL.

▶ **QuickStart**   **page 410**

Another place to find helpful hints is from the Member Services screen. Go to
Keyword: **Newmember**, where you will find the QuickStart guide for those
recently joining America Online — as well as AOL veterans who need a refresher
on the basics. This guide can also be reached via the Keyword: **QuickStart**.

▶ **Best of AOL**   **page 411**

A topic in the QuickStart guide is Best of AOL, Keyword: **Best of AOL**. This
guide gives short explanations of unique features, such as Buddy Lists, shopping on AOL, and Instant Message conversations. The AOL Tips link, Keyword:
AOL Tips, leads you to a wide range of helpful hints about getting the most
from your America Online experience.

▶ **Keyword: *Keyword***   **page 411**

Going to Keyword: **Keyword** may sound odd, but when you do, you will be
presented with a great list of the entire spectrum of AOL topics, from which
you can pick and chose the information you want to learn more about.

Chapter 15

Troubleshooting and Finding Help

IN THIS CHAPTER

Learn basic solutions to common computer problems

Learn how to be prepared when calling for technical support

Learn where to get help from AOL and online

Your computer, your America Online account, and your Internet connection can be wonderful things — exciting, enjoyable, stimulating, and fun — until you run into a problem. Some problems are easy to solve, but some become more than a momentary snag.

Perhaps you really need to do something but you can't. You're looking for a section of AOL that you know was there yesterday, but it doesn't seem to be there today. You misplaced some files that you know you saved . . . but where? Or, seemingly worst of all, your computer "freezes," completely locks up: the screen is motionless. Pressing keys and clicking mouse buttons elicits no response, and even those loud curses are of no avail.

Where can you turn for help? Don't panic! As you'll learn in this chapter, you're never far from assistance. In fact, on AOL and the Internet, almost everywhere you turn someone is offering you advice. The trick, of course, is to know where to find good advice.

Sometimes, you just need basic help with how your computer works. Other times, you want instructions for a particular software application. You might need assistance with an immediate problem, or you might suspect that a better way exists to do something you already know how to do. If your system locks up, you can minimize your damage by taking some specific precautionary steps, described in this chapter, but — with the current state of the technology — it's virtually impossible to guarantee 100-percent error-free operation of your computer.

Definition

Troubleshooting is the process of finding and correcting a computer problem.

Troubleshooting

The process of finding and correcting a computer problem is called *troubleshooting.* Sometimes, you will need professional help to troubleshoot a problem; however, you can often detect and correct the problem yourself with a few simple steps.

Basic Problems

Computer problems often express themselves in unusual ways — the computer screen goes blank, or the computer freezes and no matter which keys you press or what you click with the mouse, you get no response. You might even encounter an ominous message such as, "You have performed an illegal

15

Troubleshooting and Finding Help

Because lightning and power surges can cause major damage to your computer as well as loss of data, be sure to purchase a quality surge protector — one that protects the telephone connection for your modem as well as your computer's electrical connection.

Give your computer and your monitor room to breathe. Keep both slightly away from walls and surrounding furniture. Don't pile papers on top of either your computer or monitor.

function." Don't look over your shoulder to see whether the police are coming. Instead, just realize that the computer is having a problem, which may not even have anything to do with your actions.

The following sections describe a few of the common things that happen and provide some information on how you can correct and/or prevent them from upsetting your happy computing.

What to Do if the Screen Is Blank

A totally blank screen can be a most disconcerting sight, but the problem may not be as bad as it first seems. First of all, don't overlook the obvious. Electronic equipment needs electricity, and if power cables are not securely plugged in to *both* the wall (a surge-protector is even better) *and* the device in question (computer, monitor, and so on), nothing will happen.

As ludicrous as this sounds, you'd be surprised how many help-desk emergencies are solved by reminding the caller to reestablish electrical connections. Keyboard, mouse, and printer cables often get dislodged. Often, a friendly cat, dog, or child inadvertently loosens a cable. (Overzealous gerbils have been known to eat right through computer cables.) So, even though all the cable connections look okay, it is a good policy to check each one.

What to Do if the Screen Is Frozen

If you have power but the image on your screen freezes, don't reach for that power switch! Take a deep breath and wait a few seconds. Sometimes, your computer becomes busy and needs time to catch up with everything you've told it to do. When your computer's processor catches up with its many tasks, it likely will get back to helping you type your letter, or whatever you were in the middle of when your screen froze.

If you wait for a few minutes and still nothing happens, move on to the next step. It may be that one application has stalled, but your operating system and other applications are still stable. If you haven't yet learned the "magic key" combination (in Windows systems), now is the time: Simultaneously pressing the keys marked Ctrl, Alt, and Del (or Delete) gives you a chance to "peek under the hood" and see what's going on inside your Windows system.

Old versions of the Windows operating system were not very good at isolating problems. When one program crashed, the entire computer was affected. However, since the introduction of Windows 95, Windows systems have become better at isolating problems. When you hit the magic Ctrl+Alt+Del key combination, you are presented with a Close Program box, listing the programs currently running.

If Windows has found the offending program, it will give the message "not responding" next to the program's name. You can then highlight the name of the errant program, press the End Task button, and return to your computing. (Again, you will lose any data in that program if you have not yet saved it.) You also have the option of pressing Ctrl+Alt+Del again to restart your computer. This approach should be used only after you have tried the other options unsuccessfully.

Occasionally, even the Close Program box freezes, and the Ctrl+Alt+Del combination loses its magic. If this happens, your last resort is to restart the computer. If your computer has a Reset button, you can press it to restart the computer. If you don't have a Reset button, turn off the computer. Wait several minutes and then turn it on again. Unfortunately, restarting the computer in this way will lose

Installing a new program can sometimes interfere with a program that you already have up and running. So, before you install a new program, close all other programs. Also, install only one new program at a time. After you install a new program, use the computer for a few days, or even a week or two, to make sure that everything is running correctly before you install another new program.

After pressing the magic Ctrl+Alt+Del key combination, be patient and give your computer at least 45 seconds to bring up the Close Program box. Don't keep hitting keys. Just wait.

15

Troubleshooting and Finding Help

After you turn off the power to the computer, always wait a minute or two before turning it back on again. This will give all the internal mechanisms a chance to fully shut down before they have to restart.

any changes you made to the document you were working on since you last saved it. If you are lucky enough to have one of the newer computers, be aware that you may need to hold your power button down for about three seconds to turn your computer off. Some new computer brands do not even have on/off switches. Your only option to shut down the computer is to unplug the machine.

Apple users also have a "magic key" combination to try in a pinch. Mac users should try pressing the Control, Command, and Power buttons simultaneously. This does not work as well on the iMac as it did on older Macs, but it is worth a try. If this doesn't work, open the iMac's hinged side panel and insert a paperclip into the topmost of the two reset button holes next to the modem jack. If that fails, unplug the computer. Wait 30 seconds and then restart.

Mac users can also try pressing the Option, Command, and Escape keys simultaneously. You'll get a prompt asking whether you want to exit the program in question. Usually this works fine, and if you have more than one application open, you'll be able to save at least some of your data. It's not a cure-all, and you will have to reboot. The system doesn't like it when applications are exited in this way!

Save Your Work

It has been said that there are two kinds of computer users: those who *have* lost data, and those who *will* lose data. If you're in the first category (like me!), you've probably developed the habit of saving your work regularly. If you're in the second category, please develop that good habit now.

Improper Shutdown

You should always exit Windows properly, by clicking the Start button and choosing Shut Down from the menu. If you use Ctrl+Alt+Del to restart your computer (or if you use the Reset button or power switch), without exiting Windows normally, certain files on your hard disk can be left open or even damaged. If you are using Windows 98 or certain versions of Windows 95 and start your computer after an improper shutdown, it will automatically run through a process called ScanDisk, which will repair any damaged files. If your computer does not do this automatically, you should initiate this process yourself. See the online Windows Help system and type the word **Scandisk** (one word) for instructions.

In most programs, you can save your work either by choosing Save from the File menu, as shown in Figure

15-1, or by clicking the Save icon, which usually looks like a floppy disk. You don't have to worry about saving anything when you are on AOL. However, when you are writing a letter, working on your family tree, or adding names and addresses to your telephone directory, you should take the time to figure out how to save the file you are working on.

Many of today's software applications have built-in AutoSave features, which save your work at regular intervals (which you can adjust to your needs) in backup files, in case a power loss or a freeze occurs. Check the program's documentation or Help screens for details about this feature, but don't rely on it. No silver-bullet type of substitution exists for saving your files.

15

Troubleshooting and Finding Help

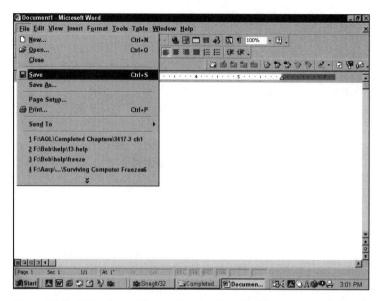

Figure 15-1. Save your work by choosing Save from the File menu or by clicking the Save icon, which looks like a floppy disk, on your toolbar.

How often should you save your work? Answer these two questions:

▸ How much of the work that you've just done can you handle doing again?

▸ How long will that take?

Check Your Connection and Transfer Speed

The speed of your AOL connection is dependent on your modem speed. To find out your modem speed on a Windows-based computer, check your owner's manual or click Start ⇨ Settings ⇨ Control Panel ⇨ Modems. For Mac users, click the Apple symbol ⇨ Apple System Profiler, and then check the Hardware tab. If you have an older, slower modem, you may want to buy a new one. Don't skimp on the modem. Buy the fastest and best one you can find. (AOL recommends using a 56K modem.)

After you have a good modem, if your connection is still slow, check out your telephone lines. Make sure that you are using a new cable to connect your computer to the telephone jack. Use a cable of the proper length. A cable that is too short may be stretched to the breaking point, whereas a cable that is too long may not give you a good connection. The 20-year-old cable that you pulled out of the garage may not be as good as it once was.

Definition

Line noise is interference in your telephone line that can cause your Internet connection to be extremely slow.

Telephone lines can also be plagued with something called *line noise,* interference in your telephone line that can cause your Internet connection to be extremely slow. If you pick up the telephone and hear a crinkling noise, you definitely have line noise, but you may also have it even if you don't hear anything. Older telephone wiring in homes can cause line noise or connection problems. If you suspect that you may have a problem with your telephone line, call the telephone company and have it checked out.

One advantage to using America Online is that it provides information that can be accessed quickly. However, when you reach out to the Internet, thousands of computers hold information and linkage to other computers, so everything may not go smoothly. Think for a moment about what must happen for an Internet page to appear on your computer screen: your computer must connect to AOL, which in turn links to a server that is perhaps hundreds or thousands of miles away. Then, all the data that comprises the page — text, graphics, sounds, and so on — must find its way back to your computer.

Any number of "invisible" causes could complicate this already tricky task. If your local telephone lines are experiencing static, you may experience

15

Troubleshooting and Finding Help

Note

URLs are very particular. In most cases, the address must be typed exactly as it was given to you. Dots and slashes are not interchangeable, and capitalization counts! When in doubt, use lowercase letters.

difficulties. If any computer in the mass network of computers goes down for some reason, your gateway to the rest of the Internet may be affected. Besides (as is becoming the case), overall traffic on the Internet may be so heavy that transmission could be slow or interrupted.

Web Address Problems

Sometimes, after clicking a hyperlink or typing a URL (short for *Uniform Resource Locator*, often simply called a "Web address"), you expect a Web page to appear in your browser window, but what you see instead is an error message. If you've manually typed the location, double-check to make sure that you haven't misspelled part of the address.

If you've avoided typos but still can't locate the page, do a little detective work. Suppose a friend tells you to check out the Computers and Technology section of the AARP Web site and gives you the URL as www.aarp.org/computers/. If you try to find that page, you'll get an error message.

But, you can still find what you're looking for if you get to the main page of the site. Click your mouse in the AOL Navigation bar (see Figure 15-2). Backspace over the last section of the address in the text box until you are left with www.aarp.org. Press Enter, and you are taken to AARP's home page, where you'll be able to locate a link to the Computers and Technology section (and, after you click this link, you can note in your location bar that the correct URL is www.aarp.org/comptech/).

Text Box

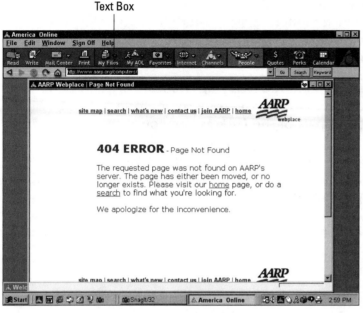

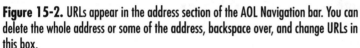

Avoid typos by adding sites you visit frequently to your list of Favorite Places, rather than reentering those long and technical addresses each time. (See Chapter 5 for more details on using Favorite Places.)

Figure 15-2. URLs appear in the address section of the AOL Navigation bar. You can delete the whole address or some of the address, backspace over, and change URLs in this box.

File Not Found Error

Sometimes, even if you click a link provided by a search engine or some other Web page, you may still get a Page Not Found error. It could be that the maintainer of that page has renamed it or moved it to another site, without providing a "forwarding address" or update notice about the new link. You may need to retry your search. For search tips, see Chapter 5.

DNS Lookup Failed Error

Another kind of error message reports that DNS Lookup Failed. A DNS is a *domain name server,* one of a special class of computers on the Internet that receives the almost-English URLs we type and translates them into the unique numerical identifiers assigned to every computer connected to the

15

Troubleshooting and Finding Help

If your URL address does not work on the first try, click the Refresh button to try again.

Internet. A DNS error could mean that the site either no longer exists, couldn't be found by the DNS computer, is temporarily offline, or is so busy that new requests can't be processed.

If the page you're trying to locate is a subsection of a larger site, try the trick of entering only the primary part of the URL, as previously explained. If that doesn't work, try one of your favorite search engines and look for the phantom Web page. (Be as complete and specific as possible when you define your search.) You may find the page you were looking for, or you might discover an even better site. The simplest solution of all is to wait a few minutes or even a few hours and try again.

Where to Find Help

The more ways you know how to find help with whatever problems occur, the more confident you'll be as a computer user and the less frustrated you'll feel when the unexpected happens. Following in this section are suggestions of where to find help when you need it.

Search AOL Help

America Online has developed an amazingly comprehensive and accessible system of online help. Much of the information available assists you with beginner, intermediate, and advanced features of the vast AOL community, but extensive sections on more general computing activities are included, too. What follows is an overview of the different kinds of help available to America Online users.

As soon as you sign on to AOL, your screen provides you with one-click access to sources of help. The last (rightmost) item on the menu bar is Help. Pull down that menu. The first two items are Member Services Online Help and Offline Help (see Figure 15-3).

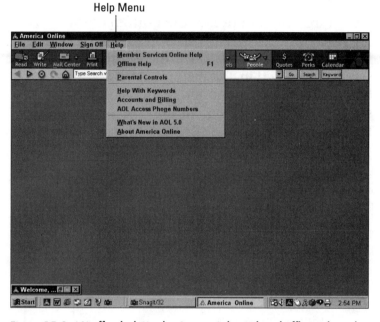

Figure 15-3. AOL offers both Member Services Online Help and Offline Help on the drop-down Help menu found on the menu bar.

Offline Help

The Offline Help choice opens a window similar to those you may have seen in other applications. These basic topics — from getting connected and using e-mail to managing your account and troubleshooting — are stored on your computer's hard drive, so you can read them even when you're not signed on to AOL.

Member Services Online Help

Member Services Online Help (which you can also reach with Keyword: **Help**) is the most complete starting point for getting assistance after you're connected to AOL. A list of Help topics covers installing new versions of AOL software, getting around the America Online world, using the Search and Find features, browsing the Internet and the Web, downloading files, and more.

The Search Help button at the bottom of the Member Services screen enables you to access a list of various AOL Help documents on the subject you're interested in. For example, if you want to learn more about the sound features of AOL, type **sounds** in the top rectangle and click Search (see Figure 15-4). You'll be given a list of more than a dozen specific topics related to sounds.

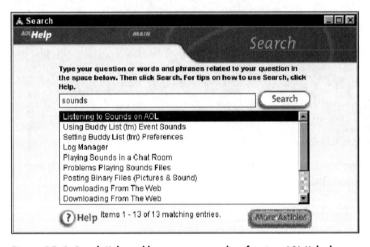

Figure 15-4. Search Help enables you to access a list of various AOL Help documents on the subject you are interested in.

QuickStart

Another choice on the Member Services screen is New Members, which takes you to the QuickStart guide for those recently joining America Online — as well as for AOL veterans who need a refresher on the basics. This guide can also be reached via the Keyword: **QuickStart**.

The QuickStart guide begins with a 5 Minute Guide to AOL, a text-and-slide presentation covering screen names and passwords, e-mail, keywords, hyperlinks, the AOL Search feature, chatting online with other AOL members, and surfing the Internet.

Another topic in the QuickStart guide is Best of AOL, Keyword: **Best of AOL**. This guide gives short explanations of unique features, such as Buddy Lists, shopping on AOL, and Instant Message conversations. The AOL Tips link, Keyword: **AOL Tips**, leads you to a wide range of helpful hints about getting the most from your America Online experience.

Keywords

Speaking of keywords, the keywords feature in itself can be a great source of help with various topics of interest. One favorite tip is to get a listing of the entire spectrum of AOL topics by going to the Keyword: **Keyword** (see Figure 15-5).

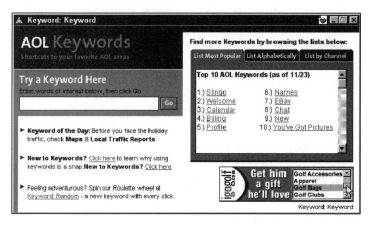

Figure 15-5. To get a listing of the entire spectrum of AOL topics, go to the Keyword: *Keyword.*

Go Online

Often, computer-related problems can be easily solved by a quick trip to a manufacturer's Web site. Most companies have a technical support area where you can e-mail your question. Most companies also have an area called FAQ, for *Frequently Asked Questions.* This is where they post the questions that have been asked most often, along with answers to these questions. You will find that, often, someone else has asked the same question you have. A quick trip through the FAQ can often answer your question. Also, if you need the most current version of a piece of software, a patch to fix a problem, or an updated driver to manage your printer or modem, you can also find that at a manufacturer's Web site.

Call Technical Support

If you have a problem that you cannot solve on your own or online, you are ready to call for technical support. Before you do, be prepared by having the following available:

> ▶ If a piece of hardware is involved, have the model and serial number handy. If you are dealing with a piece of software, note the version number.

> ▶ If any error messages have occurred, be sure to write them down.

> ▶ Get the name of the person you are talking to and also document the facts, including the telephone number you called, the date, and the length of your call.

> ▶ If you can, write down the solution to the problem, so that if it reoccurs, you can use your notes to correct it.

Some computer problems are frustrating and can also be somewhat overwhelming, but you are sure to get through them. Whether you solve the problem yourself or find help from technical support, be sure to give yourself a pat on the back. Believe it or not, every time you solve a computer problem, you are adding to your technical expertise. Even if you are not sure about how the problem was actually solved, you likely have learned something from the experience.

So, keep on plugging away! Happy computing!

Coming Up Next

Here we are at the end of the book. You have learned how to use AOL to communicate with others online, how to meet others through chatting, how to navigate AOL and the Internet, as well as where to look to pursue your favorite hobbies, where to find information, and how to deal with e-mail attachments and downloadable software. The next step in your online journey is to continue to have fun with the computer, AOL, and the Internet.

In case things don't work the way you expect them to, this chapter has discussed how to troubleshoot problems and know where to find help, including the following:

- ▶ The more ways you know how to find help, the more confident you will be as a computer user.
- ▶ If your computer freezes up, your *last* resort is to restart the computer.
- ▶ Computer users should develop a habit of periodically saving their work.
- ▶ America Online has comprehensive and easily accessible online help.
- ▶ Often, computer-related problems can be easily solved by a quick trip to a manufacturer's Web site.
- ▶ When calling for technical support, be prepared.
- ▶ Every time you solve a computer problem, you are adding to your technical expertise.

Find an assortment of online classes at keyword: **Online Classrooms.**

Also look for training courses that will be offered at local retailers, such as CompUSA.

15

Troubleshooting and Finding Help

Index

AOL Selects the Best

Protect Your PC From Internet Viruses!

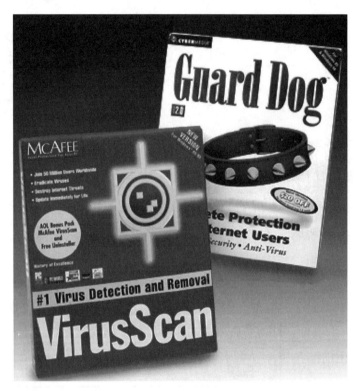

Order Today!
1-888-299-0329

VirusScan/Free Guard Dog 2.0

VirusScan detects viruses from floppy disks, Internet downloads, email attachments, Intranets, shared files, CD-ROMs and online services. In addition, we are including as a Bonus, Guard Dog 2.0. Guard Dog is reliable way to safeguard your personal files and keep your web browsing habits private. A must have duo of robust protection programs! Know the facts. AOL created a Computer Protection Center to help you learn more about viruses. For more information regarding computer protection go to AOL Keyword: Virus Info.
$29.95 (s&h $5.60)   #0010424N00011271

2 for 1 exclusive AOL offer!

AMERICA
Online

So easy to use,
no wonder it's #1

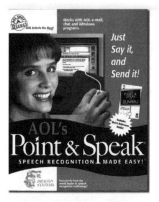

AOL Selects the Best

Express Yourself with an Electronic Smile :)

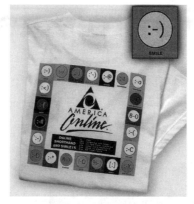

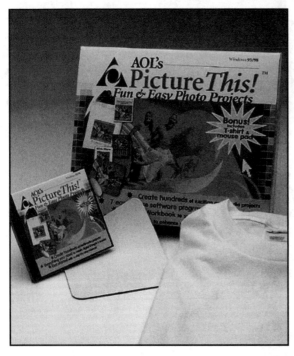

AOL Selects the Best

Visit the Great Shops at AOL Shop Direct!

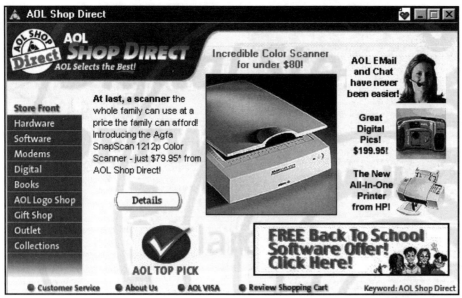

AOL Shop Direct's goal is to simplify your online and computing needs by selecting the best quality and value products available and presenting them to you in an informative easy to use store. The products in AOL Shop Direct have been pre-tested to not only ensure your 100% satisfaction, but to specifically enhance your computing and America Online experience.

Visit us today and check out our:

> Daily Specials
> Easy to use computer and Internet guides
> New Releases
> Top Picks
> And our Clearance Outlet!

All this and more is available at AOL Keyword: AOL Shop Direct

AMERICA
Online.

*So easy to use,
no wonder it's #1*

250 Hour Free Trial for One Month — Try AOL 5.0 Now!

CD-ROM Installation Instructions for Windows

1. Insert the AOL CD-ROM into your CD-ROM drive.
2. If installation does not begin automatically, click **Start** on the task bar (Windows 3.1 users click on the **File** menu of your Windows Program Manager) then select **Run**.
3. Type **D:\SETUP** (or **E:\SETUP**) and press OK. Follow the easy instructions and you'll be online in minutes!

Installation Instructions for MacIntosh

1. For AOL 4.0 for Mac, **insert** the AOL CD into your CD-ROM drive.
2. Double-click on the **Install** icon.
3. Follow the easy instructions and you'll be online in minutes!

Availability may be limited, especially during peak times.

System Requirements for AOL 5.0 for Windows: Windows 95 32-bit or Windows 98, 16 megabytes of RAM, Pentium-class processor, 38 Megabytes available hard disk space, 640x480, 256 colors or better screen (optimized for 800x600), 14.4 Kbps or faster modem

Note: You may be given the opportunity to upgrade your Web browser to Internet Explorer 5.0 while you are upgrading your AOL software. If you choose to upgrade your browser at the same time, you will need 80 additional Megabytes of available hard disk space.

System Requirements for AOL 4.0 for MAC: 68040 or better Macintosh, System 7.5 or higher recommended, 16 MB RAM, 20 MB disk space, 256 color monitor, 14.4 Kbps or faster modem. Note: AOL recommends using Virtual Memory. If you have less than 24 MB of built-in memory, you must use Virtual Memory to increase your available RAM toa a minimum of 24 MB.

Need Help? Call us toll-free at **1-800-827-6364**